CAMBRIDGE LIBRARY

Books of enduring schol.

Literary studies

This series provides a high-quality selection of early printings of literary works, textual editions, anthologies and literary criticism which are of lasting scholarly interest. Ranging from Old English to Shakespeare to early twentieth-century work from around the world, these books offer a valuable resource for scholars in reception history, textual editing, and literary studies.

Letters from Dorothy Osborne to Sir William Temple, 1652–54

Published in 1888, this work reproduced for the first time in full the letters sent by the English gentlewoman Dorothy Osborne (1627–95) to Sir William Temple (1628–99) during their courtship. Osborne first met Temple on the Isle of Wight in 1648, but both their families opposed the relationship and the couple were not able to marry until 1654. Osborne's letters are highly engaging, especially notable for their political and social commentary as well as for the details they reveal about her daily life and the clandestine courtship. Only one of Temple's letters survives, since Osborne destroyed them as soon as she had read them. While extracts of her letters had appeared in print earlier, the lawyer and author Edward Abbott Parry (1863–1943) was the first person to publish the entire collection of surviving correspondence. His edition is particularly valuable for the explanatory notes that accompany each letter.

Cambridge University Press has long been a pioneer in the reissuing of out-of-print titles from its own backlist, producing digital reprints of books that are still sought after by scholars and students but could not be reprinted economically using traditional technology. The Cambridge Library Collection extends this activity to a wider range of books which are still of importance to researchers and professionals, either for the source material they contain, or as landmarks in the history of their academic discipline.

Drawing from the world-renowned collections in the Cambridge University Library and other partner libraries, and guided by the advice of experts in each subject area, Cambridge University Press is using state-of-the-art scanning machines in its own Printing House to capture the content of each book selected for inclusion. The files are processed to give a consistently clear, crisp image, and the books finished to the high quality standard for which the Press is recognised around the world. The latest print-on-demand technology ensures that the books will remain available indefinitely, and that orders for single or multiple copies can quickly be supplied.

The Cambridge Library Collection brings back to life books of enduring scholarly value (including out-of-copyright works originally issued by other publishers) across a wide range of disciplines in the humanities and social sciences and in science and technology.

Letters from Dorothy Osborne to Sir William Temple, 1652–54

EDITED BY
EDWARD ABBOTT PARRY

CAMBRIDGE
UNIVERSITY PRESS

CAMBRIDGE
UNIVERSITY PRESS

University Printing House, Cambridge, CB2 8BS, United Kingdom

Published in the United States of America by Cambridge University Press, New York

Cambridge University Press is part of the University of Cambridge.

It furthers the University's mission by disseminating knowledge in the pursuit of education, learning and research at the highest international levels of excellence.

www.cambridge.org
Information on this title: www.cambridge.org/9781108070553

© in this compilation Cambridge University Press 2014

This edition first published 1888
This digitally printed version 2014

ISBN 978-1-108-07055-3 Paperback

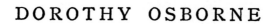

DOROTHY OSBORNE

Dorothy Daughter of Sir Peter Osborne Wife to
Sr William Temple Bart Ambasador to the
States General

Photo-engraving.-Waterlow & Sons, Limited.

notwithstanding
all your litle doubts, beleeu, that I am
very much
Your faithfull freind
& humble servant
D Osborne

March ye 25 th

LETTERS FROM

DOROTHY OSBORNE

TO

SIR WILLIAM TEMPLE

1652–54

EDITED BY

EDWARD ABBOTT PARRY

(Barrister-at-Law)

Iach.	Here are letters for you.
Post.	Their tenor good, I trust?
Iach.	'Tis very like.

Cymbeline, Act ii. Sc. 4

Printed for *Griffith, Farran, Okeden & Welsh,* successors to Newbery & Harris, at *the sign of the Bible and Sun,* West Corner of St. Paul's Churchyard, London; and Sydney, New South Wales, MDCCCLXXXVIII

TO

MY DAUGHTER

HELEN

THIS VOLUME IS DEDICATED

EXEMPLI GRATIA.

CONTENTS.

——o——

CHAPTER I.

INTRODUCTION.

"AN editor," says Dr. Johnson, is "he that revises or prepares any work for publication;" and this definition of an editor's duty seems wholly right and satisfactory. But now that the revision of these letters is apparently complete, the reader has some right to expect a formal introduction to a lady whose name he has, in all probability, never heard; and one may not be over-stepping the modest and Johnsonian limits of an editor's office, when the writing of a short introduction is included among the duties of preparation.

Dorothy Osborne was the wife of the famous Sir William Temple, and apology for her biography will be found in her own letters, here for the first time published. Some of them have indeed been printed in a *Life of Sir William Temple* by the Right Honourable Thomas Peregrine Courtenay, a man better known to the Tory politician of fifty years ago than to any world of letters in that day or this. Forty-two extracts from these letters did Courtenay transfer to an Appendix, without arrangement or any form of editing, as he candidly confesses; but not without mis-givings as to how they would be received by a people thirsting to read the details of the negotiations which took place in connection with the Triple Alliance. If Courtenay lived to learn that the world had other things

A

to do than pore over dull excerpts from inhuman State papers, we may pity his awakening ; but we can never quite forgive the apologetic paragraph with which he relegates Dorothy Osborne's letters to the mouldy obscurity of an Appendix.

When Macaulay was reviewing Courtenay's book in the *Edinburgh Review,* he took occasion to write a short but living sketch of the early history of Sir William Temple and Dorothy Osborne.   And with this account so admirably written, ready at hand, it becomes the clear duty of the Editor to quote rather than to rewrite ; which he does with the greater pleasure, remembering that it was this very passage that first led him to read the letters of Dorothy Osborne.

"William Temple, Sir John's eldest son, was born in London in the year 1628.   He received his early educa-tion under his maternal uncle, was subsequently sent to school at Bishop-Stortford, and, at seventeen, began to reside at Emmanuel College, Cambridge, where the celebrated Cudworth was his tutor.   The times were not favourable to study.   The Civil War disturbed even the quiet cloisters and bowling-greens of Cambridge, pro-duced violent revolutions in the government and dis-cipline of the colleges, and unsettled the minds of the students.   Temple forgot at Emmanuel all the little Greek which he had brought from Bishop-Stortford, and never retrieved the loss ; a circumstance which would hardly be worth noticing but for the almost incredible fact, that fifty years later he was so absurd as to set up his own authority against that of Bentley on questions of Greek history and philology.   He made no proficiency, either in the old philosophy which still lingered in the schools of Cambridge, or in the new philosophy of which Lord Bacon was the founder.   But to the end of his life he continued to speak of the former with ignorant admiration, and of the latter with equally ignorant contempt.

" After residing at Cambridge two years, he departed without taking a degree, and set out upon his travels. He seems to have been then a lively, agreeable young man of fashion, not by any means deeply read, but versed in all the superficial accomplishments of a gentleman, and acceptable in all polite societies. In politics he professed himself a Royalist. His opinions on religious subjects seem to have been such as might be expected from a young man of quick parts, who had received a rambling education, who had not thought deeply, who had been disgusted by the morose austerity of the Puritans, and who, surrounded from childhood by the hubbub of conflicting sects, might easily learn to feel an impartial contempt for them all.

" On his road to France he fell in with the son and daughter of Sir Peter Osborne. Sir Peter held Guernsey for the King, and the young people were, like their father, warm for the Royal cause. At an inn where they stopped in the Isle of Wight, the brother amused himself with inscribing on the windows his opinion of the ruling powers. For this instance of malignancy the whole party were arrested, and brought before the Governor. The sister, trusting to the tenderness which, even in those troubled times, scarcely any gentleman of any party ever failed to show where a woman was concerned, took the crime on herself, and was immediately set at liberty with her fellow-travellers.

" This incident, as was natural, made a deep impression on Temple. He was only twenty. Dorothy Osborne was twenty-one. She is said to have been handsome ; and there remains abundant proof that she possessed an ample share of the dexterity, the vivacity, and the tenderness of her sex. Temple soon became, in the phrase of that time, her servant, and she returned his regard. But difficulties, as great as ever expanded a novel to the fifth volume, opposed their wishes. When the courtship commenced, the father of the hero was sitting in the Long Parliament; the father of the heroine was commanding in Guernsey for King Charles. Even when the war ended, and Sir Peter Osborne returned to his seat at Chicksands, the prospects of the lovers were scarcely less gloomy. Sir John Temple had a more advantageous alliance in view for his son. Dorothy Osborne was in the meantime besieged by as many suitors as were drawn to Belmont by the fame of Portia. The most distinguished on the list was Henry Cromwell. Destitute of the capacity, the energy, the magnanimity of his illustrious father, destitute also of the meek and placid virtues of his elder brother, this young man was perhaps a more formidable rival in love than either of them would have been. Mrs. Hutchinson, speaking the sentiments of the grave and aged, describes him as an 'insolent foole,' and a 'debauched ungodly cavalier.' These expressions probably mean that he was one who, among young and dissipated people, would pass for a fine gentleman. Dorothy was fond of dogs, of larger and more formidable breed than those which lie on modern hearthrugs; and Henry Cromwell promised that the highest functionaries at Dublin should be set to work to procure her a fine Irish greyhound. She seems to have felt his attentions as very flattering, though his father was then only Lord General, and not yet Protector. Love, however, triumphed over ambition, and the young lady appears never to have regretted her

decision; though, in a letter written just at the time
when all England was ringing with the news of the
violent dissolution of the Long Parliament, she could
not refrain from reminding Temple with pardonable
vanity, 'how great she might have been, if she had
been so wise as to have taken hold of the offer of H. C.'

"Nor was it only the influence of rivals that Temple
had to dread. The relations of his mistress regarded
him with personal dislike, and spoke of him as an un-
principled adventurer, without honour or religion, ready
to render service to any party for the sake of preferment. This is, indeed, a very distorted view of Temple's
character. Yet a character, even in the most distorted
view taken of it by the most angry and prejudiced
minds, generally retains something of its outline. No
caricaturist ever represented Mr. Pitt as a Falstaff, or
Mr. Fox as a skeleton; nor did any libeller ever impute
parsimony to Sheridan, or profusion to Marlborough.
It must be allowed that the turn of mind which the
eulogists of Temple have dignified with the appellation
of philosophical indifference, and which, however becoming it may be in an old and experienced statesman, has
a somewhat ungraceful appearance in youth, might
easily appear shocking to a family who were ready to
fight or to suffer martyrdom for their exiled King and
their persecuted Church. The poor girl was exceed-
ingly hurt and irritated by these imputations on her
lover, defended him warmly behind his back, and
addressed to himself some very tender and anxious
admonitions, mingled with assurances of her confidence
in his honour and virtue. On one occasion she was
most highly provoked by the way in which one of her
brothers spoke of Temple. 'We talked ourselves
weary,' she says; 'he renounced me, and I defied him.'

"Near seven years did this arduous wooing continue. We are not accurately informed respecting Temple's movements during that time. But he seems to have led a rambling life, sometimes on the Continent, sometimes in Ireland, sometimes in London. He made himself master of the French and Spanish languages, and amused himself by writing essays and romances, an employment which at least served the purpose of forming his style. The specimen which Mr. Courtenay has preserved of these early compositions is by no means contemptible : indeed, there is one passage on Like and Dislike, which could have been produced only by a mind habituated carefully to reflect on its own operations, and which reminds us of the best things in Montaigne.

"Temple appears to have kept up a very active correspondence with his mistress. His letters are lost, but hers have been preserved ; and many of them appear in these volumes. Mr. Courtenay expresses some doubt whether his readers will think him justified in inserting so large a number of these epistles. We only wish that there were twice as many. Very little indeed of the diplomatic correspondence of that generation is so well worth reading."

Here Macaulay indulges in an eloquent but lengthy philippic against that "vile phrase" the "dignity of history," which we may omit,—taking up the thread of his discourse where he recurs to the affairs of our two lovers. "Thinking thus,"—concerning the "dignity of history,"—"we are glad to learn so much, and would willingly learn more about the loves of Sir William and his mistress. In the seventeenth century, to be sure, Louis the Fourteenth was a much more important person than Temple's sweetheart. But death and time equalize all things. Neither the great King nor the beauty of Bedfordshire, neither the gorgeous paradise of Marli nor Mistress Osborne's favourite walk 'in the common that lay hard by the house, where a great many young wenches used to keep sheep and cows and sit in the shade singing of ballads,' is anything to us. Louis and Dorothy are alike dust. A cotton-mill stands on the ruins of Marli ; and the Osbornes have ceased to dwell under the ancient roof of Chicksands. But of that information, for the sake of which alone it is worth while to study remote events, we find so much in the love letters which Mr. Courtenay has published, that we would gladly purchase equally interesting billets with ten times their weight in State papers taken at random. To us surely it is as useful to know how the young ladies of England employed themselves a hundred and eighty years ago, how far their minds were cultivated, what were their favourite studies, what degree of liberty was allowed to them, what use they made of that liberty, what accomplishments they most valued in men, and what proofs of tenderness delicacy permitted them to give to favoured suitors, as to know all about the seizure of Franche-Comté and the Treaty of Nimeguen. The mutual relations of the two sexes seem to us to be at least as important as the mutual relations of any two Governments in the world ; and a series of letters written by a virtuous, amiable, and sensible girl, and intended for the eye of her lover alone, can scarcely fail to throw some light on the relations of the sexes ; whereas it is perfectly possible, as all who have made any historical researches can attest, to read bale after bale of despatches and protocols, without catching one glimpse of light about the relations of Governments.

"Mr. Courtenay proclaims that he is one of Dorothy Osborne's devoted servants, and expresses a hope that the publication of her letters will add to the number. We must declare ourselves his rivals. She really seems to have been a very charming young woman, modest, generous, affectionate, intelligent, and sprightly; a Royalist, as was to be expected from her connections, without any of that political asperity which is as un-womanly as a long beard; religious, and occasionally gliding into a very pretty and endearing sort of preach-ing, yet not too good to partake of such diversions as London afforded under the melancholy rule of the Puritans, or to giggle a little at a ridiculous sermon from a divine who was thought to be one of the great lights of the Assembly at Westminster; with a little turn for coquetry, which was yet perfectly compatible with warm and disinterested attachment, and a little turn for satire, which yet seldom passed the bounds of good nature. She loved reading; but her studies were not those of Queen Elizabeth and Lady Jane Grey. She read the verses of Cowley and Lord Broghill, French Memoirs recommended by her lover, and the Travels of Fernando Mendez Pinto. But her favourite books were those ponderous French romances which modern readers know chiefly from the pleasant satire of Charlotte Lennox. She could not, however, help laughing at the vile English into which they were translated. Her own style is very agreeable; nor are her letters at all the worse for some passages in which raillery and tenderness are mixed in a very engaging namby-pamby.

"When at last the constancy of the lovers had triumphed over all the obstacles which kinsmen and rivals could oppose to their union, a yet more serious calamity befell them. Poor Mistress Osborne fell ill of the small-pox, and, though she escaped with life, lost all her beauty. To this most severe trial the affection and honour of the lovers of that age was not unfrequently subjected. Our readers probably remember what Mrs. Hutchinson tells us of herself. The lofty Cornelia-like spirit of the aged matron seems to melt into a long forgotten softness when she relates how her beloved Colonel 'married her as soon as she was able to quit the chamber, when the priest and all that saw her were affrighted to look on her. But God,' she adds, with a not ungraceful vanity, 'recompensed his justice and constancy by restoring her as well as before.' Temple showed on this occasion the same justice and constancy which did so much honour to Colonel Hutchinson. The date of the marriage is not exactly known, but Mr. Courtenay supposes it to have taken place about the end of the year 1654. From this time we lose sight of Dorothy, and are reduced to form our opinion of the terms on which she and her husband were from very slight indications which may easily mislead us."

When an editor is in the pleasant position of being able to retain an historian of the eminence of Macaulay to write a large portion of his introduction, it would ill become him to alter and correct his statements wherever there was a petty inaccuracy; still it is necessary to say, once for all, that there are occasional errors in the passage, — as where Macaulay mentions that Chicksands is no longer the property of the Osbornes, —though happily not one of these errors is in itself important. To our thinking, too, in the character that he draws of our heroine, Macaulay hardly appears to be sufficiently aware of the sympathetic womanly nature of Dorothy, and the dignity of her disposition; so that he is persuaded to speak of her too constantly from the position of a man of the world praising with patronizing emphasis the pretty qualities of a school-girl. But we must remember, that in forming our estimate of her character, we have an extended series of letters before us; and from these the reader can draw his own conclusions as to the accuracy of Macaulay's description, and the importance of Dorothy's character.

It was this passage from Macaulay that led the Editor to Courtenay's Appendix, and it was the literary and human charm of the letters themselves that suggested the idea of stringing them together into a connected story or sketch of the love affairs of Dorothy Osborne. This was published in April 1886 in the *English Illustrated Magazine*, and happened, by good luck, to fall into the hands of an admirer of Dorothy, who, having had access to the original letters, had made faithful and loving copies of each one,—accurate even to the old-world spelling. These labours had been followed up by much patient research, the fruits of which were now to be generously offered to the present Editor on condition that he would prepare the letters for the press. The owner of the letters having courteously expressed his acquiescence, nothing remained but to give to the task that patient care that it is easy to give to a labour of love.

A few words of explanation as to the arrangement of the letters. Although few of them were dated, it was found possible, by minute analysis of their contents, to place them in approximately correct order; and if one could not date each letter, one could at least assign groups of letters to specific months or seasons of the year. The fact that New Year's day was at this period March 25—a fact sometimes ignored by antiquarians of high repute—adds greatly to the difficulty of ascertaining exact dates, and as an instance of this we find in different chronicles of authority Sir Peter Osborne's death correctly, yet differently, given as happening in March 1653 and March 1654. Throughout this volume the ordinary New Year's day has been retained. The further revision and preparation that the letters have undergone is shortly this. The spelling has been modernized, the letters punctuated and arranged in paragraphs, and names indicated by initials have been, wherever it was possible, written in full. A note has been prefixed to each letter, printed in smaller type than the letter itself, and dealing with all the allusions contained in it. This system is very fit to be applied to Dorothy's letters, because, by its use, Dorothy is left to tell her own story without the constant and irritating references to footnotes or Appendix notes that other arrangements necessitate. The Editor has a holy horror of the footnote, and would have it relegated to those "*biblia a-biblia*" from which class he is sure Elia would cheerfully except Dorothy's letters. In the notes themselves the endeavour has been to obtain, where it, was possible, parallel references to letters, diaries, or memoirs, and the Editor can only regret that his researches, through both MSS. and printed records, have been so little successful. In the case of well-known men like Algernon Sydney, Lord Manchester, Edmund Waller, etc., no attempt has been made to write a complete note,—their lives and works being sufficiently well known ; but in the case of more obscure persons,—as, for instance, Dorothy's brother-in-law, Sir Thomas Peyton,—all the known details of their history have been carefully collected. Yet in spite of patience, toil, and the kindness of learned friends, the Editor is

bound to acknowledge that some names remain mere
words to him, and but too many allusions are mysteriously
dim.

The division of the letters into chapters, at first sight
an arbitrary arrangement, really follows their natural
grouping. The letters were written in the years 1653
and 1654, and form a clear and connected story of the
love affairs of the young couple during that time. The
most important group of letters, both from the number
of letters contained in it and the contents of the letters
themselves, is that entitled "Life at Chicksands, 1653."
The Editor regards this group as the very mainland of
the epistolary archipelago that we are exploring. For
it is in this chapter that a clear idea of the domestic
social life of these troublous times is obtainable, none
the less valuable in that it does not tally altogether
with our preconceived and too romantic notions. Here,
too, we find what Macaulay longed for—those social
domestic trivialities which the historians have at length
begun to value rightly. Here are, indeed, many things
of no value to Dryasdust and his friends, but of
moment to us, who look for and find true details of life
and character in nearly every line. And above all
things, here is a living presentment of a beautiful
woman, pure in dissolute days, passing quiet hours of
domestic life amongst her own family, where we may
all visit her and hear her voice, even in the very tones in
which she spoke to her lover.

And now the Editor feels he must augment Macaulay's
sketch of Dorothy Osborne with some account of the
Osborne family, of whom it consisted, what part it took
in the struggle of the day, and what was the past
position of Dorothy's ancestors. All that can be
promised is, that such account shall be as concise as

may be consistent with clearness and accuracy, and that it shall contain nothing but ascertained facts.

There were Osbornes—before there were Osbornes of Chicksands—who, coming out of the north, settled at Purleigh in Essex, where we find them in the year 1442. From this date, passing lightly over a hundred troubled years, we find Peter Osborne, Dorothy's great-grandfather, born in 1521. He was Keeper of the Purse to Edward VI., and was twice married, his second wife being Alice, sister of Sir John Cheke, a family we read of in Dorothy's letters. One of his daughters, named Catharine,—he had a well-balanced family of eleven sons and eleven daughters,—afterwards married Sir Thomas Cheke. Peter Osborne died in 1592; and Sir John Osborne, Peter's son and Dorothy's grand-father, was the first Osborne of Chicksands. It was he who settled at Chicksands, in Bedfordshire, and purchased the neighbouring rectory at Hawnes, to restore it to that Church of which he and his family were in truth militant members; and having generously built and furnished a parsonage house, he presented it in the first place to the celebrated preacher Thomas Brightman, who died there in 1607. It is this rectory that in 1653–54 is in the hands of the Rev. Edward Gibson, who appears from time to time in Dorothy's letters, and who was on occasions the medium through which Temple's letters reached their destination, and avoided falling into the hands of Dorothy's jealous brother. Sir John Osborne married Dorothy Barlee, grand-daughter of Richard Lord Rich, Lord Chancellor of England in the reign of Henry VIII. Sir John was Treasurer's Remembrancer in the Exchequer for many years during the reign of James I., and was also a Commissioner of the Navy. He died November 2, 1628, and was buried in Campton Church,—Chicksands lies between the village of Hawnes and Campton,—where a tablet to his memory still exists.

Sir John had five sons: Peter, the eldest, Dorothy's father, who succeeded him in his hereditary office of Treasurer's Remembrancer; Christopher, Thomas, Richard, and Francis,—Francis Osborne may be mentioned as having taken the side of the Parliament in the Civil Wars. He was Master of the Horse to the Earl of Pembroke, and is noticeable to us as the only known relation of Dorothy who published a book. He was the author of an *Advice to his Son*, in two parts, and some tracts published in 1722, of course long after his death.

Of Sir Peter himself we had at one time thought to write at some length. The narrative of his defence of Castle Cornet for the King, embodied in his own letters, in the letters and papers of George Carteret, Governor of Jersey, in the detailed account left behind by a native of Guernsey, and in the State papers of the period, is one of the most interesting episodes in an epoch of episodes. But though the collected material for some short life of Sir Peter Osborne lies at hand, it seems scarcely necessary for the purpose of this book, and so not without reluctance it is set aside.

Sir Peter was an ardent loyalist. In his obstinate flesh and blood devotion to the house of Stuart he was as sincere and thorough as Sir Henry Lee, Sir Geoffrey Peveril, or Kentish Sir Byng. He was the incarnation of the malignant of latter-day fiction.

> " King Charles, and who'll do him right now?
> King Charles, and who's ripe for fight now?
> Give a rouse; here's in hell's despite now,
> King Charles."

To this text his life wrote the comment.

In 1621, James I. created him Lieutenant-Governor of Guernsey. He had married Dorothy, daughter of Sir John Danvers. Sir John was the younger brother and heir to the Earl of Danby, and was a Gentleman of the Privy Chamber to the King. Clarendon tells us that he got into debt, and to get out of debt found himself in Cromwell's counsel; that he was a proud, formal, weak man, between being seduced and a seducer, and that he took it to be a high honour to sit on the same bench with Cromwell, who employed him and contemned him at once. The Earl of Danby was the Governor of Guernsey, and Sir Peter was his lieutenant until 1643, when the Earl died, and Sir Peter was made full Governor. It would be in 1643 that the siege of Castle Cornet began, the same year in which the rents of the Chicksands estate were assigned away from their rightful owner to one Mr. John Blackstone, M.P. Sir Peter was in his stronghold on a rock in the sea; he was for the King. The inhabitants of the island, more comfortably situated, were a united party for the Parliament. Thus they remained for three years; the King writing to Sir Peter to reduce the inhabitants to a state of reason; the Parliament sending instructions to the jurats of Guernsey to seize the person of Sir Peter; and the Earl of Warwick, prompted, we should suppose, by Sir John Danvers, offering terms to Sir Peter which he indignantly rejected. Meanwhile Lady Osborne —Dorothy with her, in all probability—was doing her best to victual the castle from the mainland, she living at St. Malo during the siege. At length, her money all spent, her health broken down, she returned to England, and was lost to sight. Sir Peter himself heard nothing of her, and her sons in England, who were doing all they could for their father among the King's friends, did not know of her whereabouts.

In 1646 he resigned his command. He was weary and heavy laden with unjust burdens heaped on him by those for whom and with whom he was fighting; he was worn out by the siege; by the characteristic treachery of the King, who, being unable to assist him, could not refrain from sending lying promises instead; and by the malice of his neighbour, George Carteret, Governor of Jersey, who himself made free with the Guernsey supplies, while writing home to the King that Sir Peter has betrayed his trust. Betrayed his trust, indeed, when he and his garrison are reduced to " one biscuit a day and a little porrage for supper," together with limpets and herbs in the best mess they can make; nay, more, when they have pulled up their floors for firewood, and are dying of hunger and want in the stone shell of Castle Cornet for the love of their King. However, circumstances and Sir George Carteret were too much for him, and, at the request of Prince Charles, he resigned his command to Sir Baldwin Wake in May 1646, remaining three years after this date at St. Malo, where he did what he was able to supply the wants of the castle. Sir Baldwin surrendered the castle to Blake in 1650. It was the last fortress to surrender.

In 1649 Sir Peter, finding the promises of reward made by the Prince to be as sincere as those of his father, returned to England, and probably through the intervention of his father-in-law, who was a strict Parliament man, his house and a portion of his estates at Chicksands were restored to him. To these he retired, disappointed in spirit, feeble in health, soon to be bereft of the company of his wife, who died towards the end of 1650, and, but for the constant ministering of his daughter Dorothy, living lonely and forgotten, to see the cause for which he had fought discredited and dead. He died in March 1654, after a long, weary illness. The parish register of Campton describes him as " a friend to the poor, a lover of learning, a maintainer of divine exercises." There is still an inscription to his memory on a marble monument on the north side of the chancel in Campton church.

Sir Peter had seven sons and five daughters. There were only three sons living in 1653; the others died young, one laying down his life for the King at Hartland in Devonshire, in some skirmish, we must now suppose, of which no trace remains. Of those living, Sir John, the eldest son and the first baronet, married his cousin Eleanor Danvers, and lived in Gloucestershire during his father's life. Henry, afterwards knighted, was probably the jealous brother who lived at Chicksands with Dorothy and her father, with whom she had many skirmishes, and who wished in his kind fraternal way to see his sister well — that is to say, wealthily— married. Robert is a younger brother, a year older than Dorothy, who died in September 1653, and who did not apparently live at Chicksands. Dorothy herself was born in 1627; where, it is impossible to say. Sir Peter was presumably at Castle Cornet at that date, but it is doubtful if Lady Osborne ever stayed there, the accommodation within its walls being straitened and primitive even for that day. Dorothy was probably born in England, maybe at Chicksands. Her other sisters had married and settled in various parts of England before 1653. Her eldest sister (not Anne, as Wotton conjectures) married one Sir Thomas Peyton, a Kentish Royalist of some note. What little could be gleaned of his actions from amongst Kentish antiquities

B

and history, and such letters of his as lie entombed in the MSS. of the British Museum, is set down hereafter. He appears to have acted, after her father's death, as Dorothy's guardian, and his name occurs more than once in the pages of her letters.

So much for the Osbornes of Chicksands; an obstinate, sturdy, quick-witted race of Cavaliers; linked by marriage to the great families of the land; aristocrats in blood and in spirit, of whom Dorothy was a worthy descendant. Let us try now and picture for ourselves their home. Chixon, Chikesonds, or Chicksands Priory, Bedfordshire, as it now stands,—what a pleasing various art was spelling in olden time,—was, in the reign of Edward III., a nunnery, situated then, as now, on a slight eminence, with gently rising hills at a short distance behind, and a brook running to join the river Ivel, thence the German Ocean, along the valley in front of the house. The neighbouring scenery of Bedfordshire is on a humble scale, and concerns very little those who do not frequent it and live among it, as we must do for the next year or more.

The Priory is a low-built sacro-secular edifice, well fitted for its former service. Its priestly denizens were turned out in Henry VIII.'s monk-hunting reign (1538). To the joy or sorrow of the neighbourhood, —who knows now? Granted then to one Richard Snow, of whom the records are silent; by him sold, in Elizabeth's reign, to Sir John Osborne, Knt., thus becoming the ancestral home of our Dorothy. There is a crisp etching of the house in Fisher's *Collections of Bedfordshire.* The very exterior of it is Catholic, unpuritanical; no methodism about the square windows, set here and there at undecided intervals wheresoever they may be wanted. Six attic windows jut out from

the low-tiled roof. At the corner of the house is a
high pinnacled buttress rising the full height of the
wall; five buttresses flank the side wall, built so that
they shade the lower windows from the morning sun,
—in one place reaching to the sill of an upper window.
At the further end of the wall are two Gothic windows,
claustral remnants, lighting now perhaps the dining-
hall where cousin Molle and Dorothy sat in state, or
the saloon where the latter received her servants.
There are still cloisters attached to the house, at the
other side of it maybe. Yes, a sleepy country house,
the warm earth and her shrubs creeping close up to
the very sills of the lower windows, sending in morning
fragrance, I doubt not, when Dorothy thrust back the
lattice after breakfast. A quiet place,—"slow" is the
accurate modern epithet for it—"awfully slow;" but
to Dorothy a quite suitable home, at which she never
repines.

This etching by Thomas Fisher, of December 26,
1816, is the more valuable to us since the old Chicksands Priory no longer remains, having suffered martyrdom at the bloody hands of the restorer. For through
this partly we have attained to a knowledge of
Dorothy's surroundings; and through the baronetages,
peerages, and the invincible heaps of genealogical records,
we have gathered some few actual facts necessary to be
known of Dorothy's relations, her human surroundings,
their lives and actions. And we shall not find ourselves
following Dorothy's story with the less interest that we
have mastered these details about the Osbornes of
Chicksands.

Temple, too, claims the consideration at our hands of
a few words concerning his near relatives and their position in the country. As Macaulay tells us, he was born

in 1628, the place of his birth being Blackfriars in London.

Sir John Temple, his father, was Master of the Rolls and a Privy Councillor in Ireland; he was in the confidence of Robert Sidney, Earl of Leicester, the Lord-Lieutenant of Ireland. Algernon Sydney, the Earl's son, was well known to Temple, and perhaps to Dorothy. Sir John Temple, like his son in after life, refused to look on politics as a game in which it was always advisable to play on the winning side, and thus we find him opposing the Duke of Ormond in Ireland in 1643, and suffering imprisonment as a partisan of the Parliament. In England, in 1648, when he was member for Chichester, he concurred with the Presbyterian vote, thereby causing the more advanced section to look askance at him, and he was turned out of the House, or *secluded*, to use the elegant parliamentary language of the day. From that time he lived in retirement in London until 1654, when, as we read in Dorothy's letters, he and his son go over to Ireland. He resumed his office of Master of the Rolls, and in August of that year was elected to the Irish Parliament as one of the members for Leitrim, Sligo, and Roscommon.

Temple's mother was a sister of Dr. Hammond, to whom one Dr. John Collop, a poetaster unknown in these days even by name, begins an ode—

" Seraphic Doctor, bright evangelist."

The "seraphic Doctor" was rector of Penshurst, near Tunbridge Wells, the seat of the Sydneys. From Hammond, who was a zealous adherent of Charles I., Temple received much of his early education. When the Parliament drove Dr. Hammond from his living, Temple was sent to school at Bishop-Stortford; and the rest

of his early life, with an account of his meeting with
Dorothy, has been already set down for us by Macaulay.

Anno Domini sixteen hundred and fifty - three ;—
let us look round through historic mist for landmarks, so that we may know our whereabouts. The
narrow streets of Worcester had been but lately
stained by the blood of heaped corpses. Cromwell
was meditating an abolition of the Parliament, and a
practical coronation of himself. The world had ceased
to wonder at English democracy giving laws to their
quondam rulers, and the democracy was beginning to be
a little tired of itself, to disbelieve in its own irksome
discipline, and to sigh for the flesh-pots of a modified
Presbyterian monarchy. Cromwell, indeed, was at the
height of his glory, his honours lie thick upon him, and
now, if ever, he is the regal Cromwell that Victor Hugo
has portrayed, the uncrowned King of England, tram-
pling under foot that sacred liberty, the baseless ideal
for which so many had fought and bled. He is soon to
be Lord Protector. He is second to none upon earth.
England is again at peace with herself, and takes her
position as one of the great Powers of Europe; Cromwell
is England's king. So much for our rulers and politics.
Now let us remember our friends, those whom we love
on account of the work they have done for us and
bequeathed to us, through which we have learned to
know them. One of the best beloved and gentlest of
these, who by the satire of heaven was born into
England in these troublous times, was now wander-
ing by brook and stream, scarcely annoyed by the
uproar and confusion of the factions around him. And
what he knew of England in these days he has left in
perhaps the gentlest and most peaceful volume the
world has ever read. I speak of Master Izaak Walton,

who in this year, 1653, published the first edition of his *Compleat Angler*, and left a comrade for the idle hours of all future ages. Other friends we have, then living, but none so intimate or well beloved. Mr. Waller, whom Dorothy may have known, Mr. Cowley, Sir Peter Lely, —who painted our heroine's portrait,—and Dr. Jeremy Taylor; very courtly and superior persons are some of these, and far removed from our world. Milton is too sublime to be called our friend, but he was Cromwell's friend at this time. Evelyn, too, is already making notes in his journal at Paris and elsewhere; but little prattling Pepys has not yet begun diary-making. Other names will come to the mind of every reader, but many of these are " people we know by name," as the phrase runs, mere acquaintances,—not friends. Nevertheless even these leave us some indirect description of their time, from which we can look back through the mind's eye to this year of grace 1653, in which Dorothy was living and writing. Yes, if we cannot actually visualize the past, these letters will at least convince us that the past did exist, a past not wholly unlike the present; and if we would realize the significance of it, we have the word of one of our historians, that there is no lamp by which to study the history of this period that gives a brighter and more searching light than contemporary letters. Thus he recommends their study, and we may apply his words to the letters before us: " A man intent to force for himself some path through that gloomy chaos called History of the Seventeenth Century, and to look face to face upon the same, may perhaps try it by this method as hopefully as by another. Here is an irregular row of beacon fires, once all luminous as suns; and with a certain inextinguishable erubescence still, in the abysses of the dead deep Night.

Let us look here. In shadowy outlines, in dimmer and dimmer crowding forms, the very figure of the old dead Time itself may perhaps be faintly discernible here."

   .   .   .   .

With this, I feel that I may cast off some of the forms and solemnities necessary to an editorial introduction, and, assuming a simpler and more personal pronoun, ask the reader, who shall feel the full charm of Dorothy's bright wit and tender womanly sympathy, to remember the thanks due to my fellow-servant, whose patient, single-hearted toil has placed these letters within our reach. And when the reader shall close this volume, let it not be without a feeling of gratitude to the unknown, whose modesty alone prevents me from changing the title of fellow-servant to that of fellow-editor.

CHAPTER II.

EARLY LETTERS. WINTER AND SPRING
1652–53.

THIS first chapter begins with a long letter, dated from Chicksands sometime in the autumn of 1652, when Temple has returned to England after a long absence. It takes us up to March 1653, about the end of which time Dorothy went to London and met Temple again. The engagement she mentions must have been one that her parents were forcing upon her, and it was not until the London visit, I fancy, that her friendship progressed beyond its original limits; but in this matter the reader of Dorothy's letters will be as well able to judge as myself.

Letter 1.—Goring House, where Dorothy and Temple had last parted, was in 1646 appointed by the House of Commons for the reception of the French Ambassador. In 1665 it was the town house of Mr. Secretary Bennet, afterwards Lord Arlington. Its grounds stood much in the position of the present Arlington Street, and Evelyn speaks of it as an ill-built house, but capable of being made a pretty villa.

Dorothy mentions, among other things, that she has been "drinking the waters," though she does not say at what place. It would be either at Barnet, Epsom, or Tunbridge, all of which places are mentioned by contemporary letter-writers as health resorts. At Barnet there was a calcareous spring with a small portion of sea salt in it, which, as we may gather from a later letter, had been but recently discovered. This spring was afterwards, in the year 1677, endowed by one John Owen, who left the sum of £1 to keep the well in repair " as long as it should be of service to the parish." Towards the end of last century, Lyson mentions that the well was in decay and little used. One wonders what has become of John Owen's legacy. The Epsom spring had been discovered earlier in the century. It was the first of its kind found in England. The town was already a place of fashionable resort on account of its mineral waters; they are mentioned as of European celebrity ; and as early as 1609 a ball-room was erected, avenues were planted, and neither Bath nor Tunbridge could rival Epsom in the splendour of their appointments. Towards the beginning of the last century, however, the waters gradually lost their reputation. Tunbridge Wells, the last of the three watering-places that Dorothy may have visited, is still flourishing and fashionable. Its springs are said to have been discovered by Lord North in 1606 ; and the fortunes of the place were firmly established by a visit paid to the springs by Queen Henrietta Maria, acting under medical advice, in 1630, shortly after the birth of Prince Charles. At this date there was no adequate accommodation for the royal party, and Her Majesty had to live in tents on the banks of the spring. An interesting account of the early legends and gradual growth of Tunbridge Wells is to be found in a guide-book of 1768, edited by one Mr. J. Sprange.

The elderly man who proposed to Dorothy was Sir Justinian Isham, Bart., of Lamport in Northampton-

shire.　He himself was about forty-two years of age at
this time, and had lost his first wife (by whom he had
four daughters) in 1638.　The Rev. W. Betham, with
that optimism which is characteristic of compilers of
peerages, thinks " that he was esteemed one of the
most accomplished persons of the time, being a gentleman, not only of fine learning, but famed for his piety
and exemplary life."　Dorothy thinks otherwise, and
writes of him as " the vainest, impertinent, self-conceited,
learned coxcomb that ever yet I saw."　Peerages in
Dorothy's style would perhaps be unprofitable writing.
The "Emperor," as Dorothy calls him in writing to
Temple, may feel thankful that his epitaph was in other
hands than hers.　He appears to have proposed to her
more than once, and evidently had her brother's good
offices, which I fear were not much in his favour with
Dorothy.　He ultimately married the daughter of
Thomas Lord Leigh of Stoneleigh, sometime in the
following year.

Sir Thomas Osborne, a Yorkshire baronet, afterwards
Earl of Danby, is a name not unknown in history.　He
was a cousin of Dorothy ; his mother, Elizabeth Danvers,
being Dorothy's aunt.　He afterwards married Lady
Bridget Lindsay, the Earl of Lindsay's daughter, and
the marriage is mentioned in due course, with Dorothy's
comments.　His leadership of the "Country Party,"
when the reins of government were taken from the
discredited Cabal, is not matter for these pages, neither
are we much concerned to know that he was greedy of
wealth and honours, corrupt himself, and a corrupter of
others.　This is the conventional character of all states-
men of all dates and in all ages, reflected in the mirror
of envious opposition ; no one believes the description
to be true.　Judged by the moral standard of his con-

temporaries, he seems to have been at least of average height. How near was Dorothy to the high places of the State when this man and Henry Cromwell were among her suitors! Had she been an ambitious woman, illustrious historians would have striven to do justice to her character in brilliant periods, and there would be no need at this day for her to claim her place among the celebrated women of England.

SIR,—There is nothing moves my charity like gratitude; and when a beggar is thankful for a small relief, I always repent it was not more. But seriously, this place will not afford much towards the enlarging of a letter, and I am grown so dull with living in't (for I am not willing to confess yet I was always so) as to need all helps. Yet you shall see I will endeavour to satisfy you, upon condition you will tell me why you quarrelled so at your last letter. I cannot guess at it, unless it were that you repented you told me so much of your story, which I am not apt to believe neither, because it would not become our friendship, a great part of it consisting (as I have been taught) in a mutual confidence. And to let you see that I believe it so, I will give you an account of myself, and begin my story, as you did yours, from our parting at Goring House.

I came down hither not half so well pleased as I went up, with an engagement upon me that I had little hope of shaking off, for I had made use

of all the liberty my friends would allow me to
preserve my own, and 'twould not do; he was
so weary of his, that he would part with it upon
any terms. As my last refuge I got my brother
to go down with him to see his house, who, when
he came back, made the relation I wished. He
said the seat was as ill as so good a country would
permit, and the house so ruined for want of living
in't, as it would ask a good proportion of time and
money to make it fit for a woman to confine herself to. This (though it were not much) I was
willing to take hold of, and made it considerable
enough to break the engagement. I had no
quarrel to his person or his fortune, but was in
love with neither, and much out of love with a
thing called marriage; and have since thanked
God I was so, for 'tis not long since one of my
brothers writ me word of him that he was killed
in a duel, though since I have heard that 'twas
the other that was killed, and he is fled upon 't,
which does not mend the matter much. Both
made me glad I had 'scaped him, and sorry
for his misfortune, which in earnest was the
least return his many civilities to me could
deserve.

Presently, after this was at an end, my mother
died, and I was left at liberty to mourn her loss
awhile. At length my aunt (with whom I was
when you last saw me) commanded me to wait
on her at London; and when I came, she told

me how much I was in her care, how well she loved me for my mother's sake, and something for my own, and drew out a long set speech which ended in a good motion (as she call'd it); and truly I saw no harm in't, for by what I had heard of the gentleman I guessed he expected a better fortune than mine. And it proved so. Yet he protested he liked me so well, that he was very angry my father would not be persuaded to give £1000 more with me; and I him so ill, that I vowed if I had £1000 less I should have thought it too much for him. And so we parted. Since, he has made a story with a new mistress that is worth your knowing, but too long for a letter. I'll keep it for you.

After this, some friends that had observed a gravity in my face which might become an elderly man's wife (as they term'd it) and a mother-in-law, proposed a widower to me, that had four daughters, all old enough to be my sisters; but he had a great estate, was as fine a gentleman as ever England bred, and the very pattern of wisdom. I that knew how much I wanted it, thought this the safest place for me to engage in, and was mightily pleased to think I had met with one at last that had wit enough for himself and me too. But shall I tell you what I thought when I knew him (you will say nothing on't): 'twas the vainest, impertinent, self-conceited, learned coxcomb that ever yet I saw; to say more were to spoil his marriage, which I hear is towards with a daughter of my Lord Coleraine's; but for his sake I shall take care of a fine gentleman as long as I live.

Before I have quite ended with him, coming to town about that and some other occasions of my own, I fell in Sir Thomas's way; and what humour took I cannot imagine, but he made very formal addresses to me, and engaged his mother and my brother to appear in't. This bred a story pleasanter than any I have told you yet, but so long a one that I must reserve it till we meet, or make it a letter of itself.

The next thing I designed to be rid on was a scurvy spleen that I have been subject to, and to that purpose was advised to drink the waters. There I spent the latter end of the summer, and at my coming home found that a gentleman (who has some estate in this country) had been treating with my brother, and it yet goes on fair and softly. I do not know him so much as to give you much of his character : 'tis a modest, melancholy, reserved man, whose head is so taken up with little philosophic studies, that I admire how I found a room there. 'Twas sure by chance; and unless he is pleased with that part of my humour which other people think the worst, 'tis very possible the next new experiment may crowd me out again. Thus you have all my late adventures, and almost as much as this paper will hold. The rest shall be employed in telling you how sorry I am you have got such a cold. I am the more sensible of your trouble by my own, for I have newly got one myself. But I will send you that which was to cure me. 'Tis like the rest of my medicines : if it do no good, 'twill be sure to do no harm, and 'twill be no great trouble to take a little on't now and then; for the taste on't, as it is not excellent, so 'tis not very ill. One thing more I must tell you, which is that you are not to take it ill that I mistook your age by my computation of your journey through this country; for I was persuaded t'other day that I could not be less than thirty years old by one that believed it himself, because he was sure it was a great while since he had heard of such a one as

Your humble servant.

Letter 2.—This letter, which is dated, comes, I think, at some distance of time from the first letter. Dorothy may have dated her letters to ordinary folk ; but as she writes to her servant once a week at least, she seems to have considered dates to be superfluous. When Temple is in Ireland, her letters are generally dated with the day of the month. Temple had probably returned from a journey into Yorkshire,—his travels in Holland were over some time ago,—and passing through Bedford within ten miles of Chicksands, he neglected to pay his respects to Dorothy, for which he is duly called to account in Letter 3.

December 24, 1652.

SIR,—You may please to let my old servant (as you call him) know that I confess I owe much to his merits and the many obligations his kindness and civilities has laid upon me; but for the ten pound he claims, it is not yet due, and I think you may do well to persuade him (as a friend) to put it in the number of his desperate debts, for 'tis a very uncertain one. In all things else, pray say I am his servant. And now, sir, let me tell you that I am extremely glad (whosoever gave you the occasion) to hear from you, since (without compliment) there are very few persons in the world I am more concerned in; to find that you have overcome your long journey, and that you are well and in a place where 'tis possible for me to see you, is such a satisfaction as I, who have not been used to many, may be allowed to doubt of. Yet I will hope my eyes do not deceive me, and that I have not forgot to read; but if you please to confirm it to me by another, you know how to direct it, for I am where I was, still the same, and always

　　　　　　　Your humble servant,

　　　　　　　　　　D. OSBORNE.

For Mrs. Paynter,
　　In Covent Garden.

(Keep this letter till it be called for.)

Letter 3.

January 2nd, 1653.

SIR,—If there were anything in my letter that pleased you I am extremely glad on't, 'twas all due to you, and made it but an equal return for the satisfaction yours gave me. And whatsoever you may believe, I shall never repent the good opinion I have with so much reason taken up. But I forget myself; I meant to chide, and I think this is nothing towards it. Is it possible you came so near me as Bedford and would not see me? Seriously, I should not have believed it from another; would your horse had lost all his legs instead of a hoof, that he might not have been able to carry you further, and you, something that you valued extremely, and could not hope to find anywhere but at Chicksands. I could wish you a thousand little mischances, I am so angry with you; for my life I could not imagine how I had lost you, or why you should call that a silence of six or eight weeks which you intended so much longer. And when I had wearied myself with thinking of all the unpleasing accidents that might cause it, I at length sat down with a resolution to choose the best to believe, which was that at the end of one journey you had begun another (which I had heard you say you intended), and that your haste, or something else, had hindered you from letting me know it. In this

C

ignorance your letter from Breda found me. But for God's sake let me ask you what you have done all this while you have been away; what you have met with in Holland that could keep you there so long; why you went no further; and why I was not to know you went so far? You may do well to satisfy me in all these. I shall so persecute you with questions else, when I see you, that you will be glad to go thither again to avoid me; though when that will be I cannot certainly say, for my father has so small a proportion of health left him since my mother's death, that I am in continual fear of him, and dare not often make use of the leave he gives me to be from home, lest he should at some time want such little services as I am able to lend him. Yet I think to be in London in the next term, and am sure I shall desire it because you are there.

Sir, your humble servant.

Letter 4.—The story of the king who renounced the league with his too fortunate friend is told in the third book of Herodotus. Amasis is the king, and Polycrates the confederate. Dorothy may have read the story in one of the French translations, either that of Pierre Saliat, a cramped duodecimo published in 1580, or that of P. du Ryer, a magnificent folio published in 1646.

My Lord of Holland's daughter, Lady Diana Rich, was one of Dorothy's dearest and most intimate friends. Dorothy had a high opinion of her excel-

lent wit and noble character, which she is never tired
of repeating. We find allusions to her in many of
these letters; she is called "My lady," and her name is
always linked to expressions of tenderness and esteem.
Her father, Henry Rich, Lord Holland, the second son
of the Earl of Warwick, has found place in sterner
history than this. He was concerned in a rising in
1648, when the King was in the Isle of Wight, the object
of which was to rescue and restore the royal prisoner.
This rising, like Sir Thomas Peyton's, miscarried, and
he suffered defeat at Kingston-on-Thames, on July 7th
of that year. He was pursued, taken prisoner, and
kept in the Tower until after the King's execution.
Then he was brought to trial, and, in accordance with
the forms and ceremonies of justice, adjudged to death.
His head was struck off before the gate of Westminster
Hall one cold March morning in the following year, and
by his side died Capel and the Duke of Hamilton.
By marriage he acquired Holland House, Kensington,
which afterwards passed by purchase into the hands of
a very different Lord Holland, and has become famous
among the houses of London. Of his daughter, Lady
Diana, I can learn nothing but that she died unmarried.
She seems to have been of a lively, vivacious tempera-
ment, and very popular with the other sex. There is a
slight clue to her character in the following scrap of
letter-writing still preserved among some old manuscript
papers of the Hutton family. She writes to Mr. Hutton
to escort her in the Park, adding—"This, I am sure, you
will do, because I am a friend to the tobacco-box, and
such, I am sure, Mr. Hutton will have more respect for
than for any other account that could be pretended
unto by

"Your humble servant."

This, with Dorothy's praise, gives us a cheerful opinion of Lady Diana, of whom we must always wish to know more.

January 22nd [1653].

Sir,—Not to confirm you in your belief in dreams, but to avoid your reproaches, I will tell you a pleasant one of mine.   The night before I received your first letter, I dreamt one brought me a packet, and told me it was from you.   I, that remembered you were by your own appointment to be in Italy at that time, asked the messenger where he had it, who told me my lady, your mother, sent him with it to me; then my memory failed me a little, for I forgot you had told me she was dead, and meant to give her many humble thanks if ever I were so happy as to see her. When I had opened the letter I found in it two rings; one was, as I remember, an emerald doublet, but broken in the carriage, I suppose, as it might well be, coming so far; t'other was plain gold, with the longest and the strangest posy that ever was; half on't was Italian, which for my life I could not guess at, though I spent much time about it; the rest was "*there was a Marriage in Cana of Galilee,*" which, though it was Scripture, I had not that reverence for it in my sleep that I should have had, I think, if I had been awake; for in earnest the oddness on't put me into that violent laughing that I waked myself with it; and as a just punishment upon me from that hour to this I could never learn whom those rings were for, nor what was in the letter besides. This is but as extravagant as yours, for it is as likely that your mother should send me letters as that I should make a journey to see poor people hanged, or that your teeth should drop out at this age.

And to remove the opinions you have of my niceness, or being hard to please, let me assure you I am far from desiring my husband should be fond of me at threescore, that I would not have him so at all. 'Tis true I should be glad to have him always kind, and know no reason why he should be wearier of being my master, than he was of being my servant. But it is very possible I may talk ignorantly of marriage; when I come to make sad experiments on it in my own person I shall know more, and say less, for fear of disheartening others (since 'tis no advantage to foreknow a misfortune that cannot be avoided), and for fear of being pitied, which of all things I hate. Lest you should be of the same humour I will not pity you, lame as you are; and to speak truth, if you did like it, you should not have it, for you do not deserve it. Would any one in the world, but you, make such haste for a new cold before the old had left him; in a year, too, when mere colds kill as many as a plague used to do? Well, seriously, either resolve to have more care of yourself, or I renounce my friendship; and as a certain king (that my learned knight is very well acquainted with), who, seeing one of his confederates in so happy a condition as it was not likely to last, sent his ambassador presently to break off the league betwixt them, lest he should be obliged to mourn the change of his fortune if he continued his friend; so I, with a great deal more reason, do declare that I will no longer be a friend to one that's none to himself, nor apprehend the loss of what you hazard every day at tennis. They had served you well enough if they had crammed a dozen ounces of that medicine down your throat to have made you remember a quinzy.

But I have done, and am now at leisure to tell you that it is that daughter of my Lord of Holland (who makes, as you say, so many sore eyes with looking on her) that is here; and if I know her at all, or have any judgment, her beauty is the least of her excellences. And now I speak of her, she has given me the occasion to make a request to you; it will come very seasonably after my chiding, and I have great reason to expect you should be in the humour of doing anything for me. She says that seals are much in fashion, and by showing me some that she has, has set me a-longing for some too; such as are oldest and oddest are most prized, and if you know anybody that is lately come out of Italy, 'tis ten to one but they have a store, for they are very common there. I do remember you once sealed a letter to me with as fine a one as I have seen. It was a

Neptune, I think, riding upon a dolphin; but I'm afraid it was not yours, for I saw it no more. My old Roman head is a present for a prince. If such things come in your way, pray remember me. I am sorry my new carrier makes you rise so early, 'tis not good for your cold; how might we do that you might lie a-bed and yet I have your letter? You must use to write before he comes, I think, that it may be sure to be ready against he goes. In earnest consider on't, and take some course that your health and my letters may be both secured, for the loss of either would be very sensible to

Your humble.

Letter 5.—Sir Justinian is the lover here described. He had four daughters, and it is one of Dorothy's favourite jests to offer Temple a mother-in-law's good word if he will pay court to one of them when she has married the "Emperor."

SIR,—Since you are so easy to please, sure I shall not miss it, and if my idle dreams and thoughts will satisfy you, I am to blame if you want long letters. To begin this, let me tell you I had not forgot you in your absence. I always meant you one of my daughters. You should have had your choice, and, trust me, they say some of them are handsome; but since things did not succeed, I thought to have said nothing on't, lest you should imagine I expected thanks for my good intention, or rather lest you should be too much affected with the thought of what you have lost by my imprudence. It would have been a good strengthening to my Party (as you say); but, in earnest, it was not that I aimed at, I only desired to have it in my power to oblige you; and 'tis certain I had proved a most excellent mother-in-law. Oh, my conscience! we should all have joined against him as the common enemy, for those poor young wenches are as weary of his government as I could have been. He gives them such precepts, as they say my Lord of Dorchester gives his wife, and keeps them so much prisoners to a vile house he has in North-amptonshire, that if but once I had let them loose, they and his learning would have been sufficient to have made him mad without my help; but his good fortune would have it otherwise, to which I will leave him, and proceed to give you some reasons why the other motion was not accepted on. The truth is, I had not that longing to ask a mother-in-law's blessing which you say you should have had, for I knew mine too well to think she could make a good one; besides, I was not so certain of his nature as not to doubt whether she might not corrupt it, nor so confident of his kindness as to assure myself that it would last longer than other people of his age and humour. I am sorry to hear he looks ill, though I think there is no great danger of him. 'Tis but a fit of an ague he has got; that the next charm cures, yet he will be apt to fall into it again upon a new occasion, and one knows not how it may work upon his thin body if it comes too often; it spoiled his beauty, sure, before I knew him, for I could never see it, or else (which is as likely) I do not know it when I see it; besides that, I never look for it in men. It was nothing that I expected made me refuse these, but something that I feared; and, seriously, I find I want courage to marry where I do not like. If we should once come to disputes I know who would have the worst on't, and I have not faith enough to believe a doctrine that is often preach'd, which is, that though at first one has no kindness for *them*, yet it will grow strongly after marriage. Let them trust to it that think good; for my part, I am clearly of opinion (and shall die in't), that, as the more one sees and knows a person that one likes, one has still the more kindness for them, so, on the other side, one is but the more weary of, and the more averse to, an unpleasant humour for having it perpetually by one. And though I easily believe that to marry one for whom we have already some affection will infinitely increase that kindness, yet I shall never be persuaded that marriage has a charm to raise love out of nothing, much less out of dislike.

This is next to telling you what I dreamed and when I rise, but you have promised to be content

with it. I would now, if I could, tell you when
I shall be in town, but I am engaged to my Lady
Diana Rich, my Lord of Holland's daughter (who
lies at a gentlewoman's hard by me for sore eyes),
that I will not leave the country till she does.
She is so much a stranger here, and finds so little
company, that she is glad of mine till her eyes
will give her leave to look out better. They are
mending, and she hopes to be at London before
the end of this next term; and so do I, though
I shall make but a short stay, for all my business
there is at an end when I have seen you, and told
you my stories. And, indeed, my brother is so
perpetually from home, that I can be very little,
unless I would leave my father altogether alone,
which would not be well. We hear of great
disorders at your masks, but no particulars, only
they say the Spanish gravity was much discomposed. I shall expect the relation from you at
your best leisure, and pray give me an account
how my medicine agrees with your cold. This
if you can read it, for 'tis strangely scribbled, will
be enough to answer yours, which is not very
long this week; and I am grown so provident
that I will not lay out more than I receive, but
I am just withal, and therefore you know how to
make mine longer when you please; though, to
speak truth, if I should make this so, you would
hardly have it this week, for 'tis a good while since
'twas call'd for.   Your humble servant.

Letter 6.—The journey that Temple is about to take may be a projected journey with the Swedish Embassy, which was soon to set out. Temple was, apparently, on the look-out for some employment, and we hear at different times of his projected excursions into foreign lands. As a matter of fact, he stayed in and near London until the spring of 1654, when he went to Ireland with his father, who was then reinstated in his office of Master of the Rolls.

Whether the Mr. Grey here written of made love to one or both of the ladies—Jane Seymour and Anne Percy—it is difficult now to say. I have been able to learn nothing more on the subject than Dorothy tells us. This, however, we know for certain, that they both married elsewhere; Lady Jane Seymour, the Duke of Somerset's daughter, marrying Lord Clifford of Lonesborough, the son of the Earl of Burleigh, and living to 1679, when she was buried in Westminster Abbey. Poor Lady Anne Percy, daughter of the Earl of Northumberland, and niece of the faithless Lady Carlisle of whom we read in these letters, was already married at this date to Lord Stanhope, Lord Chesterfield's heir. She died — probably in childbed — in November of next year (1654), and was buried at Petworth with her infant son.

Lady Anne Wentworth was the daughter of the famous and ill-fated Earl of Strafford. She married Lord Rockingham.

The reader will remember that "my lady" is Lady Diana Rich.

March 5th [1653].

SIR,—I know not how to oblige so civil a person as you are more than by giving you the

occasion of serving a fair lady. In sober earnest,
I know you will not think it a trouble to let your
boy deliver these books and this enclosed letter
where it is directed for my lady, whom I would,
the fainest in the world, have you acquainted with,
that you might judge whether I had not reason to
say somebody was to blame. But had you reason
to be displeased that I said a change in you
would be much more pardonable than in him?
Certainly you had not. I spake it very innocently, and out of a great sense how much she
deserves more than anybody else. I shall take
heed though hereafter what I write, since you
are so good at raising doubts to persecute yourself withal, and shall condemn my own easy faith
no more; for me 'tis a better-natured and a less
fault to believe too much than to distrust where
there is no cause. If you were not so apt to
quarrel, I would tell you that I am glad to hear
your journey goes forwarder, but you would
presently imagine that 'tis because I would be
glad if you were gone; need I say that 'tis
because I prefer your interest much before my
own, because I would not have you lose so good
a diversion and so pleasing an entertainment (as
in all likelihood this voyage will be to you), and
because the sooner you go, the sooner I may
hope for your return. If it be necessary, I will
confess all this, and something more, which is,
that notwithstanding all my gallantry and resolu-

tion, 'tis much for my credit that my courage is put to no greater a trial than parting with you at this distance. But you are not going yet neither, and therefore we'll leave the discourse on't till then, if you please, for I find no great entertainment in't. And let me ask you whether it be possible that Mr. Grey makes love, they say he does, to my Lady Jane Seymour? If it were expected that one should give a reason for their passions, what could he say for himself? He would not offer, sure, to make us believe my Lady Jane a lovelier person than my Lady Anne Percy. I did not think I should have lived to have seen his frozen heart melted, 'tis the greatest conquest she will ever make; may it be happy to her, but in my opinion he has not a good-natured look. The younger brother was a servant, a great while, to my fair neighbour, but could not be received; and in earnest I could not blame her. I was his confidante and heard him make his addresses; not that I brag of the favour he did me, for anybody might have been so that had been as often there, and he was less scrupulous in that point than one would have been that had had less reason. But in my life I never heard a man say more, nor less to the purpose; and if his brother have not a better gift in courtship, he will owe my lady's favour to his fortune rather than to his address. My Lady Anne Wentworth I hear is marrying, but

I cannot learn to whom; nor is it easy to guess
who is worthy of her. In my judgment she is,
without dispute, the finest lady I know (one
always excepted); not that she is at all handsome, but infinitely virtuous and discreet, of a
sober and very different humour from most of
the young people of these times, but has as
much wit and is as good company as anybody
that ever I saw. What would you give that I
had but the wit to know when to make an end
of my letters? Never anybody was persecuted
with such long epistles; but you will pardon my
unwillingness to leave you, and notwithstanding
all your little doubts, believe that I am very
much

Your faithful friend

and humble servant,

D. Osborne.

Letter 7. — There seem to have been two carriers
bringing letters to Dorothy at this time, Harrold and
Collins; we hear something of each of them in the
following letters. Those who have seen the present-
day carriers in some unawakened market-place in the
Midlands, — heavy, rumbling, two-horse cars of huge
capacity, whose three miles an hour is fast becoming
too sluggish for their enfranchised clients; those who
have jolted over the frozen ruts of a fen road, behind
their comfortable Flemish horses, and heard the gossip
of the farmers and their wives, the grunts of the
discontented baggage pig, and the encouraging shouts
of the carrier; those, in a word, who have travelled

in a Lincolnshire carrier's cart, have, I fancy, a more correct idea of Dorothy's postmen and their conveyances than any I could quote from authority or draw from imagination.

Lord Lisle was the son of Robert Sidney, Earl of Leicester, and brother of the famous Algernon. He sat in the Long Parliament for Yarmouth, in the Isle of Wight, and afterwards became a member of the Upper House. Concerning his embassage to Sweden this is again proposed to him in September 1653, but, as we read in the minutes of the Council, "when he was desired to proceed, finding himself out of health, he desired to be excused, whereupon Council still wishing to send the embassy—the Queen of Sweden being favourably inclined to the Commonwealth — pitched upon Lord Whitelocke, who was willing to go."

To Lady Sunderland and Mr. Smith there are several amusing references in these letters. Lady Sunderland was the daughter of the Earl of Leicester, and sister of Algernon Sydney. She was born in 1620, and at the age of nineteen married Henry Lord Spencer, who was killed in the battle of Newbury in 1642. After her husband's death, she retired to Brington in Northamptonshire, until, wearied with the heavy load of housekeeping, she came to live with her father and mother at Penshurst. In the Earl of Leicester's journal, under date Thursday, July 8th, 1652, we find :—"My daughter Spencer was married to Sir Robert Smith at Penshurst, my wife being present with my daughters Strangford, and Lacy Pelham, Algernon and Robin Sydney, etc. ; but I was in London." From this we may imagine the Earl did not greatly approve the match. The ubiquitous Evelyn was there, too, to see "ye marriage of my old fellow collegian Mr. Robt. Smith ;" and the place being full of company, he probably enjoyed himself vastly. Lady Sunderland was the Sacharissa of Waller the poet.

SIR,—I am so great a lover of my bed myself that I can easily apprehend the trouble of rising at four o'clock these cold mornings. In earnest, I'm troubled that you should be put to it, and have chid the carrier for coming out so soon; he swears to me he never comes out of town before eleven o'clock, and that my Lady Paynter's footman (as he calls him) brings her letters two hours sooner than he needs to do. I told him he was gone one day before the letter came; he vows he was not, and that your old friend Collins never brought letters of my Lady Paynter's in his life; and, to speak truth, Collins did not bring me that letter. I had it from this Harrold two hours before Collins came. Yet it is possible all that he says may not be so, for I have known better men than he lie; therefore if Collins be more for your ease or conveniency, make use of him hereafter. I know not whether my letter were kind or not, but I'll swear yours was not, and am sure mine was meant to be so. It is not kind in you to desire an increase of my friendship; that is to doubt it is not as great already as it can be, than which you cannot do me a greater injury. 'Tis my misfortune indeed that it lies not in my power to give

you better testimony on't than words, otherwise
I should soon convince you that 'tis the best
quality I have, and that where I own a friendship, I mean so perfect a one, as time can neither
lessen nor increase. If I said nothing of my
coming to town, 'twas because I had nothing
to say that I thought you would like to hear.
For I do not know that ever I desired anything
earnestly in my life, but 'twas denied me, and I
am many times afraid to wish a thing merely lest
my Fortune should take that occasion to use me
ill. She cannot see, and therefore I may venture
to write that I intend to be in London if
it be possible on Friday or Saturday come
sennight. Be sure you do not read it aloud,
lest she hear it, and prevent me, or drive you
away before I come. It is so like my luck,
too, that you should be going I know not whither
again; but trust me, I have looked for it ever
since I heard you were come home. You will
laugh, sure, when I shall tell you that hearing
that my Lord Lisle was to go ambassador into
Sweden, I remember'd your father's acquaintance
in that family with an apprehension that he might
be in the humour of sending you with him. But
for God's sake whither is it that you go? I
would not willingly be at such a loss again as
I was after your Yorkshire journey. If it prove
as long a one, I shall not forget you; but in
earnest I shall be so possessed with a strong

splenetic fancy that I shall never see you more
in this world, as all the waters in England will
not cure. Well, this is· a sad story; we'll have
no more on't.

I humbly thank you for your offer of your
head; but if you were an emperor, I should not
be so bold with you as to claim your promise;
you might find twenty better employments for't.
Only with your gracious leave, I think I should
be a little exalted with remembering that you
had been once my friend; 'twould more endanger
my growing proud than being Sir Justinian's
mistress, and yet he thought me pretty well
inclin'd to't then. Lord! what would I give
that I had a Latin letter of his for you, that
he writ to a great friend at Oxford, where he
gives him a long and learned character of me;
'twould serve you to laugh at this seven years.
If I remember what was told me on't, the
worst of my faults was a height (he would not
call it pride) that was, as he had heard, the
humour of my family; and the best of my com-
mendations was, that I was capable of being
company and conversation for him. But you
do not tell me yet how you found him out. If
I had gone about to conceal him, I had been
sweetly serv'd. I shall take heed of you hereafter; because there is no very great likelihood
of your being an emperor, or that, if you were, I
should have your head.

I have sent into Italy for seals; 'tis to be hoped by that time mine come over, they may be of fashion again, for 'tis an humour that your old acquaintance Mr. Smith and his lady have brought up; they say she wears twenty strung upon a ribbon, like the nuts boys play withal, and I do not hear of anything else. Mr. Howard presented his mistress but a dozen such seals as are not to be valued as times now go. But *à propos* of Monsr. Smith, what a scape has he made of my Lady Barbury; and who would e'er have dreamt he should have had my Lady Sunderland, though he be a very fine gentleman, and does more than deserve her. I think I shall never forgive her one thing she said of him, which was that she married him out of pity; it was the pitifullest saying that ever I heard, and made him so contemptible that I should not have married him for that reason. This is a strange letter, sure, I have not time to read it over, but I have said anything that came into my head to put you out of your dumps. For God's sake be in better humour, and assure yourself I am as much as you can wish,

Your faithful friend and servant.

Letter 8. — The name of Algernon Sydney occurs more than once in these pages, and it is therefore only right to remind the reader of some of the leading facts in his life. He was born in 1622, and was the second son of Robert Earl of Leicester. He was educated in

Paris and Italy, and first served in the army in Ireland.
On his recall to England he espoused the popular
cause, and fought on that side in the battle of Marston
Moor.   In 1651 he was elected a member of the
Council of State, and in this situation he continued to
act until 1653.   It is unnecessary to mention his
republican sympathies, and after the dismissal of the
Parliament, his future actions concern us but little.
He was arrested, tried, and executed in 1683, on
the pretence of being concerned in the Rye House
Plot.

Arundel Howard was Henry, second son of the Earl
of Arundel.   His father died July 12, 1652.   Dorothy
would call him Arundel Howard, to distinguish him
from the Earl of Berkshire's family.

SIR,—You have made me so rich as I am able
to help my neighbours.   There is a little head
cut in an onyx that I take to be a very good one,
and the dolphin is (as you say) the better for
being cut less; the oddness of the figures makes
the beauty of these things.   If you saw one that
my brother sent my Lady Diana last week, you
would believe it were meant to fright people
withal; 'twas brought out of the Indies, and cut
there for an idol's head : they took the devil himself for their pattern that did it, for in my life I
never saw so ugly a thing, and yet she is as fond
on't as if it were as lovely as she herself is.   Her
eyes have not the flames they have had, nor is
she like (I am afraid) to recover them here; but
were they irrecoverably lost, the beauty of her

mind were enough to make her outshine everybody else, and she would still be courted by all
that knew how to value her, like *la belle aveugle* that
was Philip the 2nd of France his mistress. I am
wholly ignorant of the story you mention, and am
confident you are not well inform'd, for 'tis impossible she should ever have done anything that
were unhandsome. If I knew who the person
were that is concern'd in't, she allows me so
much freedom with her, that I could easily put
her upon the discourse, and I do not think she
would use much of disguise in it towards me. I
should have guessed it Algernon Sydney, but
that I cannot see in him that likelihood of a
fortune which you seem to imply by saying 'tis
not present. But if you should mean by that,
that 'tis possible his wit and good parts may raise
him to one, you must pardon if I am not of your
opinion, for I do not think these are times for
anybody to expect preferment in that deserves
it, and in the best 'twas ever too uncertain for a
wise body to trust to. But I am altogether of
your mind, that my Lady Sunderland is not to be
followed in her marrying fashion, and that Mr.
Smith never appear'd less her servant than in
desiring it; to speak truth, it was convenient for
neither of them, and in meaner people had been
plain undoing one another, which I cannot understand to be kindness of either side. She has lost
by it much of the repute she had gained by

keeping herself a widow; it was then believed that wit and discretion were to be reconciled in her person that have so seldom been persuaded to meet in anybody else. But we are all mortal.

I did not mean that Howard. 'Twas Arundel Howard. And the seals were some remainders that showed his father's love to antiquities, and therefore cost him dear enough if that would make them good. I am sorry I cannot follow your counsel in keeping fair with Fortune. I am not apt to suspect without just cause, but in earnest if I once find anybody faulty towards me, they lose me for ever; I have forsworn being twice deceived by the same person. For God's sake do not say she has the spleen, I shall hate it worse than ever I did, nor that it is a disease of the wits, I shall think you abuse me, for then I am sure it would not be mine; but were it certain that they went together always, I dare swear there is nobody so proud of their wit as to keep it upon such terms, but would be glad after they had endured it a while to let them both go as they came. I know nothing yet that is likely to alter my resolution of being in town on Saturday next; but I am uncertain where I shall be, and therefore it will be best that I send you word when I am there. I should be glad to see you sooner, but that I do not know myself what company I may have with me. I meant this letter longer when I begun it, but an extreme cold that I have taken lies so in my head, and makes it ache so violently, that I hardly see what I do. I'll e'en to bed as soon as I have told you that I am very much

Your faithful friend

and servant,

D. OSBORNE.

CHAPTER III.

LIFE AT CHICKSANDS. 1653.

Letter 9.—Temple's sister here mentioned was his only sister Martha, who married Sir Thomas Giffard in 1662, and was left a widow within two months of her marriage. She afterwards lived with Temple and his wife, was a great favourite with them, and their confidential friend. Lady Giffard has left a manuscript life of her brother from which the historian Courtenay deigned to extract some information, whereby we in turn have benefited. She outlived both her brother and his wife, to carry on a warlike encounter with her brother's amanuensis, Mr. Jonathan Swift, over Temple's literary remains. Esther Johnson, the unfortunate Stella, was Lady Giffard's maid.

Cléopâtre and *Le Grand Cyrus* appear to have been Dorothy's literary companions at this date. She would read these in the original French; and, as she tells us somewhere, had a scorn of translations. Both these romances were much admired, even by people of taste; a thing difficult to understand, until we remember that Fielding, the first and greatest English novelist, was yet unborn, and novels, as we know them, non-existing. Both the romances found translators; *Cyrus*, in one mysterious F. G. *Gent*—the translation was published in this year; *Cléopâtre*, in Richard Loveday, an elegant letter-writer of this time.

Artamenes, or *Le Grand Cyrus*, the masterpiece of Mademoiselle Madeleine de Scudéri, is contained in no less than ten volumes, each of which in its turn has many books; it is, in fact, more a collection of romances than a single romance. *La Cléopâtre*, a similar work, was originally published in twenty-three volumes of twelve parts, each part containing three or four books. It is but a collection of short stories. Its author rejoiced in the romantic title of Gauthier de Costes Chevalier Seigneur de la Calprenede; he published *Cléopâtre* in 1642; he was the author of other romances, and some tragedies, noted only for their worthlessness. Even Richelieu, "quoiqu' admirateur indulgent de la médiocrité," could not stand Calprenede's tragedies. *Reine Marguerite* is probably the translation by Robert Codrington of the Memorials of Margaret of Valois, first wife of Henri IV. Bussy is a servant of the Duke of Avenson, Margaret's brother, with whom Margaret is very intimate.

Of Lady Sunderland and Mr. Smith we have already sufficient knowledge. As for Sir Justinian, we are not to think he was already married; the reference to his "new wife" is merely jocular, meaning his new wife when he shall get one; for Sir Justinian is still wife-hunting, and comes back to renew his suit with Dorothy after this date. "Your fellow-servant," who is as often called Jane, appears to have been a friend and companion of Dorothy, in a somewhat lower rank of life. Mrs. Goldsmith, mentioned in a subsequent letter,— wife of Daniel Goldsmith, the rector of Campton, in which parish Chicksands was situated, — acted as chaperon or duenna companion to Dorothy, and Jane was, it seems to me, in a similar position; only, being a younger woman than the rector's wife, she was more the companion and less the duenna. The servants and companions of ladies of that date were themselves gentlewomen of good breeding. Waller writes verses to Mrs. Braughton, servant to Sacharissa, commencing his lines, " Fair fellow-servant." Temple, had he written verse to his mistress, would probably have left us some " Lines to Jane."

There is in Campton Church a tablet erected to Daniel Goldsmith, " Ecclesiæ de Campton Pastor idem et Patronus;" also to Maria Goldsmith, " uxor dilec-tissima." This is erected by Maria's faithful sister, Jane Wright; and if the astute reader shall think fit to agree with me in believing Temple's " fellow-servant" to be this Jane Wright on such slender evidence and slight thread of argument, he may well do so. Failing this, all search after Jane will, I fear, prove futile at this distant date. There are constant references to Jane in the letters. " Her old woman," in the same passage, is, of course, a jocular allusion to Dorothy herself; and " the old knight" is, I believe, Sir Robert Cook, a Bedfordshire gentleman, of whom nothing is known except that he was knighted at Ampthill, July 21st, 1621. We hear some little more of him from Dorothy.

Note well the signature of this and following letters; it will help us to discover what passed between the friends in London. For my own part, I do not think Dorothy means that she has ceased to be *faithful* in that she has become " his *affectionate* friend and servant."

SIR,—I was so kind as to write to you by the coachman, and let me tell you I think 'twas the greatest testimony of my friendship that I could give you; for, trust me, I was so tired with my journey, so *dowd* with my cold, and so out of humour with our parting, that I should have done it with great unwillingness to anybody else. I lay abed all next day to recover myself, and rised a Thursday to receive your letter with the more ceremony. I found no fault with the ill writing, 'twas but too easy to read, methought, for I am sure I had done much sooner than I could have wished. But, in earnest, I was heartily troubled to find you in so much disorder. I would not have you so kind to me as to be cruel to yourself, in whom I am more concerned. No; for God's sake, let us not make afflictions of such things as these; I am afraid we shall meet with too many real ones.

I am glad your journey holds, because I think 'twill be a good diversion for you this summer; but I admire your father's patience, that lets you rest with so much indifference when there is such a fortune offered. I'll swear I have great scruples of conscience myself on the point, and am much afraid I am not your friend if I am any part of the occasion that hinders you from accepting it. Yet I am sure my intentions towards you are very innocent and good, for you are one of those whose interests I shall ever prefer much above my own; and you are not to thank me for it, since, to speak truth, I secure my own by it; for I defy my ill fortune to make me miserable, unless she does it in the persons of my friends. I wonder how your father came to know I was in town, unless my old friend, your cousin Hammond, should tell him. Pray, for my sake, be a very obedient son; all your faults will be laid to my charge else, and, alas! I have too many of my own.

You say nothing how your sister does, which makes me hope there is no more of danger in her sickness. Pray, when it may be no trouble to her, tell her how much I am her servant; and have a care of yourself this cold weather. I have read your *Reine Marguerite*, and will return it you when you please. If you will have my opinion of her, I think she had a good deal of wit, and a great deal of patience for a woman of so high a spirit. She speaks with too much indifference of her husband's several amours, and commends Bussy as if she were a little concerned in him. I think her a better sister than a wife, and believe she might have made a better wife to a better husband. But the story of Mademoiselle de Tournon is so sad, that when I had read it I was able to go no further, and was fain to take up something else to divert myself withal. Have you read *Cléopâtre?* I have six tomes on't here that I can lend you if you have not; there are some stories in't you will like, I believe. But what an ass am I to think you can be idle enough at London to read romance! No, I'll keep them till you come hither; here they may be welcome to you for want of better company. Yet, that you may not imagine we are quite out of the world here, and so be frighted from coming, I can assure you we are seldom without news, such as it is; and at this present we do abound with stories of my Lady Sunderland and Mr. Smith; with what reverence he approaches her, and how like a gracious princess she receives him, that they say 'tis worth one's going twenty miles to see it. All our ladies are mightily pleased with the example, but I do not find that the men intend to follow it, and I'll undertake Sir Solomon Justinian wishes her in the Indias, for fear she should pervert his new wife.

Your fellow-servant kisses your hands, and says, "If you mean to make love to her old woman this is the best time you can take, for she is dying; this cold weather kills her, I think." It has undone me, I am sure, in killing an old knight that I have been waiting for this seven year, and now he dies and will leave me nothing, I believe, but leaves a rich widow for somebody. I think you had best come awooing to her; I have a good interest in her, and it shall be all employed in your service if you think fit to make any addresses there. But to be sober now again, for God's sake send me word how your journey goes forward, when you think you shall begin it, and how long it may last, when I may expect your coming this way; and of all things, remember to provide a safe address for your letters when you are abroad.

This is a strange, confused one, I believe; for I have been called away twenty times, since I sat down to write it, to my father, who is not well; but you will pardon it—we are past ceremony, and excuse me if I say no more now but that I am *toujours le mesme*, that is, ever

Your affectionate
friend and servant.

Letter 10.—Dorothy is suffering from *the spleen*, a disease as common to-day as then, though we have lost the good name for it. This and the ague plague her continually. My Lord Lisle's proposed embassy to Sweden is, we see, still delayed; ultimately Bulstrode Whitelocke is chosen ambassador.

Dorothy's cousin Molle, here mentioned, seems to have been an old bachelor, who spent his time at one country house or another, visiting his country friends; and playing the bore not a little, I should fear, with his gossip and imaginary ailments.

Temple's father was at this time trying to arrange a match for him with a certain Mrs. Ch. as Dorothy calls her. Courtenay thinks she may be one Mistress Chambers, an heiress, who ultimately married Temple's brother John, and this conjecture is here followed.

SIR,—Your last letter came like a pardon to one upon the block. I had given over the hopes on't, having received my letters by the other carrier, who was always [wont] to be last. The loss put me hugely out of order, and you would have both pitied and laughed at me if you could

have seen how woodenly I entertained the widow,
who came hither the day before, and surprised
me very much. Not being able to say anything,
I got her to cards, and there with a great deal
of patience lost my money to her;—or rather I
gave it as my ransom. In the midst of our play,
in comes my blessed boy with your letter, and,
in earnest, I was not able to disguise the joy it
gave me, though one was by that is not much
your friend, and took notice of a blush that for
my life I could not keep back. I put up the
letter in my pocket, and made what haste I could
to lose the money I had left, that I might take
occasion to go fetch some more; but I did not
make such haste back again, I can assure you. I
took time enough to have coined myself some
money if I had had the art on't, and left my brother
enough to make all his addresses to her if he
were so disposed. I know not whether he was
pleased or not, but I am sure I was.

You make so reasonable demands that 'tis not
fit you should be denied. You ask my thoughts·
but at one hour; you will think me bountiful, I
hope, when I shall tell you that I know no hour
when you have them not. No, in earnest, my
very dreams are yours, and I have got such a
habit of thinking of you that any other thought
intrudes and proves uneasy to me. I drink
your health every morning in a drench that would
poison a horse I believe, and 'tis the only way

I have to persuade myself to take it. 'Tis the infusion of steel, and makes me so horridly sick, that every day at ten o'clock I am making my will and taking leave of all my friends. You will believe you are not forgot then. They tell me I must take this ugly drink a fortnight, and then begin another as bad; but unless you say so too, I do not think I shall. 'Tis worse than dying by the half.

I am glad your father is so kind to you. I shall not dispute it with him, because it is much more in his power than in mine, but I shall never yield that 'tis more in his desire, since he was much pleased with that which was a truth when you told it him, but would have been none if he had asked the question sooner. He thought there was no danger of you since you were more ignorant and less concerned in my being in town than he. If I were Mrs. Chambers, he would be more my friend; but, however, I am much his servant as he is your father. I have sent you your book. And since you are at leisure to consider the moon, you may be enough to read *Cléopâtre*, therefore I have sent you three tomes; when you have done with these you shall have the rest, and I believe they will please. There is a story of Artemise that I will recommend to you; her disposition I like extremely, it has a great deal of practical wit; and if you meet with one Brittomart, pray send me word how you like him.

I am not displeased that my Lord [Lisle] makes no more haste, for though I am very willing you should go the journey for many reasons, yet two or three months hence, sure, will be soon enough to visit so cold a country, and I would not have you endure two winters in one year. Besides, I look for my eldest brother and cousin Molle here shortly, and I should be glad to have nobody to entertain but you, whilst you are here. Lord! that you had the invisible ring, or Fortunatus his wishing hat; now, at this instant, you should be here.

My brother has gone to wait upon the widow homewards,—she that was born to persecute you and I, I think. She has so tired me with being here but two days, that I do not think I shall accept of the offer she made me of living with her in case my father dies before I have disposed of myself. Yet we are very great friends, and for my comfort she says she will come again about the latter end of June and stay longer with me. My aunt is still in town, kept by her business, which I am afraid will not go well, they do so delay it; and my precious uncle does so visit her, and is so kind, that without doubt some mischief will follow. Do you know his son, my cousin Harry? 'Tis a handsome youth, and well-natured, but such a goose; and she has bred him so strangely, that he needs all his ten thousand a year. I would fain have him marry my Lady

E

Diana, she was his mistress when he was a boy.
He had more wit then than he has now, I think,
and I have less wit than he, sure, for spending my
paper upon him when I have so little.   Here is
hardly room for

Your affectionate
friend and servant.

Letter 11.—It is a curious thing to find the Lord
General's son among our loyal Dorothy's servants; and
to find, moreover, that he will be as acceptable to
Dorothy as any other, if she may not marry Temple.
Henry Cromwell was Oliver Cromwell's second son.
How Dorothy became acquainted with him it is impossible to say.   Perhaps they met in France.   He seems
to have been entirely unlike his father.   Good Mrs.
Hutchinson calls him " a debauched ungodly Cavalier,"
with other similar expressions of Presbyterian abhor-
rence; from which we need not draw any unkinder conclusion than that he was no solemn puritanical soldier,
but a man of the world, brighter and more courteous
than the frequenters of his father's Council, and therefore more acceptable to Dorothy.   He was born at
Huntingdon in 1627, the year of Dorothy's birth.   He
was captain under Harrison in 1647; colonel in Ireland
with his father in 1649; and married at Kensington
Church, on May 10th, 1653, to Elizabeth, daughter of
Sir Francis Russell of Chippenham, Cambridgeshire.
He was made Lord-Deputy in Ireland in 1657, but he
wearied of the work of transplanting the Irish and
planting the new settlers, which, he writes, only brought
him disquiet of body and mind.   This led to his retirement from public life in 1658.   Two years afterwards, at

the Restoration, he came to live at Spinney Abbey, near Isham, Cambridgeshire, and died on the 23rd of March 1673. These are shortly the facts which remain to us of the life of Henry Cromwell, Dorothy's favoured servant.

SIR,—I am so far from thinking you ill-natured for wishing I might not outlive you, that I should not have thought you at all kind if you had done otherwise; no, in earnest, I was never yet so in love with my life but that I could have parted with it upon a much less occasion than your death, and 'twill be no compliment to you to say it would be very uneasy to me then, since 'tis not very pleasant to me now. Yet you will say I take great pains to preserve it, as ill as I like it; but no, I'll swear 'tis not that I intend in what I do; all that I aim at is but to keep myself from proving a beast. They do so fright me with strange stories of what the spleen will bring me to in time, that I am kept in awe with them like a child; they tell me 'twill not leave me common sense, that I shall hardly be fit company for my own dogs, and that it will end either in a stupidness that will make me incapable of anything, or fill my head with such whims as will make me ridiculous. To prevent this, who would not take steel or anything,—though I am partly of your opinion that 'tis an ill kind of physic. Yet I am confident that I take it the safest way, for I do not take the powder, as many do, but only lay a piece of steel in white wine over night and drink the infusion next morning, which one would think were nothing, and yet 'tis not to be imagined how sick it makes me for an hour or two, and, which is the misery, all that time one must be using some kind of exercise. Your fellow-servant has a blessed time on't that ever you saw. I make her play at shuttlecock with me, and she is the veriest bungler at it ever you saw. Then am I ready to beat her with the battledore, and grow so peevish as I grow sick, that I'll undertake she wishes there were no steel in England. But then to recompense the morning, I am in good humour all the day after for joy that I am well again. I am told 'twill do me good, and am content to believe it; if it does not, I am but where I was.

I do not use to forget my old acquaintances. Almanzor is as fresh in my memory as if I had visited his tomb but yesterday, though it be at least seven year agone since. You will believe I had not been used to great afflictions when I made his story such a one to me, as I cried an hour together for him, and was so angry with Alcidiana that for my life I could never love her after it. You do not tell me whether you received the books I sent you, but I will hope you did, because you say nothing to the contrary. They are my dear Lady Diana's, and therefore I am much concerned that they should be safe. And now I speak of her, she is acquainted with your aunt, my

Lady B., and says all that you say of her. If her niece has so much wit, will you not be persuaded to like her; or say she has not quite so much, may not her fortune make it up? In earnest, I know not what to say, but if your father does not use all his kindness and all his power to make you consider your own advantage, he is not like other fathers. Can you imagine that he that demands £5000 besides the reversion of an estate will like bare £4000? Such miracles are seldom seen, and you must prepare to suffer a strange persecution unless you grow conformable; therefore consider what you do, 'tis the part of a friend to advise you. I could say a great deal to this purpose, and tell you that 'tis not discreet to refuse a good offer, nor safe to trust wholly to your own judgment in your disposal. I was never better provided in my life for a grave admonishing discourse. Would you had heard how I have been catechized for you, and seen how soberly I sit and answer to interrogatories. Would you think that upon examination it is found that you are not an indifferent person to me? But the mischief is, that what my intentions or resolutions are, is not to be discovered, though much pains has been taken to collect all scattering circumstances; and all the probable conjectures that can be raised from thence has been urged, to see if anything would be confessed. And all this done with so much ceremony and

compliment, so many pardons asked for undertaking to counsel or inquire, and so great kindness and passion for all my interests professed,
that I cannot but take it well, though I am very
weary on't.   You are spoken of with the reverence
due to a person that I seem to like, and for as
much as they know of you, you do deserve a very
good esteem; but your fortune and mine can
never agree, and, in plain terms, we forfeit our
discretions and run wilfully upon our own ruins if
there be such a thought.   To all this I make no
reply, but that if they will needs have it that I
am not without kindness for you, they must conclude withal that 'tis no part of my intention to
ruin you, and so the conference breaks up for that
time.   All this is [from] my friend, that is not
yours; and the gentleman that came up-stairs in
a basket, I could tell him that he spends his
breath to very little purpose, and has but his
labour for his pains.   Without his precepts my
own judgment would preserve me from doing
anything that might be prejudicial to you or
unjustifiable to the world; but if these be secured,
nothing can alter the resolution I have taken of
settling my whole stock of happiness upon the
affection of a person that is dear to me, whose
kindness I shall infinitely prefer before any other
consideration whatsoever, and I shall not blush to
tell you that you have made the whole world
besides so indifferent to me that, if I cannot be

yours, they may dispose of me how they please. Henry Cromwell will be as acceptable to me as any one else. If I may undertake to counsel, I think you shall do well to comply with your father as far as possible, and not to discover any aversion to what he desires further than you can give reason for. What his disposition may be I know not; but 'tis that of many parents to judge their children's dislikes to be an humour of approving nothing that is chosen for them, which many times makes them take up another of denying their children all they choose for themselves. I find I am in the humour of talking wisely if my paper would give me leave. 'Tis great pity here is room for no more but—

Your faithful friend and servant.

Letter 12.

Sir,—There shall be two posts this week, for my brother sends his groom up, and I am resolved to make some advantage of it. Pray, what the paper denied me in your last, let me receive by him. Your fellow-servant is a sweet jewel to tell tales of me. The truth is, I cannot deny but that I have been very careless of myself, but, alas! who would have been other? I never thought my life worth my care whilst nobody was concerned in't but myself; now I shall look upon't as something that you would

not lose, and therefore shall endeavour to keep
it for you.   But then you must return my kindness with the same care of a life that's much
dearer to me.   I shall not be so unreasonable as
to desire that, for my satisfaction, you should
deny yourself a recreation that is pleasing to you,
and very innocent, sure, when 'tis not used in
excess, but I cannot consent you should disorder
yourself with it, and Jane was certainly in the
right when she told you I would have chid if I
had seen you so endanger a health that I am so
much concerned in.   But for what she tell you
of my melancholy you must not believe; she
thinks nobody in good humour unless they laugh
perpetually, as Nan and she does, which I was
never given to much, and now I have been so
long accustomed to my own natural dull humour
that nothing can alter it.   'Tis not that I am sad
(for as long as you and the rest of my friends are
well), I thank God I have no occasion to be so,
but I never appear to be very merry, and if I had
all that I could wish for in the world, I do not
think it would make any visible change in my
humour.   And yet with all my gravity I could
not but laugh at your encounter in the Park,
though I was not pleased that you should leave
a fair lady and go lie upon the cold ground.
That is full as bad as overheating yourself at
tennis, and therefore remember 'tis one of the
things you are forbidden.   You have reason to

think your father kind, and I have reason to think him very civil; all his scruples are very just ones, but such as time and a little good fortune (if we were either of us lucky to it) might satisfy. He may be confident I can never think of disposing myself without my father's consent; and though he has left it more in my power than almost anybody leaves a daughter, yet certainly I were the worst natured person in the world if his kindness were not a greater tie upon me than any advantage he could have reserved. Besides that, 'tis my duty, from which nothing can ever tempt me, nor could you like it in me if I should do otherwise, 'twould make me unworthy of your esteem; but if ever that may be obtained, or I left free, and you in the same condition, all the advantages of fortune or person imaginable met together in one man should not be preferred before you. I think I cannot leave you better than with this assurance. 'Tis very late, and having been abroad all this day, I knew not till e'en now of this messenger. Good-night to you. There need be no excuse for the conclusion of your letter. Nothing can please me better. Once more good-night. I am half in a dream already.

Your

Letter 13.—There is some allusion here to an inconstant lover of my Lady Diana Rich, who seems to have deserted his mistress on account of the sore eyes with which, Dorothy told us in a former letter, her friend was afflicted.

I cannot find any account of the great shop above the Exchange, " The Flower Pott." There were two or three "Flower Pots" in London at this time, one in Leadenhall Street and another in St. James' Market. An interesting account of the old sign is given in a work on London tradesmen's tokens, in which it is said to be " derived from the earlier representations of the salutations of the angel Gabriel to the Virgin Mary, in which either lilies were placed in his hand, or they were set as an accessory in a vase. As Popery declined, the angel disappeared, and the lily-pot became a vase of flowers; subsequently the Virgin was omitted, and there remained only the vase of flowers. Since, to make things more unmistakeable, two debonair gentlemen, with hat in hand, have superseded the floral elegancies of the olden time, and the poetry of the art seems lost."

SIR,—I am glad you 'scaped a beating, but, in earnest, would it had lighted on my brother's groom. I think I should have beaten him myself if I had been able. I have expected your letter all this day with the greatest impatience that was possible, and at last resolved to go out and meet the fellow; and when I came down to the stables, I found him come, had set up his horse, and was sweeping the stable in great order. I could not imagine him so very a beast as to think his horses were to be serv'd before me, and therefore was presently struck with an apprehension he had no

letter for me: it went cold to my heart as ice, and
hardly left me courage enough to ask him the
question; but when he had drawled it out that he
thought there was a letter for me in his bag, I
quickly made him leave his broom. 'Twas well
'tis a dull fellow, he could not [but] have discern'd
else that I was strangely overjoyed with it, and
earnest to have it; for though the poor fellow
made what haste he could to untie his bag, I did
nothing but chide him for being so slow. Last
I had it, and, in earnest, I know not whether an
entire diamond of the bigness on't would have
pleased me half so well; if it would, it must be
only out of this consideration, that such a jewel
would make me rich enough to dispute you with
Mrs. Chambers, and perhaps make your father
like me as well. I like him, I'll swear, and
extremely too, for being so calm in a business
where his desires were so much crossed. Either
he has a great power over himself, or you have
a great interest in him, or both. If you are
pleased it should end thus, I cannot dislike it; but
if it would have been happy for you, I should
think myself strangely unfortunate in being the
cause that it went not further. I cannot say that
I prefer your interest before my own, because all
yours are so much mine that 'tis impossible for
me to be happy if you are not so; but if they
could be divided I am certain I should. And
though you reproached me with unkindness for

advising you not to refuse a good offer, yet I
shall not be discouraged from doing it again when
there is occasion, for I am resolved to be your
friend whether you will or no.   And, for example,
though I know you do not need my counsel, yet
I cannot but tell you that I think 'twere very well
that you took some care to make my Lady B.
your friend, and oblige her by your civilities to
believe that you were sensible of the favour was
offered you, though you had not the grace to
make good use on't.   In very good earnest now,
she is a woman (by all that I have heard of her)
that one would not lose; besides that, 'twill become you to make some satisfaction for downright
refusing a young lady—'twas unmercifully done.

Would to God you would leave that trick of
making excuses!   Can you think it necessary to
me, or believe that your letters can be so long as
to make them unpleasing to me?   Are mine so to
you?   If they are not, yours never will be so to me.
You see I say anything to you, out of a belief that,
though my letters were more impertinent than they
are, you would not be without them nor wish them
shorter.   Why should you be less kind?   If your
fellow-servant has been with you, she has told you
I part with her but for her advantage.   That I
shall always be willing to do; but whensoever she
shall think fit to serve again, and is not provided
of a better mistress, she knows where to find me.

I have sent you the rest of *Cléopâtre*, pray keep

them all in your hands, and the next week I will
send you a letter and directions where you shall
deliver that and the books for my làdy. Is it
possible that she can be indifferent to anybody ?
Take heed of telling me such stories ; if all those
excellences she is rich in cannot keep warm a
passion without the sunshine of her eyes, what
are poor people to expect ; and were it not a
strange vanity in me to believe yours can be long-
lived ? It would be very pardonable in you to
change, but, sure, in him 'tis a mark of so great
inconstancy as shows him of an humour that
nothing can fix. When you go into the Exchange, pray call at the great shop above, " The
Flower Pott." I spoke to Heams, the man of
the shop, when I was in town, for a quart of
orange-flower water ; he had none that was good
then, but promised to get me some. Pray put
him in mind of it, and let him show it you before
he sends it me, for I will not altogether trust to
his honesty ; you see I make no scruple of giving
you little idle commissions, 'tis a freedom you
allow me, and that I should be glad you would
take. The Frenchman that set my seals lives
between Salisbury House and the Exchange, at
a house that was not finished when I was there,
and the master of the shop, his name is Walker,
he made me pay 50s. for three, but twas too
dear. You will meet with a story in these parts
of *Cléopâtre* that pleased me more than any that

ever I read in my life; 'tis of one Délie, pray give
me your opinion of her and her prince. This
letter is writ in great haste, as you may see; 'tis
my brother's sick day, and I'm not willing to
leave him long alone. I forgot to tell you in my
last that he was come hither to try if he can lose
an ague here that he got in Gloucestershire. He
asked me for you very kindly, and if he knew I
writ to you I should have something to say from
him besides what I should say for myself if I had
room.

Yrs.

Letter 14.—This letter contains the most interesting
political reference of the whole series. Either Temple
has written Dorothy an account of Cromwell's dissolv-
ing the Long Parliament, or perhaps some news-letter
has found its way to Chicksands with the astounding
news. All England is filled with intense excitement
over Cromwell's *coup d'état;* and it cannot be unin-
teresting to quote a short contemporary account of
the business. Algernon Sydney's father, the Earl of
Leicester, whose journal has already been quoted, under
date Wednesday, April 20th, 1653, writes as follows :—
"My Lord General came into the House clad in plain
black clothes with grey worsted stockings, and sat down,
as he used to do, in an ordinary place." Then he began
to speak, and presently " he put on his hat, went out of
his place, and walked up and down the stage or floor in
the midst of the House, with his hat on his head, and
chid them soundly." After this had gone on for some
time, Colonel Harrison was called in to remove the

Speaker, which he did; "and it happened that Algernon Sydney sat next to the Speaker on the right hand.
The Géneral said to Harrison, 'Put him out!'

"Harrison spake to Sydney to go out, but he said he
would not go out and waited still.

"The General said again, 'Put him out!' Then
Harrison and Wortley [Worsley] put their hands upon
Sydney's shoulders as if they would force him to go out.
Then he rose and went towards the door."

Such is the story which reaches Dorothy, and startles
all England at this date.

SIR,—That you may be sure it was a dream
that I writ that part of my letter in, I do not now
remember what it was I writ, but seems it was
very kind, and possibly you owe the discovery
on't to my being asleep. But I do not repent it,
for I should not love you if I did not think you
discreet enough to be trusted with the knowledge
of all my kindness. Therefore 'tis not that I
desire to hide it from you, but that I do not love
to tell it; and perhaps if you could read my heart,
I should make less scruple of your seeing on't
there than in my letters.

I can easily guess who the pretty young lady is,
for there are but two in England of that fortune,
and they are sisters, but I am to seek who the
gallant should be. If it be no secret, you may tell
me. However, I shall wish him all good success
if he be your friend, as I suppose he is by his confidence in you. If it be neither of the Spencers,

I wish it were; I have not seen two young men that looked as if they deserved better fortunes so much as those brothers.

But, bless me, what will become of us all now? Is not this a strange turn? What does my Lord Lisle? Sure this will at least defer your journey? Tell me what I must think on't; whether it be better or worse, or whether you are at all concern'd in't? For if you are not I am not, only if I had been so wise as to have taken hold of the offer was made me by Henry Cromwell, I might have been in a fair way of preferment, for, sure, they will be greater now than ever. Is it true that Algernon Sydney was so unwilling to leave the House, that the General was fain to take the pains to turn him out himself? Well, 'tis a pleasant world this. If Mr. Pim were alive again, I wonder what he would think of these proceedings, and whether this would appear so great a breach of the Privilege of Parliament as the demanding the 5 members? But I shall talk treason by and by if I do not look to myself. 'Tis safer talking of the orange-flower water you sent me. The carrier has given me a great charge to tell you that it came safe, and that I must do him right. As you say, 'tis not the best I have seen, nor the worst.

I shall expect your Diary next week, though this will be but a short letter: you may allow me to make excuses too sometimes; but, seriously, my father is now so continuously ill, that I have hardly time for anything. 'Tis but an ague that he has, but yet I am much afraid that is more than his age and weakness will be able to bear; he keeps his bed, and never rises but to have it made, and most times faints with that. You ought in charity to write as much as you can, for, in earnest, my life here since my father's sickness is so sad that, to another humour than mine, it would be unsupportable; but I have been so used to misfortunes, that I cannot be much surprised with them, though perhaps I am as sensible of them as another. I'll leave you, for I find these thoughts begin to put me in ill humour; farewell, may you be ever happy. If I am so at all, it is in being

Your

Letter 15. — What Temple had written about Mr. Arbry's prophecy and " the falling down of the form," we cannot know. Mr. Arbry was probably William Erbury, vicar of St. Mary's, Cardiff, a noted schismatic. He is said to have been a " holy, harmless man," but incurred both the hate and ridicule of his opponents. Many of his tracts are still extant, and they contain extravagant prophecies couched in the peculiar phraseology of the day.

The celebrated Sir Samuel Luke was a near neighbour of the Osbornes, and Mr. Luke was one of his numerous family. Sir Samuel was Lord of the Manor of Hawnes, and in the Hawnes parish register there are notices of

F

the christenings of his sons and daughters. Sir Samuel
was not only a colonel in the Parliament Army, but
Scout-Master-General in the counties of Bedford and
Surrey. Samuel Butler, the author of *Hudibras*, lived
with Sir Samuel Luke as his secretary, at some date
prior to the Restoration; and Dr. Grey, his learned
editor, believes that he wrote *Hudibras* about that time,
"because he had then the opportunity to converse
with those living characters of rebellion, nonsense, and
hypocrisy which he so lively and pathetically exposes
throughout the whole work." Sir Samuel is said himself
to be the original "Hudibras;" and if Dr. Grey's conjecture on this matter is a right one, we have already
in our minds a very complete portrait of Dorothy's
neighbour.

The old ballad that Dorothy encloses to her lover
has not been preserved with her letter. If it is older
than the ballad of "The Lord of Lorne," it must have
been composed before Henry VIII.'s reign; for
Edward Guilpin, in his *Skialethia* [1598], speaks of

> Th' olde ballad of the Lord of Lorne,
> Whose last line in King Harrie's day was borne.

"The Lord of Learne" (this was the old spelling) may
be found in Bishop Percy's well-known collection of
Ballads and Romances.

SIR,—You must pardon me, I could not burn
your other letter for my life; I was so pleased to
see I had so much to read, and so sorry I had
done so soon, that I resolved to begin them again,
and had like to have lost my dinner by it. I
know not what humour you were in when you

writ it; but Mr. Arbry's prophecy and the falling down of the form did a little discompose my gravity. But I quickly recovered myself with thinking that you deserved to be chid for going where you knew you must of necessity lose your time. In earnest, I had a little scruple when I went with you thither, and but that I was assured it was too late to go any whither else, and believed it better to hear an ill sermon than none, I think I should have missed his *Belles remarques.* You had repented you, I hope, of that and all other your faults before you thought of dying.

What a satisfaction you had found out to make me for the injuries you say you have done me! And yet I cannot tell neither (though 'tis not the remedy I should choose) whether that were not a certain one for all my misfortunes; for, sure, I should have nothing then to persuade me to stay longer where they grow, and I should quickly take a resolution of leaving them and the world at once. I agree with you, too, that I do not see any great likelihood of the change of our fortunes, and that we have much more to wish than to hope for; but 'tis so common a calamity that I dare not murmur at it; better people have endured it, and I can give no reason why (almost) all are denied the satisfaction of disposing themselves to their own desires, but that it is a happiness too great for this world, and might endanger one's forgetting the next; whereas if we are crossed in that which only can make the world pleasing to us, we are quickly tired with the length of our journey and the disquiet of our inns, and long to be at home. One would think it were I who had heard the three sermons and were trying to make a fourth; these are truths that might become a pulpit better than Mr. Arbry's predictions. But lest you should think I have as many worms in my head as he, I'll give over in time, and tell you how far Mr. Luke and I are acquainted. He lives within three or four miles of me, and one day that I had been to visit a lady that is nearer him than me, as I came back I met a coach with some company in't that I knew, and thought myself obliged to salute. We all lighted and met, and I found more than I looked for by two damsels and their squires. I was afterwards told they were of the Lukes, and possibly this man might be there, or else I never saw him; for since these times we have had no commerce with that family, but have kept at great distance, as having on several occasions been disobliged by them. But of late, I know not how, Sir Sam has grown so kind as to send to me for some things he desired out of this garden, and withal made the offer of what was in his, which I had reason to take for a high favour, for he is a nice florist; and since this we are insensibly come to as good degrees of civility for one another as can be expected from people that never meet.

Who those demoiselles should be that were at Heamses I cannot imagine, and I know so few that are concerned in me or my name that I admire you should meet with so many that seem to be acquainted with it. Sure, if you had liked them you would not have been so sullen, and a less occasion would have served to make you entertain their discourse if they had been handsome. And yet I know no reason I have to believe that beauty is any argument to make you like people; unless I had more on't myself. But be it what it will that displeased you, I am glad they did not fright you away before you had the orange-flower water, for it is very good, and I am so sweet with it a days that I despise roses. When I have given you humble thanks for it, I mean to look over your other letter and take the heads, and to treat of them in order as my time and your patience shall give me leave.

And first for my Sheriff, let me desire you to believe he has more courage than to die upon a denial. No (thanks be to God!), none of my servants are given to that; I hear of many every day that do marry, but of none that do worse. My brother sent me word this week that my fighting servant is married too, and with the news this ballad, which was to be sung in the grave that you dreamt of, I think ; but because you tell me I shall not want company then, you may dispose of this piece of poetry as you please when you have sufficiently admired with me where he found it out, for 'tis much older than that of my " Lord of Lorne." You are altogether in the right that my brother will never be at quiet till he sees me disposed of, but he does not mean to lose me by it ; he knows that if I were married at this present, I should not be persuaded to leave my father as long as he lives ; and when this house breaks up, he is resolved to follow me if he can, which he thinks he might better do to a house where I had some power than where I am but upon courtesy myself. Besides that, he thinks it would be to my advantage to be well bestowed, and by that he understands richly. He is much of your sister's humour, and many times wishes me a husband that loved me as well as he does (though he seems to doubt the possibility on't), but never desires that I should love that husband with any passion, and plainly tells me so. He says it would not be so well for him, nor perhaps for me, that I should; for he is of opinion that all passions have more of trouble than satisfaction in them, and therefore they are happiest that have least of them. You think him kind from a letter that you met with of his ; sure, there was very little of anything in that, or else I should not have employed it to wrap a book up. But, seriously, I many times receive letters from him, that were they seen without an address to me or his name, nobody would believe they were from a brother ;

and I cannot but tell him sometimes that, sure, he mistakes and sends me letters that were meant to his mistress, till he swears to me that he has none.

Next week my persecution begins again; he comes down, and my cousin Molle is already cured of his imaginary dropsy, and means to meet here. I shall be baited most sweetly, but sure they will not easily make me consent to make my life unhappy to satisfy their importunity. I was born to be very happy or very miserable, I know not which, but I am very certain that you will never read half this letter 'tis so scribbled; but 'tis no matter, 'tis not much worth it.

Your most faithful friend and servant.

Letter 16.—The trial of Lord Chandos for killing Mr. Compton in a duel was, just at this moment, exciting the fickle attention of the town, which had probably said its say on the subject of Cromwell's *coup d'état,* and was only too ready for another subject of conversation. The trial is not reported among the State Trials, but our observant friend the Earl of Leicester has again taken note of the matter in his journal, and can give us at least his own ideas of the trial and its political and social importance. Under date May 1653, he writes :—
" Towards the end of Easter Term, the Lord Chandos, for killing in duel Mr. Compton the year before," that is to say, in March ; the new year begins on March 25th, "and the Lord Arundel of Wardour, one of his seconds, were brought to their trial for their lives at the Upper Bench in Westminster Hall, when it was found man-

slaughter only, as by a jury at Kingston-upon-Thames it had been found formerly. The Lords might have had the privilege of peerage (Justice Rolles being Lord Chief Justice), but they declined it by the advice of Mr. Maynard and the rest of their counsel, least by that means the matter might have been brought about again, therefore they went upon the former verdict of manslaughter, and so were acquitted ; yet to be burned in the hand, which was done to them both a day or two after, but very favourably." These were the first peers that had been burned in the hand, and the democratic Earl of Leicester expresses at the event some satisfaction, and derives from the whole circumstances of the trial comfortable assurance of the power and stability of the Government. The Earl, however, misleads us in one particular. Lord Arundel was Henry Compton's second. He had married Cecily Compton, and naturally enough acted as his brother-in-law's second. It is also interesting to remember that Lord Chandos was known to the world as something other than a duellist. He was an eminent loyalist, among the first of those nobles who left Westminster, and at Newbury fight had his three horses killed under him. Lady Carey was Mary, natural daughter of Lord Scrope, who married Henry Carey, commonly called Lord Leppington. Lady Leppington (or Carey) lost her husband in 1649, and her son died May 24, 1653. This helps us to date the letter. Of her "kindness to Compton," of which Dorothy writes in her next letter, nothing is known, but she married Charles Paulet, Lord St. John, afterwards the Duke of Bolton, early in 1654.

The jealous Sir T—— here mentioned may be Sir Thomas Osborne, who, we may suppose, was not well pleased at the refusal of his offer.

Sir Peter Lely did paint a portrait of Lady Diana Rich some months after this date. It is somewhat curious that he should remain in England during the Civil Wars; but his business was to paint all men's portraits. He had painted Charles I.; now he was painting Cromwell. It was to him Cromwell is said to have shouted: " Paint the warts! paint the warts!" when the courtly Sir Peter would have made a presentable picture even of the Lord General himself. Cromwell was a sound critic in this, and had detected the main fault of Sir Peter's portraits, whose value to us is greatly lessened by the artist's constant habit of flattery.

SIR,—If it were the carrier's fault that you stayed so long for your letters, you are revenged, for I have chid him most unreasonably. But I must confess 'twas not for that, for I did not know it then, but going to meet him (as I usually do), when he gave me your letter I found the upper seal broken open, and underneath where it uses to be only closed with a little wax, there was a seal, which though it were an anchor and a heart, methought it did not look like yours, but less, and much worse cut. This suspicion was so strong upon me, that I chid till the poor fellow was ready to cry, and swore to me that it had never been touched since he had it, and that he was careful of it, as he never put it with his other letters, but by itself, and that now it come amongst his money, which perhaps might break the seal; and lest I should think it was his curiosity, he told me very ingenuously he could not read, and so we parted for the present. But since, he has been with a neighbour of mine whom he sometimes delivers my letters to, and begged her that she would go to me and desire my worship to write to your worship to know how the letter was sealed, for it has so grieved him that he has neither eat nor slept (to do him any good) since he came home, and in grace of God this shall be a warning to him as long as he lives. He takes it so heavily that I think I must be friends with him again; but pray hereafter seal your letters, so that the difficulty of opening them may dishearten anybody from attempting it.

It was but my guess that the ladies at Heams' were unhandsome; but since you tell me they were remarkably so, sure I know them by it; they are two sisters, and might have been mine if the Fates had so pleased. They have a brother that is not like them, and is a baronet besides. 'Tis strange that you tell me of my Lords Shandoys [Chandos] and Arundel; but what becomes of young Compton's estate? Sure my Lady Carey cannot neither in honour nor conscience keep it; besides that, she needs it less now than ever, her son (being, as I hear) dead.

Sir T., I suppose, avoids you as a friend of mine. My brother tells me they meet sometimes, and have the most ado to pull off their hats to one another that can be, and never speak. If I were in town, I'll undertake he would venture the being choked for want of air rather than stir out of doors for fear of meeting me. But did you not say in your last that you took something very ill from me? If 'twas my humble thanks, well, you shall have no more of them then, nor no more servants. I think that they are not necessary among friends.

I take it very kindly that your father asked for me, and that you were not pleased with the question he made of the continuance of my friendship. I can pardon it him, because he does not know me, but I should never forgive you if you could doubt it. Were my face in no more danger of changing than my mind, I should be worth the seeing at threescore; and that which is but very ordinary now, would then be counted handsome for an old woman; but, alas! I am more likely to look old before my time with grief. Never anybody had such luck with servants; what with marrying and what with dying, they all leave me. Just now I have news brought me of the death of an old rich knight that has promised me this seven years to marry me whensoever his wife died, and now he's dead before her, and has left her such a widow, it makes me mad to think on't, £1200 a year jointure and £20,000 in money and personal estate, and all this I might have had if Mr. Death had been pleased to have taken her

instead of him. Well, who can help these things?
But, since I cannot have him, would you had her!
What say you? Shall I speak a good word for
you? She will marry for certain, and perhaps,
though my brother may expect I should serve
him in it, yet if you give me commission I'll say
I was engaged beforehand for a friend, and leave
him to shift for himself. You would be my
neighbour if you had her, and I should see you
often. Think on't, and let me know what you
resolve? My lady has writ me word that she
intends very shortly to sit at Lely's for her picture
for me; I give you notice on't, that you may have
the pleasure of seeing it sometimes whilst 'tis
there. I imagine 'twill be so to you, for I am
sure it would be a great one to me, and we do
not use to differ in our inclinations, though I
cannot agree with you that my brother's kindness
to me has anything of trouble in't; no, sure, I may
be just to you and him both, and to be a kind
sister will take nothing from my being a perfect
friend.

Letter 17.—Lady Newcastle was Margaret Duchess of
Newcastle. " The thrice noble, chaste, and virtuous, but
again somewhat fantastical and original-brained, generous
Margaret Newcastle," as Elia describes her. She was the
youngest daughter of Sir Charles Lucas, and was born at
Colchester towards the end of the reign of James I. Her
mother appears to have been remarkably careful of her
education in all such lighter matters as dancing, music,

and the learning of the French tongue ; but she does not seem to have made any deep study of the classics. In 1643 she joined the Court at Oxford, and was made one of the Maids of Honour to Henrietta Maria, whom she afterwards attended in exile. At Paris she met the Marquis of Newcastle, who married her in that city in 1645. From Paris they went to Rotterdam, she leaving the Queen to follow her husband's fortunes ; and after stopping at Rotterdam and Brabant for short periods, they settled at Antwerp.

At the Restoration she returned to England with her husband, and employed her time in writing letters, plays, poems, philosophical discourses, and orations. There is a long catalogue of her works in Ballard's *Memoirs*, but all published at a date subsequent to 1653. However, from Anthony Wood and other sources one gathers somewhat different details of her life and writings ; and the book to which Dorothy refers here and in Letter 21, is probably the *Poems and Fancies*, an edition of which was published, I believe, in this year [1653]. Many of her verses are more strangely incomprehensible than anything even in the poetry of to-day. Take, for instance, a poem of four lines, from the *Poems and Fancies*, entitled—

THE JOINING OF SEVERAL FIGUR'D ATOMS MAKES
OTHER FIGURES.

> Several figur'd Atoms well agreeing
> When joined, do give another figure being.
> For as those figures joined several ways
> The fabrick of each several creature raise.

This seems to be a rhyming statement of the Atomic theory, but whether it is a poem or a fancy we should find it hard to decide. It is not, however, an unfair

example of Lady Newcastle's fantastic style. Lady
Newcastle died in 1673, when she was buried in Westminster Abbey,—"A wise, witty, and learned Lady,
which her many books do well testify."

SIR,—I received your letter to-day, when I
thought it almost impossible that I should be
sensible of anything but my father's sickness and
my own affliction in it. Indeed, he was then so
dangerously ill that we could not reasonably hope
he should outlive this day; yet he is now, I thank
God, much better, and I am come so much to
myself with it, as to undertake a long letter to
you whilst I watch by him. Towards the latter
end it will be excellent stuff, I believe; but, alas!
you may allow me to dream sometimes. I have
had so little sleep since my father was sick that
I am never thoroughly awake. Lord, how I have
wished for you! Here do I sit all night by a
poor moped fellow that serves my father, and
have much ado to keep him awake and myself
too. If you heard the wise discourse that is
between us, you would swear we wanted sleep;
but I shall leave him to-night to entertain himself, and try if I can write as wisely as I talk. I
am glad all is well again. In earnest, it would
have lain upon my conscience if I had been the
occasion of making your poor boy lose a service,
that if he has the wit to know how to value it,
he would never have forgiven me while he had
lived.

But while I remember it, let me ask you if you did not send my letter and *Cléopâtre* where I directed you for my lady? I received one from her to-day full of the kindest reproaches, that she has not heard from me this three weeks. I have writ constantly to her, but I do not so much wonder that the rest are lost, as that she seems not to have received that which I sent to you nor the books. I do not understand it, but I know there is no fault of yours in't. But, mark you! if you think to 'scape with sending me such bits of letters, you are mistaken. You say you are often interrupted, and I believe it; but you must use then to begin to write before you receive mine, and whensoever you have any spare time allow me some of it. Can you doubt that anything can make your letters cheap? In earnest, 'twas unkindly said, and if I could be angry with you it should be for that. No, certainly they are, and ever will be, dear to me as that which I receive a huge contentment by. How shall I long when you are gone your journey to hear from you! how shall I apprehend a thousand accidents that are not likely nor will never happen, I hope! Oh, if you do not send me long letters, then you are the cruellest person that can be! If you love me you will; and if you do not, I shall never love myself. You need not fear such a command as you mention. Alas! I am too much concerned that you should love me ever to forbid it you; 'tis all that I propose of happiness to myself in the world. The burning of my paper has waked me; all this while I was in a dream. But 'tis no matter, I am content you should know they are of you, and that when my thoughts are left most at liberty they are the kindest. I swear my eyes are so heavy that I hardly see what I write, nor do I think you will be able to read it when I have done; the best on't is 'twill be no great loss to you if you do not, for, sure, the greatest part on't is not sense, and yet on my conscience I shall go on with it. 'Tis like people that talk in their sleep, nothing interrupts them but talking to them again, and that you are not like to do at this distance; besides that, at this instant you are, I believe, more asleep than I, and do not so much as dream that I am writing to you. My fellow-watchers have been asleep too, till just now they begin to stretch and yawn; they are going to try if eating and drinking can keep them awake, and I am kindly invited to be of their company; and my father's man has got one of the maids to talk nonsense to to-night, and they have got between them a bottle of ale. I shall lose my share if I do not take them at their first offer. Your patience till I have drunk, and then I'll for you again.

And now on the strength of this ale, I believe I shall be able to fill up this paper that's left with something or other; and first let me ask you if

you have seen a book of poems newly come out,
made by my Lady Newcastle? For God's sake
if you meet with it send it to me; they say 'tis
ten times more extravagant than her dress. Sure,
the poor woman is a little distracted, she could
never be so ridiculous else as to venture at writing
books, and in verse too. If I should not sleep
this fortnight I should not come to that. My
eyes grow a little dim though, for all the ale, and
I believe, if I could see it this is most strangely
scribbled. Sure, I shall not find fault with your
writing in haste, for anything but the shortness of
your letter; and 'twould be very unjust in me
to tie you to a ceremony that I do not observe
myself. No, for God's sake let there be no
such thing between us; a real kindness is so far
beyond all compliment, that it never appears more
than when there is least of t'other mingled with
it. If, then, you would have me believe yours to
be perfect, confirm it to me by a kind freedom.
Tell me if there be anything that I can serve you
in, employ me as you would do that sister that
you say you love so well. Chide me when I do
anything that is not well, but then make haste to
tell me that you have forgiven me, and that you
are what I shall ever be, a faithful friend.

Letter 18.—I cannot pass by this letter without saying that the first part of it is, to my thinking, the most
dainty and pleasing piece of writing that Dorothy has
G

left us. The account of her life, one day and every
day, is like a gust of fresh country air clearing away
the mist of time and enabling one to see Dorothy at
Chicksands quite clearly. It is fashionable to deny
Macaulay everything but memory ; but he had the good
taste and discernment to admire this letter, and quote
from it in his Essay on Sir William Temple,—a quotation for which I shall always remain very grateful to
him.

Sir Thomas Peyton, "Brother Peyton," was born in
1619, being, I believe, the second baronet of that name ;
his seat was at Knowlton, in the county of Kent.
Early in the reign of Charles I. we find him as Member
of Parliament for Sandwich, figuring in a Committee
side by side with the two Sir Harry Vanes ; the Committee having been sent into Kent to prevent the
dispersal of rumours to the scandal of Parliament,—no
light task, one would think. In 1643 he is in prison,
charged among other things with being a malignant.
An unjust charge, as he thinks ; for he writes to his
brother, "If to wish on earth peace, goodwill towards
men, be a malignant, none is greater than your affectionate brother, Thomas Peyton." But in spite of these
peaceful thoughts in prison, in May 1648 he is heading
a loyalist rising in Kent. The other counties not joining in at the right moment, in accordance with the
general procedure at Royalist risings, it is defeated by
Fairfax. Sir Thomas's house is ransacked, he himself is
taken prisoner near Bury St. Edmunds, brought to the
House of Commons, and committed to the Tower. A
right worthy son-in-law of good Sir Peter. We are
glad to find him at large again in 1653, his head safe on
his shoulders, and do not grudge him his grant of duties
on sea-coal, dated 1660 ; nor are we sorry that he should'

once again grace the House of Commons with his presence as one of the members for loyal Kent in the good days when the King enjoyed his own again.

Sir,—I have been reckoning up how many faults you lay to my charge in your last letter, and I find I am severe, unjust, unmerciful, and unkind. Oh me, how should one do to mend all these! 'Tis work for an age, and 'tis to be feared I shall be so old ˌbefore I am good, that 'twill not be considerable to anybody but myself whether I am so or not. I say nothing of the pretty humour you fancied me in, in your dream, because 'twas but a dream. Sure, if it had been anything else, I should have remembered that my Lord L. loves to have his chamber and his bed to himself. But seriously, now, I wonder at your patience. How could you hear me talk so senselessly, though 'twere but in your sleep, and not be ready to beat me? What nice mistaken points of honour I pretended to, and yet could allow him room in the same bed with me! Well, dreams are pleasant things to people whose humours are so; but to have the spleen, and to dream upon't, is a punishment I would not wish my greatest enemy. I seldom dream, or never remember them, unless they have been so sad as to put me into such disorder as ˈI can hardly recover when I am awake, and some of those I am confident I shall never forget.

You ask me how I pass my time here. I can give you a perfect account not only of what I do for the present, but of what I am likely to do this seven years if I stay here so long. I rise in the morning reasonably early, and before I am ready I go round the house till I am weary of that, and then into the garden till it grows too hot for me. About ten o'clock I think of making me ready, and when that's done I go into my father's chamber, from whence to dinner, where my cousin Molle and I sit in great state in a room, and at a table that would hold a great many more. After dinner we sit and talk till Mr. B. comes in question, and then I am gone. The heat of the day is spent in reading or working, and about six or seven o'clock I walk out into a common that lies hard by the house, where a great many young wenches keep sheep and cows, and sit in the shade singing of ballads. I go to them and compare their voices and beauties to some ancient shepherdesses that I have read of, and find a vast difference there; but, trust me, I think these are as innocent as those could be. I talk to them, and find they want nothing to make them the happiest people in the world but the knowledge that they are so. Most commonly, when we are in the midst of our discourse, one looks about her, and spies her cows going into the corn, and then away they all run as if they had wings at their heels. I, that am not so nimble, stay behind; and when I see them driving home their cattle, I think 'tis time for me to return too. When I have supped, I go into the garden, and so to the side of a small river that runs by it, when I sit down and wish you were with me (you had best say this is not kind neither). In earnest, 'tis a pleasant place, and would be much more so to me if I had your company. I sit there sometimes till I am lost with thinking; and were it not for some cruel thoughts of the crossness of our fortunes that will not let me sleep there, I should forget that there were such a thing to be done as going to bed.

Since I writ this my company is increased by two, my brother Harry and a fair niece, the eldest of my brother Peyton's children. She is so much a woman that I am almost ashamed to say I am her aunt; and so pretty, that, if I had any design to gain of servants, I should not like her company; but I have none, and therefore shall endeavour to keep her here as long as I can persuade her father to spare her, for she will easily consent to it, having so much of my humour (though it be the worst thing in her) as to like a melancholy place and little company. My brother John is not come down again, nor am I certain when he will be here. He went from London into Gloucestershire to my sister who was very ill, and his youngest girl, of which he

was very fond, is since dead. But I believe by
that time his wife has a little recovered her sickness and loss of her child, he will be coming this
way. My father is reasonably well, but keeps his
chamber still, and will hardly, I am afraid, ever be
so perfectly recovered as to come abroad again.

I am sorry for poor Walker, but you need not
doubt of what he has of yours in his hands, for
it seems he does not use to do his work himself.
I speak seriously, he keeps a Frenchman that
sets all his seals and rings. If what you say of
my Lady Leppington be of your own knowledge,
I shall believe you, but otherwise I can assure
you I have heard from people that pretend to
know her very well, that her kindness to Compton
was very moderate, and that she never liked him
so well as when he died and gave her his estate.
But they might be deceived, and 'tis not so
strange as that you should imagine a coldness
and an indifference in my letters when I so little
meant it; but I am not displeased you should
desire my kindness enough to apprehend the loss
of it when it is safest. Only I would not have
you apprehend it so far as to believe it possible,
—that were an injury to all the assurances I have
given you, and if you love me you cannot think
me unworthy. I should think myself so, if I
found you grew indifferent to me, that I have had
so long and so particular a friendship for; but,
sure, this is more than I need to say. You are

enough in my heart to know all my thoughts, and if so, you know better than I can tell you how much I am

Yours.

Letter 19. — Lady Ruthin is Susan, daughter and heiress of Charles Longueville Lord Grey de Ruthin. She married Sir Harry Yelverton, a match of which Dorothy thoroughly approved. We hear more of Dorothy's beautiful friend at the time when the treaty with Sir Harry Yelverton is going forward. Of Mr. Talbot I find nothing; we must rest contented in knowing him to be a fellow-servant.

R. Spencer is Robert Spencer, Earl of Sunderland, Lady Sunderland's brother-in-law. He was afterwards one of the inner council of four in Temple's Scheme of Government. "In him," says Macaulay, in a somewhat highly-coloured character-sketch, "the political immorality of his age was personified in the most lively manner. Nature had given him a keen understanding, a restless and mischievous temper, a cold heart, and an abject spirit. His mind had undergone a training by which all his vices had been nursed up to the rankest maturity."

ᐧ Lady Lexington was Mary, daughter of Sir Anthony Leger; she was the third wife of Robert Sutton, Earl of Lexington. I cannot find that her daughter married one of the Spencers.

SIR,—If to know I wish you with me pleases you, 'tis a satisfaction you may always have, for I do it perpetually; but were it really in my power to make you happy, I could not miss being so

myself, for I know nothing else I want towards it.
You are admitted to all my entertainments; and
'twould be a pleasing surprise to me to see you
amongst my shepherdesses. I meet some there
sometimes that look very like gentlemen (for 'tis
a road), and when they are in good humour they
give us a compliment as they go by; but you
would be so courteous as to stay, I hope, if we
entreated you; 'tis in your way to this place,
and just before the house. 'Tis our Hyde Park,
and every fine evening, anybody that wanted a
mistress might be sure to find one there. I have
wondered often to meet my fair Lady Ruthin
there alone; methinks it should be dangerous for
an heir. I could find in my heart to steal her
away myself, but it should be rather for her
person than her fortune. My brother says not a
word of you, nor your service, nor do I expect he
should; if I could forget you, he would not help
my memory. You would laugh, sure, if I could
tell you how many servants he has offered me
since he came down; but one above all the rest I
think he is in love with himself, and may marry
him too if he pleases, I shall not hinder him.
'Tis one Talbot, the finest gentleman he has seen
this seven year; but the mischief on't is he has
not above fifteen or sixteen hundred pound a year,
though he swears he begins to think one might
bate £500 a year for such a husband. I tell him
I am glad to hear it; and if I was as much taken

LELY.

Sir William Temple Baronet
Ambassador Extraordinary
to the States of Holland &c.
Married Dorothy Daughter
of Sir Peter Osborn. H
Was born was d. ed

Photo-engraving _Waterlow & Sons.Ld

humble servant
W Temple

(as he) with Mr. Talbot, I should not be less
gallant; but I doubted the first extremely. I have
spleen enough to carry me to Epsom this summer;
but yet I think I shall not go. If I make one
journey, I must make more, for then I have no
excuse. Rather than be obliged to that, I'll make
none. You have so often reproached me with
the loss of your liberty, that to make you some
amends I am contented to be your prisoner this
summer; but you shall do one favour for me
into the bargain. When your father goes into
Ireland, lay your commands upon some of his
servants to get you an Irish greyhound. I have
one that was the General's; but 'tis a bitch, and
those are always much less than the dogs. I got
it in the time of my favour there, and it was all
they had. Henry Cromwell undertook to write
to his brother Fleetwood for another for me; but
I have lost my hopes there. Whomsoever it is
that you employ, he will need no other instructions but to get the biggest he can meet with;
'tis all the beauty of those dogs, or of any kind, I
think. A masty [mastif] is handsomer to me than
the most exact little dog that ever lady played
withal. You will not offer to take it ill that I
employ you in such a commission, since I have
told you that the General's son did not refuse it;
but I shall take it ill if you do not take the same
freedom with me whensoever I am capable of
serving you. The town must needs be unplea-

sant now, and, methinks, you might contrive some way of having your letters sent to you without giving yourself the trouble of coming to town for them when you have no other business; you must pardon me if I think they cannot be worth it.

I am told that R. Spencer is a servant to a lady of my acquaintance, a daughter of my Lady Lexington's. Is it true? And if it be, what is become of the £2500 lady? Would you think it, that I have an ambassador from the Emperor Justinian that comes to renew the treaty? In earnest, 'tis true, and I want your counsel extremely, what to do in it. You told me once that of all my servants you liked him the best. If I could do so too, there were no dispute in't. Well, I'll think on't, and if it succeed I will be as good as my word; you shall take your choice of my four daughters. Am not I beholding to him, think you? He says that he has made addresses, 'tis true, in several places since we parted, but could not fix anywhere; and, in his opinion, he sees nobody that would make so fit a wife for him as I. He has often inquired after me to hear if I were marrying, and somebody told him I had an ague, and he presently fell sick of one too, so natural a sympathy there is between us; and yet for all this, on my conscience, we shall never marry. He desires to know whether I am at liberty or not. What shall I tell him? Or shall I send him to you to know? I think that will be best. I'll say that you are much my friend, and that I have resolved not to dispose of myself but with your consent and approbation, and therefore he must make all his court to you; and when he can bring me a certificate under your hand, that you think him a fit husband for me, 'tis very likely I may have him. Till then I am his humble servant and your faithful friend.

Letter 20.—In this letter the journey into Sweden is given up finally, and Temple is once more without employment or the hope of employment. This was probably brought about by the alteration of the Government plans; and as Lord Lisle was not to go to Sweden, there was no chance of Temple's being attached to the Embassy.

SIR,—I am sorry my last letter frighted you so; 'twas no part of my intention it should; but I am more sorry to see by your first chapter that your humour is not always so good as I could wish it. 'Twas the only thing I ever desired we might differ in, and therefore I think it is denied me. Whilst I read the description on't, I could not believe but that I had writ it myself, it was so much my own. I pity you in earnest much more than I do myself; and yet I may deserve yours when I shall have told you, that besides all that you speak of, I have gotten an ague that with two fits has made me so very weak, that I doubted extremely yesterday whether I should be able to sit up to-day to write to you. But you must not be troubled at this; that's the way to kill me indeed. Besides, it is impossible I should keep it long, for here is my eldest brother, and my cousin Molle, and two or three more that have great understanding in agues, as people that have been long acquainted with them, and they do so tutor and govern me, that I am neither to eat, drink, nor sleep without their leave; and, sure, my obedience deserves they should cure me, or else they are great tyrants to very little purpose. You cannot imagine how cruel they are to me, and yet will persuade me 'tis for my good. I know they mean it so, and therefore say nothing on't, I admit, and sigh to think those are not here that would be kinder to me. But you were cruel yourself when you seemed to apprehend I might oblige you to make good your last offer. Alack! if I could purchase the empire of the world at that rate, I should think it much too dear; and though, perhaps, I am too unhappy myself ever to make anybody else happy, yet, sure, I shall take heed that my misfortunes may not prove infectious to my friends. You ask counsel of a person that is very little able to give it. I cannot imagine whither you should go, since this journey is broke. You must e'en be content to stay at home, I think, and see what will become of us, though I expect nothing of good; and, sure, you never made a truer remark in your life than that all changes are for the worse. Will it not stay your father's journey too? Methinks it should. For God's sake write me all that you hear or can think of, that I may have something to entertain myself withal. I have a scurvy head that will not let me write longer.

I am your.

[Directed]—

For Mrs. Paynter, at her house
in Bedford Street, next ye Goate,
In Covent Garden.

Letter 21.—Sir Thomas Osborne is Dorothy's " Cousin Osborne " here mentioned. He was, you remember, a suitor for Dorothy's hand, but has now married Lady Bridget Lindsay.

The "squire that is as good as a knight," is, in all probability, Richard Bennet. Thomas Bennet, his father, an alderman of the city of London, had bought a seat near Cambridge, called Babraham or Babram, that had belonged to Sir Toby Palavicini. The alderman appears to have been a loyal citizen, as he was created baronet in 1660. His two sons, Sir Richard and Sir Thomas, married daughters of Sir Lavinius Munck ;—so we need not accuse Dorothy of irretrievably breaking hearts by her various refusals.

When Dorothy says she will "sit like the lady of the lobster, and give audience at Babram," she simply means that she will sit among magnificent surroundings unsuited to her modest disposition. The "lady" of a

lobster is a curious-shaped substance in the head of
that fish, bearing some distant resemblance to the figure
of a woman.   The expression is still known to fish-
mongers and others, who also refer to the "Adam and
Eve" in a shrimp, a kindred formation.   Curiously
enough, this very phrase has completely puzzled Dr.
Grosart, the learned editor of Herrick, who confesses
that he can make nothing of the allusion in the following passage from *The Fairie Temple :*—

> "The saint to which the most he prayes,
>   And offers Incense Nights and Dayes,
>   The Lady of the Lobster is
>   Whose foot-pace he doth stroak and kiss."

Swift, too, uses the phrase in his *Battle of the Books* in
describing the encounter between Virgil and Dryden,
where he says, "The helmet was nine times too large
for the head, which appeared situate far in the hinder
part, even like the lady in a lobster, or a mouse under
a canopy of state, or like a shrivelled beau from within
the pent-house of a modern periwig."

SIR,—I do not know that anybody has frighted
me, or beaten me, or put me into more passion
than what I usually carry about me, but yesterday
I missed my fit, and am not without hope I shall
hear no more on't.   My father has lost his too,
and my eldest brother, but we all look like people
risen from the dead.   Only my cousin Molle
keeps his still; and, in earnest, I am not certain
whether he would lose it or not, for it gives him
a lawful occasion of being nice and cautious about
himself, to which he in his own humour is so
much inclined that 'twere not easy for him to

forbear it. You need not send me my Lady Newcastle's book at all, for I have seen it, and am satisfied that there are many soberer people in Bedlam. I'll swear her friends are much to blame to let her go abroad.

But I am hugely pleased that you have seen my Lady. I knew you could not choose but like her; but yet, let me tell you, you have seen but the worst of her. Her conversation has more charms than can be in mere beauty, and her humour and disposition would make a deformed person appear lovely. You had strange luck to meet my brother so soon. He went up but last Tuesday. I heard from him on Thursday, but he did not tell me he had seen you; perhaps he did not think it convenient to put me in mind of you; besides, he thought he told me enough in telling me my cousin Osborne was married. Why did you not send me that news and a garland? Well, the best on't is I have a squire now that is as good as a knight. He was coming as fast as a coach and six horses could carry him, but I desired him to stay till my ague was gone, and give me a little time to recover my good looks; for I protest if he saw me now he would never deign to see me again. Oh, me! I can but think how I shall sit like the lady of the lobster, and give audience at Babram. You have been there, I am sure. Nobody that is at Cambridge 'scapes it. But you were never so welcome thither as you shall be when I am mistress on't. In the meantime, I have sent you the first tome of *Cyrus* to read; when you have done with it, leave it at Mr. Hollingsworth's, and I'll send you another. I have had ladies with me all the afternoon that are for London to-morrow, and now I have as many letters to write as my Lord General's Secretary. Forgive me that this is no longer, for

I am your.

Addressed—
For Mrs. Paynter, at her house in
Bedford Street, next ye Goate,
In Covent Garden.

Letter 22.—Mr. Fish and Mr. Freeman were probably neighbours of Dorothy. There is a Mr. Ralph Freeman of Aspedon Hall, in Hertfordshire, mentioned in contemporary chronicles; he died in 1714, aged 88, and was therefore about 37 years of age at this time. His father seems to have been an ideal country gentleman, "who," says Sir Henry Chauncy, "made his house neat, his gardens pleasant, his groves delicious, his children cheerful, his servants easy, and kept excellent order in his family."

SIR,—You are more in my debt than you imagine. I never deserved a long letter so much as now, when you sent me a short one. I could tell you such a story ('tis too long to be written)

as would make you see (what I never discover'd
in myself before) that I am a valiant lady. In
earnest, we have had such a skirmish, and upon
so foolish an occasion, as I cannot tell which is
strangest. The Emperor and his proposals began
it; I talked merrily on't till I saw my brother
put on his sober face, and could hardly then
believe he was in earnest. It seems he was, for
when I had spoke freely my meaning, it wrought
so with him as to fetch up all that lay on his
stomach. All the people that I had ever in my
life refused were brought again upon the stage,
like Richard the III.'s ghosts, to reproach me
withal; and all the kindness his discoveries could
make I had for you was laid to my charge. My
best qualities (if I have any that are good) served
but for aggravations of my fault, and I was
allowed to have wit and understanding and discretion in other things, that it might appear I had
none in this. Well, 'twas a pretty lecture, and I
grew warm with it after a while; in short, we came
so near an absolute falling out, that 'twas time to
give over, and we said so much then that we
have hardly spoken a word together since. But
'tis wonderful to see what curtseys and legs pass
between us; and as before we were thought the
kindest brother and sister, we are certainly the
most complimental couple in England. 'Tis a
strange change, and I am very sorry for it, but
I'll swear I know not how to help it. I look

H

upon't as one of my great misfortunes, and I must
bear it, as that which is not my first nor likely to
be my last. 'Tis but reasonable (as you say) that
you should see me, and yet I know not now how
it can well be. I am not for disguises, it looks like
guilt, and I would not do a thing I durst not
own. I cannot tell whether (if there were a
necessity of your coming) I should not choose to
have it when he is at home, and rather expose
him to the trouble of entertaining a person whose
company (here) would not be pleasing to him,
and perhaps an opinion that I did it purposely to
cross him, than that your coming in his absence
should be thought a concealment. 'Twas one
reason more than I told you why I resolv'd not
to go to Epsom this summer, because I knew he
would imagine it an agreement between us, and
that something besides my spleen carried me
thither; but whether you see me or not you may
be satisfied I am safe enough, and you are in no
danger to lose your prisoner, since so great a
violence as this has not broke her chains. You
will have nothing to thank me for after this; my
whole life will not yield such another occasion to
let you see at what rate I value your friendship,
and I have been much better than my word in
doing but what I promised you, since I have
found it a much harder thing not to yield to the
power of a near relation, and a greater kindness
than I could then imagine it.

To let you see I did not repent me of the last commission, I'll give you another. Here is a seal that Walker set for me, and 'tis dropt out; pray give it him to mend. If anything could be wonder'd at in this age, I should very much how you came by your informations.

'Tis more than I know if Mr. Freeman be my servant. I saw him not long since, and he told me no·such thing. Do you know him? In earnest, he's a pretty gentleman, and has a great deal of good nature, I think, which may oblige him perhaps to speak well of his acquaintances without design. Mr. Fish is the Squire of Dames, and has so many mistresses that anybody may pretend a share in him and be believed; but though I have the honour to be his near neighbour, to speak freely, I cannot brag much that he makes any court to me ; and I know no young woman in the country that he does not visit often.

I have sent you another tome of *Cyrus*, pray send the first to Mr. Hollingsworth for my Lady. My cousin Molle went from hence to Cambridge on Thursday, and there's an end of Mr. Bennet. I have no company now but my niece Peyton, and my brother will be shortly for the term, but will make no long stay in town. I think my youngest brother comes down with him. Remember that you owe me a long letter and something for forgiving your last. I have no room for more than your.

Letter 23.

SIR,—I will tell you no more of my servants. I can no sooner give you some little hints whereabouts they live, but you know them presently, and I meant you should be beholding to me for your acquaintance. But it seems this gentleman is not so easy access, but you may acknowledge something due to me, if I incline him to look graciously upon you, and therefore there is not much harm done. What has kept him from marrying all this time, or how the humour comes so furiously upon him now, I know not; but if he may be believed, he is resolved to be a most romance squire, and go in quest of some enchanted damsel, whom if he likes, as to her person (for fortune is a thing below him),—and we do not read in history that any knight or squire was ever so discourteous as to inquire what portions their ladies had,—then he comes with the power of the county to demand her (which for the present he may dispose of, being Sheriff), so I do not see who is able to resist him. All that is to be hoped is, that since he may reduce whomsoever he pleases to his obedience, he will be very curious in his choice, and then I am secure.

It may be I dreamt it that you had met my brother, or else it was one of the reveries of my ague; if so, I hope I shall fall into no more

of them. I have missed four fits, and had but
five, and have recovered so much strength as
made me venture to meet your letter on Wednesday, a mile from home. Yet my recovery will
be nothing towards my leaving this place, where
many reasons will oblige me to stay at least all
this summer, unless some great alteration should
happen in this family; that which I most own is
my father's ill-health, which, though it be not in
that extremity it has been, yet keeps him still a
prisoner in his chamber, and for the most part to
his bed, which is reason enough. But, besides, I
can give you others. I am here much more out
of people's way than in town, where my aunt and
such as pretend an interest in me, and a power
over me, do so persecute me with their good
nature, and take it so ill that they are not accepted, as I would live in a hollow tree to avoid
them. Here I have nobody but my brother to
torment me, whom I can take the liberty to dispute with, and whom I have prevailed with
hitherto to bring none of his pretenders to this
place, because of the noise all such people make
in a country, and the tittle-tattle it breeds
among neighbours that have nothing to do but
to inquire who marries and who makes love. If
I can but keep him still in that humour, Mr.
Bennet and I are likely to preserve our state and
treat at distance like princes; but we have not sent
one another our pictures yet, though my cousin

Molle, who was his agent here, begged mine very earnestly.   But, I thank God, an imagination took him one morning that he was falling into a dropsy, and made him in such haste to go back to Cambridge to his doctor, that he never remembers anything he has to ask of me, but the coach to carry him away.   I lent it most willingly, and gone he is.   My eldest brother goes up to town on Monday too; perhaps you may see him, but I cannot direct you where to find him, for he is not yet resolved himself where to lie; only 'tis likely Nan may tell you when he is there.   He will make no stay, I believe.   You will think him altered (and, if it be possible) more melancholy than he was.   If marriage agrees no better with other people than it does with him, I shall pray that all my friends may 'scape it.   Yet if I were my cousin, H. Danvers, my Lady Diana should not, if I could help it, as well as I love her: I would try if ten thousand pound a year with a husband that doted on her, as I should do, could not keep her from being unhappy.   Well, in earnest, if I were a prince, that lady should be my mistress, but I can give no rule to any one else, and perhaps those that are in no danger of losing their hearts to her may be infinitely taken with one I should not value at all; for (so says the Justinian) wise Providence has ordained it that by their different humours everybody might find something to please themselves withal, without envying their neighbours. And now I have begun to talk gravely and wisely, I'll try if I can go a little further without being out. No, I cannot, for I have forgot already what 'twas I would have said; but 'tis no matter, for, as I remember, it was not much to the purpose, and, besides, I have paper little enough left to chide you for asking so unkind a question as whether you were still the same in my thoughts. Have you deserved to be otherwise; that is, am I no more in yours? For till that be, it's impossible the other should; but that will never be, and I shall always be the same I am. My heart tells me so, and I believe it; for were it otherwise, Fortune would not persecute me thus. Oh, me! she's cruel, and how far her power may reach I know not, only I am sure, she cannot call back time that is past, and it is long since we resolved to be for ever

Most faithful friends.

Letter 24.—Tom Cheeke is Sir Thomas Cheeke, Knight, of Purgo, in the county of Essex, or more probably his son, from the way Dorothy speaks of him; but it is difficult to discriminate among constant generations of Toms after a lapse of two hundred years. We find Sir Thomas's daughter was at this time the third wife of Lord Manchester; and it appears that Dorothy's great-grandfather married Catherine Cheeke, daughter of the then Sir Thomas. This will assist us to the connection between Dorothy, Tom Cheeke, and Lord

Manchester. Sir Richard Franklin, Knight, married a daughter of Sir Thomas Cheeke. He purchased Moor Park, Hertfordshire, about this time. The park and the mansion he bought in 1652 from the Earl of Monmouth, and the manor in 1655 from Sir Charles Harbord. The gardens had been laid out by the Countess of Bedford, who had sold the place in 1626 to the Earl of Pembroke. The house was well known to Temple, who describes the gardens in his Essay on Gardening; and when he retired in later years to an estate near Farnham in Surrey, he gave to it the name of Moor Park.

Lord Manchester was Edward Montagù, second Earl of Manchester. He was educated at Sidney Sussex College, Cambridge, and sat for Huntingdonshire in the first two Parliaments of Charles I. He was called to the Upper House as Lord Kimbolton in 1626, and succeeded his father in 1642. His name is well known in history as that of the leader of the Puritans in the House of Lords, and as the only peer joined with the five members impeached by the King. He raised a regiment and fought under Essex at Edgehill, reconquered Lincolnshire, and took part in the battle of Marston Moor. At this time Cromwell was his subordinate, and to his directions Lord Manchester's successes are in all probability due. At the second battle of Newbury, Lord Manchester showed some hesitation in following up his success, and Cromwell accused him of lukewarmness in the cause from his place in the House of Commons. An inquiry was instituted, but the Committee never carried out their investigations, and in parliamentary language the matter then dropped. He afterwards held, among other offices, that of Chancellor of the University of Cambridge, and inducted a visitation and reform of that University. He resisted the trial of the King and the foundation of the Commonwealth, refused to sit in Cromwell's new House of Lords, and was among those Presbyterians who helped to bring about the Restoration.

Cooper and Hoskins were famous miniature painters of the day. Samuel Cooper was a nephew of John Hoskins, who instructed him in the art of miniature painting, in which he soon out-rivalled his master. Cooper, who is styled by contemporary eulogists the " prince of limners," gave a strength and freedom to the art which it had not formerly possessed; but where he attempted to express more of the figure than the head, his drawing is defective. His painting was famous for the beauty of his carnation tints, and the loose flowing lines in which he described the hair of his model. He was a friend of the famous Samuel Butler. Hoskins, though a painter of less merit, had had the honour of painting His Majesty King Charles I., his Queen, and many members of the Court; and had passed through the varying fortunes of a fashionable portrait-painter, whose position, leaning as it does on the fickle approbation of the connoisseurs, is always liable to be wrested from him by a younger rival.

It is noticeable that this is the first letter in which we have intimation of the world's gossip about Dorothy's love affairs. We may, perhaps not unfairly, trace the growth of Dorothy's affection for Temple by the actions of others. First her brother raises his objections, and then her relations begin to gossip ; meanwhile the letters do not grow less kind.

Sir,—You amaze me with your story of Tom Cheeke. I am certain he could not have had it where you imagine, and 'tis a miracle to me that he remember that there is such a one in the world as his cousin D. O. I am sure he has not seen her this six year, and I think but once in his life. If he has spread his opinion in that family, I shall quickly hear on't, for my cousin Molle is now gone to Kimbolton to my Lord Manchester, and from there he goes to Moor Park to my cousin Franklin's, and in one, or both, he will be sure to meet with it. The matter is not great, for I confess I do naturally hate the noise and talk of the world, and should be best pleased never to be known in't upon any occasion whatsoever; yet, since it can never be wholly avoided, one must satisfy oneself by doing nothing that one need care who knows. I do not think *à propos* to tell anybody that you and I are very good friends, and it were better, sure, if nobody knew it but we ourselves. But if, in spite of all our caution, it be discovered, 'tis no treason nor anything else that's ill; and if anybody should tell me that I have had a greater kindness and esteem for you than for any one besides, I do not think I should deny it; howsoever you do, oblige me by not owning any such thing, for as you say, I have no reason to take it ill that you endeavour to preserve me a liberty, though I'm never likely to make use on't. Besides that, I agree with you too that certainly 'tis much better you should owe my kindness to nothing but your own merit and my inclination, than that there should lie any other necessity upon me of making good my words to you.

For God's sake do not complain so that you do not see me ; I believe I do not suffer less in't than you, but 'tis not to be helped. If I had a picture that were fit for you, you should have it. I have but one that's anything like, and that's a great one, but I will send it some time or other to Cooper or Hoskins, and have a little one drawn by it, if I cannot be in town to sit myself. You undo me by but dreaming how happy we might have been, when I consider how far we are from it in reality. Alas ! how can you talk of defying fortune ; nobody lives without it, and therefore why should you imagine you could ? I know not how my brother comes to be so well informed as you say, but I am certain he knows the utmost of the injuries you have received from her. 'Tis not possible she should have used you worse than he says. We have had another debate, but much more calmly. 'Twas just upon his going up to town, and perhaps he thought it not fit to part in anger. Not to wrong him, he never said to me (whate'er he thought) a word in prejudice of you in your own person, and I never heard him accuse any but your fortune and my indiscretion. And whereas I did expect that (at least in compliment to me) he should have said we had been a couple of fools well met, he says by his troth he

does not blame you, but bids me not deceive myself to think you have any great passion for me.

If you have done with the first part of *Cyrus*, I
should be glad Mr. Hollingsworth had it, because
I mentioned some such thing in my last to my
Lady; but there is no haste of restoring the other
unless she should send to me for it, which I
believe she will not.   I have a third tome here
against you have done with that second; and to
encourage you, let me assure you that the more
you read of them you will like them still better.
Oh, me! whilst I think on't, let me ask you one
question seriously, and pray resolve me truly;—do
I look so stately as people apprehend?   I vow to
you I made nothing on't when Sir Emperor said
so, because I had no great opinion of his judgment, but Mr. Freeman makes me mistrust myself
extremely, not that I am sorry I did appear so
to him (since it kept me from the displeasure of
refusing an offer which I do not perhaps deserve),
but that it is a scurvy quality in itself, and I am
afraid I have it in great measure if I showed any
of it to him, for whom I have so much respect
and esteem.   If it be so you must needs know it;
for though my kindness will not let me look so upon
you, you can see what I do to other people.   And,
besides, there was a time when we ourselves were
indifferent to one another;—did I do so then, or
have I learned it since?   For God's sake tell me,
that I may try to mend it.   I could wish, too, that

you would lay your commands on me to forbear fruit: here is enough to kill 1000 such as I am, and so extremely good, that nothing but your power can secure me; therefore forbid it me, that I may live to be

Your.

Letter 25. — Dorothy's dissertations on love and marriage are always amusing in their demureness. Who Cousin Peters was we cannot now say, but she was evidently a relation and a gossip. The episode concerning Mistress Harrison and the Queen is explained by the following quotation from the autobiography of the Countess of Warwick.

She is writing of Mr. Charles Rich, and says: " He was then in love with a Maid of Honour to the Queen, one Mrs. Hareson, that had been chamber-fellow to my sister-in-law whilst she lived at Court, and that brought on the acquaintance between him and my sister. He continued to be much with us for about five or six months, till my brother Broghill then (afterwards Earl of Orrery) grew also to be passionately in love with the same Mrs. Hareson. My brother then having a quarrel with Mr. Thomas Howard, second son to the Earl of Berkshire, about Mrs. Hareson (with whom he also was in love), Mr. Rich brought my brother a challenge from Mr. Howard, and was second to him against my brother when they fought, which they did without any great hurt of any side, being parted. This action made Mr. Rich judge it not civil to come to our house, and so for some time forbore doing it; but at last my brother's match with Mrs. Hareson being unhandsomely (on her side) broken off, when they were so near being married as the wedding clothes were to be made, and she after married Mr. Thomas Howard (to my father's great satisfaction), who always was averse to it, though, to comply with my brother's passion, he consented to it." There is a reference to the duel in a letter of Lord Cork, which fixes the date as 1639–40, but Mr. Nevile's name is nowhere mentioned.

Lord Broghill is well known to the history of that time, both literary and political. He was Roger Boyle, afterwards Earl of Orrery, the fifth son of the "great Earl of Cork." He acted for the Parliament against the Catholics in Ireland, but was still thought to retain some partiality for the King's party. Cromwell, however, considered himself secure in Lord Broghill's attachment; and, indeed, he continued to serve not only Cromwell during his lifetime, but his son Richard, after his father's death, with great fidelity. Lord Broghill was active in forwarding the Restoration in Ireland, and in reward of his services was made Earl of Orrery. He died in 1679.

SIR,—You have furnished me now with arguments to convince my brother, if he should ever enter on the dispute again. In earnest, I believed all this before, but 'twas something an ignorant kind of faith in me. I was satisfied myself, but could not tell how to persuade another of the truth on't; and to speak indifferently, there are such multitudes that abuse the names of love and friendship, and so very few that either understand or practise it in reality, that it may raise great doubts whether there is any such thing in the world or not, and such as do not find it in them-

selves will hardly believe 'tis anywhere. But it
will easily be granted, that most people make
haste to be miserable; that they put on their
fetters as inconsiderately as a woodcock runs into
a noose, and are carried by the weakest considerations imaginable to do a thing of the
greatest consequence of anything that concerns
this world. I was told by one (who pretends to
know him very well) that nothing tempted my
cousin Osborne to marry his lady (so much) as
that she was an Earl's daughter; which methought
was the prettiest fancy, and had the least of sense
in it, of any I had heard on, considering that it
was no addition to her person, that he had honour
enough before for his fortune, and how little it is
esteemed in this age,—if it be anything in a better,
—which for my part I am not well satisfied in.
Beside that, in this particular it does not sound
handsomely. My Lady Bridget Osborne makes
a worse name a great deal, methinks, than plain
my Lady Osborne would do.

I have been studying how Tom Cheeke might
come by his intelligence, and I verily believe he
has it from my cousin Peters. She lives near
them in Essex, and in all likelihood, for want of
other discourse to entertain him withal, she has
come out with all she knows. The last time I
saw her she asked me for you before she had
spoke six words to me; and I, who of all things do
not love to make secrets of trifles, told her I had

seen you that day. She said no more, nor I neither;
but perhaps it worked in her little brain.   The best
on't is, the matter is not great, for though I confess I had rather nobody knew it, yet 'tis that I
shall never be ashamed to own.

How kindly do I take these civilities of your
father's ; in earnest, you cannot imagine how his
letter pleased me.   I used to respect him merely
as he was your father, but I begin now to owe it
to himself; all that he says is so kind and so
obliging, so natural and so easy, that one may see
'tis perfectly his disposition, and has nothing to
disguise in it. 'Tis long since that I knew
how well he writ, perhaps you have forgot that
you showed me a letter of his (to a French
Marquis, I think, or some such man of his
acquaintance) when I first knew you ; I remember
it very well, and that I thought it as handsome a
letter as I had seen ; but I have not skill it seems,
for I like yours too.

I can pardon all my cousin Franklin's little
plots of discovery, if she believed herself when
she said she was confident our humours would
agree extremely well.   In earnest, I think they do ;
for I mark that I am always of your opinion,
unless it be when you will not allow that you
write well, for there I am too much concerned.
Jane told me t'other day very soberly that we
write very much alike.   I think she said it with
an intent to please me, and did not fail in't ; but

if you write ill, 'twas no great compliment to me. *A propos de* Jane, she bids me tell you that, if you liked your marmalade of quince, she would send you more, and she thinks better, that has been made since.

'Twas a strange caprice, as you say, of Mrs. Harrison, but there is fate as well as love in those things. The Queen took the greatest pains to persuade her from it that could be ; and (as somebody says, I know not who) " Majesty is no ill orator ; " but all would not do. When she had nothing to say for herself, she told her she had rather beg with Mr. Howard than live in the greatest plenty that could be with either my Lord Broghill, Charles Rich, or Mr. Nevile,—for all these were dying for her then. I am afraid she has altered her opinion since 'twas too late, for I do not take Mr. Howard to be a person that can deserve one should neglect all the world for him. And where there is no reason to uphold a passion, it will sink of itself ; but where there is, it may last eternally.—I am yours.

Letter 26.

SIR,—The day I should have received your letter I was invited to dine at a rich widow's (whom I think I once told you of, and offered my service in case you thought fit to make addresses there) ; and she was so kind, and in so good

I

humour, that if I had had any commission I should
have thought it a very fit time to speak. We
had a huge dinner, though the company was only
of her own kindred that are in the house with her
and what I brought; but she is broke loose from
an old miserable husband that lived so long, she
thinks if she does not make haste she shall not
have time to spend what he left. She is old and
was never handsome, and yet is courted a thousand times more than the greatest beauty in the
world would be that had not a fortune. We could
not eat in quiet for the letters and presents that
came in from people that would not have looked
upon her when they had met her if she had been
left poor. I could not but laugh to myself at the
meanness of their humour, and was merry enough
all day, for the company was very good; and
besides, I expected to find when I came home a
letter from you that would be more a feast and
company to me than all that was there. But
never anybody was so defeated as I was to find
none. I could not imagine the reason, only I
assured myself it was no fault of yours, but
perhaps a just punishment upon me for having
been too much pleased in a company where you
were not.

After supper my brother and I fell into dispute
about riches, and the great advantages of it; he
instanced in the widow that it made one respected
in the world. I said 'twas true, but that was a

respect I should not at all value when I owed it only to my fortune. And we debated it so long till we had both talked ourselves weary enough to go to bed. Yet I did not sleep so well but that I chid my maid for waking me in the morning, till she stopped my mouth with saying she had letters for me. I had not patience to stay till I could rise, but made her tie up all the curtains to let in light; and among some others I found my dear letter that was first to be read, and which made all the rest not worth the reading. I could not but wonder to find in it that my cousin Franklin should want a true friend when 'tis thought she has the best husband in the world; he was so passionate for her before he had her, and so pleased with her since, that, in earnest, I did not think it possible she could have anything left to wish for that she had not already in such a husband with such a fortune. But she can best tell whether she is happy or not; only if she be not, I do not see how anybody else can hope it. I know her the least of all the sisters, and perhaps 'tis to my advantage that she knows me no more, since she speaks so obligingly of me. But do you think it was altogether without design she spoke it to you? When I remember she is Tom Cheeke's sister, I am apt to think she might have heard his news, and meant to try whether there was anything of truth in't. My cousin Molle, I think, means to end the summer there. They say, indeed, 'tis a very fine seat, but if I did not mistake Sir Thomas Cheeke, he told me there was never a good room in the house. I was wondering how you came by an acquaintance there, because I had never heard you speak that you knew them. I never saw him in my life, but he is famous for a kind husband. Only 'twas found fault with that he could not forbear kissing his wife before company, a foolish trick that young married men are apt to; he has left it long since, I suppose. But, seriously, 'tis as ill a sight as one would wish to see, and appears very rude, methinks, to the company.

What a strange fellow this goldsmith is, he has a head fit for nothing but horns. I chid him once for a seal he set me just of this fashion and the same colours. If he were to make twenty they should be all so, his invention can stretch no further than blue and red. It makes me think of the fellow that could paint nothing but a flower-de-luce, who, when he met with one that was so firmly resolved to have a lion for his sign that there was no persuading him out on't, "Well," says the painter, "let it be a lion then, but it shall be as like a flower-de-luce as e'er you saw." So, because you would have it a dolphin, he consented to it, but it is like an ill-favoured knot of ribbon. I did not say anything of my father's being ill of late; I think I told you before, he kept his chamber ever since his last sickness, and so he does still. Yet I cannot say that he is at all sick, but has so general a weakness upon him that I am much afraid their opinion of him has too much of truth in it, and do extremely apprehend how the winter may work upon him. Will you pardon this strange scribbled letter, and the disorderliness on't? I know you would, though I should not tell you that I am not so much at leisure as I used to be. You can forgive your friends anything, and when I am not the faithfulest of those, never forgive me. You may direct your letters how you please, here will be nobody to receive it but

Your.

Letter 27.—Althorp, in Northamptonshire, was the seat of Lady Sunderland's first husband, Robert Lord Spencer.

SIR,—Your last came safe, and I shall follow your direction for the address of this, though, as you say, I cannot imagine what should tempt anybody to so severe a search for them, unless it be that he is not yet fully satisfied to what degree our friendship is grown, and thinks he may best inform himself from them. In earnest, 'twould not be unpleasant to hear our discourse. He forms his with so much art and design, and is so pleased with the hopes of making some discovery, and I [who] know him as well as he does himself, cannot but give myself the recreation sometimes of confounding him and destroying

all that his busy head had been working on since
the last conference.   He gives me some trouble
with his suspicions; yet, on my conscience, he is
a greater to himself, and I deal with so much
franchise as to tell him so; and yet he has no
more the heart to ask me directly what he
would so fain know, than a jealous man has to
ask (one that might tell him) whether he were a
cuckold or not, for fear of being resolved of that
which is yet a doubt to him.   My eldest brother
is not so inquisitive; he satisfies himself with
persuading me earnestly to marry, and takes
no notice of anything that may hinder me, but
a carelessness of my fortune, or perhaps an
aversion to a kind of life that appears to have
less of freedom in't than that which at present
I enjoy.   But, sure, he gives himself another
reason, for 'tis not very long since he took
occasion to inquire for you very kindly of me;
and though I could then give but little account
of you, he smiled as if he did not altogether
believe me, and afterwards maliciously said he
wondered you did not marry.   And I seemed to
do so too, and said, if I knew any woman that
had a great fortune, and were a person worthy of
you, I should wish her you with all my heart.
" But, sister," says he, " would you have him
love her?"   "Do you doubt it?" did I say;
"he were not happy in't else."   He laughed,
and said my humour was pleasant; but he made

some question whether it was natural or not. He cannot be so unjust as to let me lose him, sure, I was kind to him though I had some reason not to take it very well when he made that a secret to me which was known to so many that did not know him ; but we shall never fall out, I believe, we are not apt to it, neither of us.

If you are come back from Epsom, I may ask you how you like drinking water ? I have wished it might agree as well with you as it did with me ; and if it were as certain that the same tning would do us good as 'tis that the same thing would please us, I should not need to doubt it. Otherwise my wishes do not signify much, but I am forbid complaints, or to express my fears. And be it so, only you must pardon me if I cannot agree to give you false hopes ; I must be deceived myself before I can deceive you, and I have so accustomed myself to tell you all that I think, that I must either say nothing, or that which I believe to be true.

I cannot say but that I have wanted Jane ; but it has been rather to have somebody to talk with of you, than that I needed anybody to put me in mind of you, and with all her diligence I should have often prevented her in that discourse. Were you at Althorp when you saw my Lady Sunderland and Mr. Smith, or are they in town ? I have heard, indeed, that they are very happy ; but withal that, as she is a very extraordinary person herself, so she aimed at doing extraordinary things, and when she had married Mr. Smith (because some people were so bold as to think she did it because she loved him) she undertook to convince the world that what she had done was in mere pity to his sufferings, and that she could not go a step lower to meet anybody than that led her, though when she thought there were no eyes on her, she was more gracious to him. But perhaps this might not be true, or it may be she is now grown weary of that constraint she put upon herself. I should have been sadder than you if I had been their neighbour to have seen them so kind; as I must have been if I had married the Emperor. He used to brag to me always of a great acquaintance he had there, what an esteem my lady had for him, and had the vanity (not to call it impudence) to talk sometimes as if he would have had me believe he might have had her, and would not; I'll swear I blushed for him when I saw he did not. He told me too, that though he had carried his addresses to me with all the privacy that was possible, because he saw I liked it best, and that 'twas partly his own humour too, yet she had discovered it, and could tell that there had been such a thing, and that it was broke off again, she knew not why; which certainly was a lie, as well as the other, for I do not think she ever heard there was such a one in the world as

Your faithful friend.

Letter 28.—Dorothy's allusion to the " Seven Sleepers "
refers to a story which occurs in the *Golden Legend* and
other places, of seven noble youths of Ephesus, who fled
from persecution to a cave in Mount Celion.   After two
hundred and thirty years they awoke, but only to die soon
afterwards.   The fable is said to have arisen from a mis-
interpretation of the text, "They fell asleep in the Lord."

Sir,—I did not lay it as a fault to your charge
that you were not good at disguise ; if it be one,
I am too guilty on't myself to accuse another.
And though I have been told it shows an un-
practisedness in the world, and betrays to all
that understand it better, yet since it is a
quality I was not born with, nor ever like to get,
I have always thought good to maintain that it
was better not to need it than to have it.

I give you many thanks for your care of my
Irish dog, but I am extremely out of countenance
your father should be troubled with it. Sure, he
will think I have a most extravagant fancy ; but
do me the right as to let him know I am not
so possessed with it as to consent he should be
employed in such a commission.

Your opinion of my eldest brother is, I think,
very just, and when I said maliciously, I meant a
French malice, which you know does not signify
the same with an English one.   I know not
whether I told it you or not, but I concluded (from
what you said of your indisposition) that it was
very like the spleen ; but perhaps I foresaw you

would not be willing to own a disease that the severe part of the world holds to be merely imaginary and affected, and therefore proper only to women. However, I cannot but wish you had stayed longer at Epsom and drunk the waters with more order though in a less proportion. But did you drink them immediately from the well ? I remember I was forbid it, and methought with a great deal of reason, for (especially at this time of year) the well is so low, and there is such a multitude to be served out on't, that you can hardly get any but what is thick and troubled ; and I have marked that when it stood all night (for that was my direction) the bottom of the vessel it stood in would be covered an inch thick with a white clay, which, sure, has no great virtue in't, and is not very pleasant to drink.

What a character of a young couple you give me ! Would you would ask some one who knew him, whether he be not much more of an ass since his marriage than he was before. I have some reason to doubt that it alters people strangely. I made a visit t'other day to welcome a lady into this country whom her husband had newly brought down, and because I knew him, though not her, and she was a stranger here, 'twas a civility I owed them. But you cannot imagine how I was surprised to see a man that I had known so handsome, so capable of being made a pretty gentleman (for though he was no proud philosopher, as the Frenchmen say, he was that which good company and a little knowledge of the world would have made equal to many that think themselves very well, and are thought so), transformed into the direct shape of a great boy newly come from school. To see him wholly taken up with running on errands for his wife, and teaching her little dog tricks! And this was the best of him; for when he was at leisure to talk, he would suffer no one else to do it, and what he said, and the noise he made, if you had heard it, you would have concluded him drunk with joy that he had a wife and a pack of hounds. I was so weary on't that I made haste home, and could not but think of the change all the way till my brother (who was with me) thought me sad, and so, to put me in better humour, said he believed I repented me I had' not this gentleman, now I saw how absolutely his wife governed him. But I assured him, that though I thought it very fit such as he should be governed, yet I should not like the employment by no means. It becomes no woman, and did so ill with this lady that in my opinion it spoiled a good face and a very fine gown. Yet the woman you met upon the way governed her husband and did it handsomely. It was, as you say, a great example of friendship, and much for the credit of our sex.

You are too severe to Walker. I'll undertake he would set me twenty seals for nothing rather

than undergo your wrath.   I am in no haste for
it, and so he does it well we will not fall out;
perhaps he is not in the humour of keeping his
word at present, and nobody can blame him if he
be often in an ill one.   But though I am merciful
to him, as to one that has suffered enough already,
I cannot excuse you that profess to be my friend
and yet are content to let me live in such ignorance, write to me every week, and yet never send
me any of the new phrases of the town.   I could
tell you, without abandoning the truth, that it is
part of your *devoyre* to correct the imperfections
you find under my hand, and that my trouble
resembles my wonder you can let me be dis-
satisfied.   I should never have learnt any of these
fine things from you; and, to say truth, I know
not whether I shall from anybody else, if to learn
them be to understand them.   Pray what is meant
by *wellness* and *unwellness ;* and why is *to some
extreme* better than *to some extremity?*   I believe
I shall live here till there is quite a new language
spoke where you are, and shall come out like one
of the Seven Sleepers, a creature of another age.
But 'tis no matter so you understand me, though
nobody else do, when I say how much I am

Your faithful.

Letter 29.

SIR,—I can give you leave to doubt anything
but my kindness, though I can assure you I spake

as I meant when I said I had not the vanity to
believe I deserv'd yours, for I am not certain
whether 'tis possible for anybody to deserve that
another should love them above themselves,
though I am certain many may deserve it more
than me. But not to dispute this with you, let
me tell you that I am thus far of your opinion,
that upon some natures nothing is so powerful as
kindness, and that I should give that to yours
which all the merit in the world besides would
not draw from me. I spake as if I had not done
so already; but you may choose whether you will
believe me or not, for, to say truth, I do not much
believe myself in that point. No, all the kindness
I have or ever had is yours; nor shall I ever repent
it so, unless you shall ever repent yours. Without
telling you what the inconveniences of your coming
hither are, you may believe they are considerable,
or else I should not deny you or myself the
happiness of seeing one another; and if you dare
trust me where I am equally concerned with you,
I shall take hold of the first opportunity that may
either admit you here or bring me nearer you.
Sure you took somebody else for my cousin
Peters? I can never believe her beauty able to
smite anybody. I saw her when I was last in
town, but she appear'd wholly the same to me,
she was at St. Malo, with all her innocent good
nature too, and asked for you so kindly, that I am
sure she cannot have forgot you; nor do I think

she has so much address as to do it merely in compliment to me. No, you are mistaken certainly; what should she do amongst all that company, unless she be towards a wedding? She has been kept at home, poor soul, and suffer'd so much of purgatory in this world that she needs not fear it in the next; and yet she is as merry as ever she was, which perhaps might make her look young, but that she laughs a little too much, and that will bring wrinkles, they say. Oh, me! now I talk of laughing, it makes me think of poor Jane. I had a letter from her the other day; she desired me to present her humble service to her master,— she did mean you, sure, for she named everybody else that she owes any service to,—and bid me say that she would keep her word with him. God knows what you have agreed on together. She tells me she shall stay long enough there to hear from me once more, and then she is resolved to come away.

Here is a seal, which pray give Walker to set for me very handsomely, and not of any of those fashions he made my others, but of something that may differ from the rest. 'Tis a plain head, but not ill cut, I think. My eldest brother is now here, and we expect my youngest shortly, and then we shall be altogether, which I do not think we ever were twice in our lives. My niece is still with me, but her father threatens to fetch her away. If I can keep her to Michaelmas I may

perhaps bring her up to town myself, and take
that occasion of seeing you; but I have no other
business that is worth my taking a journey, for I
have had another summons from my aunt, and I
protest I am afraid I shall be in rebellion there;
but 'tis not to be helped. The widow writes me
word, too, that I must expect her here about a
month hence; and I find that I shall want no
company, but only that which I would have, and
for which I could willingly spare all the rest.
Will it be ever thus? I am afraid it will. There
has been complaints made on me already to my
eldest brother (only in general, or at least he takes
notice of no more), what offers I refuse, and what
a strange humour has possessed me of being deaf
to the advice of all my friends. I find I am to be
baited by them all by turns. They weary themselves, and me too, to very little purpose, for to
my thinking they talk the most impertinently that
ever people did; and I believe they are not in my
debt, but think the same of me. Sometimes I tell
them I will not marry, and then they laugh at
me; sometimes I say, "Not yet," and they laugh
more, and would make me believe I shall be old
within this twelvemonth. I tell them I shall be
wiser then. They say 'twill be to no purpose.
Sometimes we are in earnest and sometimes in
jest, but always saying something since my
brother Henry found his tongue again. If you
were with me I could make sport of all this; but

"patience is my penance" is somebody's motto, and I think it must be mine.

I am your.

Letter 30.—Here is Lord Lisle's embassage discussed again ! We know that in the end it comes to nothing; Whitelocke going, but without Temple. The statute commanding the marriage ceremony to be conducted before Justices of the Peace was passed in August 1653; it is to some extent by such references as these that the letters have been dated and grouped. The Marriage Act of 1653, with the other statutes of this period, have been erased from the Statute Book ; but a draft of it in Somers' Tracts remains to us for reference. It contained provisions for the names of those who intended being joined together in holy matrimony to be posted, with certain other particulars, upon the door of the common meeting-house, commonly called the parish church or chapel; and after the space of three weeks the parties, with two witnesses, might go before a magistrate, who, having satisfied himself, by means of examining witnesses on oath or otherwise, that all the preliminaries commanded by the Act had been properly fulfilled, further superintended the proceedings to perfect the said intended marriage as follows :—The man taking the woman by the hand pronounced these words, " I, A. B., do hereby in the presence of God take thee C. D. to my wedded wife, and do also in the presence of God, and before these witnesses, promise to be unto thee a loving and faithful husband." Then the woman in similar formula promised to be a "loving, faithful, and obedient wife," and the magistrate pronounced the parties to be man and wife. This ceremony, and this only, was to be a legal marriage. It is probable that parties might and did add a voluntary religious rite to this compulsory civil ceremony, as is done at this day in many foreign countries.

SIR,—You cannot imagine how I was surpris'd to find a letter that began " Dear brother;" I thought sure it could not belong at all to me, and was afraid I had lost one by it; that you intended me another, and in your haste had mistook this for that. Therefore, till I found 'the permission you gave me, I had laid it by with a resolution not to read it, but to send it again. If I had done so, I had missed a great deal of satisfaction which I received from it. In earnest, I cannot tell you how kindly I take all the obliging things you say in it of me; nor how pleased I should be (for your sake) if I were able to make good the character you give me to your brother, and that I did not owe a great part of it wholly to your friendship for me. I dare call nothing on't my own but faithfulness; that I may boast of with truth and modesty, since 'tis but a simple virtue; and though some are without it, yet 'tis so absolutely necessary, that nobody wanting it can be worthy of any esteem. I see you speak well of me to other people, though you complain always to me. I know not how to believe I should misuse your heart as you pretend; I never had any quarrel to it, and since our friendship it has been dear to me as my own. 'Tis rather, sure, that you have a mind to try another, than

K

that any dislike of yours makes you turn it over to me; but be it as it will, I am contented to stand to the loss, and perhaps when you have changed you will find so little difference that you'll be calling for your own again. Do but assure me that I shall find you almost as merry as my Lady Anne Wentworth is always, and nothing shall fright me from my purpose of seeing you as soon as I can with any conveniency. I would not have you insensible of our misfortunes, but I would not either that you should revenge them on yourself; no, that shows a want of constancy (which you will hardly yield to be your fault); but 'tis certain that there was never anything more mistaken than the Roman courage, when they killed themselves to avoid misfortunes that were infinitely worse than death. You confess 'tis an age since our story began, as is not fit for me to own. Is it not likely, then, that if my face had ever been good, it might be altered since then; or is it as unfit for me to own the change as the time that makes it? Be it as you please, I am not enough concerned in't to dispute it with you; for, trust me, if you would not have my face better, I am satisfied it should be as it is; since if ever I wished it otherwise, 'twas for your sake.

I know not how I stumbled upon a news-book this week, and, for want of something else to do, read it; it mentions my Lord Lisle's embassage again. Is there any such thing towards? I met with somebody else too in't that may concern anybody that has a mind to marry; 'tis a new form for it, that, sure, will fright the country people extremely, for they apprehend nothing like going before a Justice; they say no other marriage shall stand good in law.   In conscience, I believe the old one is the better; and for my part I am resolved to stay till that comes in fashion again.

Can your father have so perfectly forgiven already the injury I did him (since you will not allow it to be any to you), in hindering you of Mrs. Chambers, as to remember me with kindness? 'Tis most certain that I am obliged to him, and, in earnest, if I could hope it might ever be in my power to serve him I would promise something for myself.   But is it not true, too, that you have represented me to him rather as you imagine me than as I am; and have you not given him an expectation that I shall never be able to satisfy?   If you have, I can forgive you, because I know you meant well in't; but I have known some women that have commended others merely out of spite, and if I were malicious enough to envy anybody's beauty, I would cry it up to all that had not seen them; there's no such way to make anybody appear less handsome than they are.

You must not forget that you are some letters in my debt, besides the answer to this.   If there were not conveniences of sending, I should persecute you strangely.   And yet you cannot wonder at it; the constant desire I have to hear from you, and the satisfaction your letters give me, would oblige one that has less time to write often.   But yet I know what 'tis to be in the town.   I could never write a letter from thence in my life of above a dozen lines; and though I see as little company as anybody that comes there, yet I always met with something or other that kept me idle.   Therefore I can excuse it, though you do not exactly pay all that you owe, upon condition you shall tell me when I see you all that you should have writ if you had had time, and all that you can imagine to say to a person that is

Your faithful friend.

Letter 31.—Dorothy is in mourning for her youngest brother, Robert, who died about this time.   As she does not mention his death to Temple, we may take it that he was, though her brother, practically a stranger to her, living away from Chicksands, and rarely visiting her.

General Monk's brother, to whom Dorothy refers, was Mr. Nicholas Monk, vicar of Kelkhampton, in Cornwall. General Monk's misfortune is no less a calamity than his marriage.   The following extract from Guizot's *Life of Monk* will fully explain the allusion : " The return of the new admiral [Monk] was marked by a domestic event which was not without its influence on his public conduct and reputation.   Unrefined tastes, and that need of repose in his private life which usually accompanies activity in public affairs, had consigned him to the dominion of a woman of low character, destitute even of the charms which seduce, and whose manners did not belie the rumour which gave her for extraction a market stall, or even, according to some, a much less respectable profession. She had lived for some time past with Monk, and united to the influence of habit an impetuosity of will and words difficult to be resisted by the tranquil apathy of her lover. It is asserted that she had managed, as long since as 1649, to force him to a marriage ; but this marriage was most certainly not declared until 1653." M. Guizot then quotes a letter, dated September 19, 1653, announcing the news of General Monk's marriage, and this would about correspond with the presumed date of Dorothy's letter. Greenwich Palace was probably occupied by Monk at this time, and Dorothy meant to say that Ann Clarges would be as much at home in Greenwich Palace as, say, the Lord Protector's wife at Whitehall.

Sir,—It was, sure, a less fault in me to make a scruple of reading your letter to your brother, which in all likelihood I could not be concerned in, than for you to condemn the freedom you take of giving me directions in a thing where we are equally concerned. Therefore, if I forgive you this, you may justly forgive me t'other ; and upon these terms we are friends again, are we not ? No, stay ! I have another fault to chide you for. You doubted whether you had not writ too much, and whether I could have the patience to read it or not. Why do you dissemble so abominably; you cannot think these things ? How I should love that plain-heartedness you speak of, if you would use it; nothing is civil but that

amongst friends.   Your kind sister ought to chide
you, too, for not writing to her, unless you have
been with her to excuse it.   I hope you have;
and pray take some time to make her one visit
from me, and carry my humble service with you,
and tell her that 'tis not my fault that you are no
better.   I do not think I shall see the town
before Michaelmas, therefore you may make what
sallies you please.   I am tied here to expect my
brother Peyton, and then possibly we may go up
together, for I should be at home again before
the term.   Then I may show you my niece; and
you may confess that I am a kind aunt to desire
her company, since the disadvantage of our being
together will lie wholly upon me.   But I must
make it my bargain, that if I come you will not
be frighted to see me; you think, I'll warrant,
you have courage enough to endure a worse
sight.   You may be deceived, you never saw me
in mourning yet; nobody that has will e'er desire
to do it again, for their own sakes as well as mine.
Oh, 'tis a most dismal dress,—I have not dared
to look in the glass since I wore it; and certainly
if it did so ill with other people as it does with
me, it would never be worn.

You told me of writing to your father, but you
did not say whether you had heard from him, or
how he did.   May not I ask it?   Is it possible
that he saw me?   Where were my eyes that I
did not see him, for I believe I should have

guessed at least that 'twas he if I had? They
say you are very like him; but 'tis no wonder
neither that I did not see him, for I saw not you
when I met you there. 'Tis a place I look upon
nobody in; and it was reproached to me by a
kinsman, but a little before you came to me, that
he had followed me to half a dozen shops to see
when I would take notice of him, and was at last
going away with a belief 'twas not I, because I
did not seem to know him. Other people make
it so much their business to gape, that I'll swear
they put me so out of countenance I dare not
look up for my life.

I am sorry for General Monk's misfortunes,
because you say he is your friend; but otherwise
she will suit well enough with the rest of the
great ladies of the times, and become Greenwich
as well as some others do the rest of the King's
houses. If I am not mistaken, that Monk has a
brother lives in Cornwall; an honest gentleman,
I have heard, and one that was a great acquaintance of a brother of mine who was killed there
during the war, and so much his friend that upon
his death he put himself and his family into
mourning for him, which is not usual, I think,
where there is no relation of kindred.

I will take order that my letters shall be left
with Jones, and yours called for there. As long
as your last was, I read it over thrice in less than
an hour, though, to say truth, I had skipped some

on't the last time. I could not read my own confession so often. Love is a terrible word, and I should blush to death if anything but a letter accused me on't. Pray be merciful, and let it run friendship in my next charge. My Lady sends me word she has received those parts of *Cyrus* I lent you. Here is another for you which, when you have read, you know how to dispose. There are four pretty stories in it, " *L'Amant Absente,*" " *L'Amant non Aimé,*" " *L'Amant Jaloux,*" et " *L'Amant dont La Maitresse est mort.*" Tell me which you have most compassion for when you have read what every one says for himself. Perhaps you will not think it so easy to decide which is the most unhappy, as you may think by the titles their stories bear. Only let me desire you not to pity the jealous one, for I remember I could do nothing but laugh at him as one that sought his own vexation. This, and the little journeys (you say) you are to make, will entertain you till I come; which, sure, will be as soon as possible I can, since 'tis equally desired by you and your faithful.

Letter 32.—Things being more settled in that part of the world, Sir John Temple is returning to Ireland, where he intends taking his seat as Master of the Rolls once again. Temple joins his father soon after this, and stays in Ireland a few months.

Lady Ormond was the wife of the first Duke of

Ormond. She had obtained her pass to go over to Ireland on August 24th, 1653. The Ormonds had indeed been in great straits for want of money, and in August 1652 Lady Ormond had come over from Caen, where they were then living, to endeavour to claim Cromwell's promise of reserving to her that portion of their estate which had been her inheritance. After great delays she obtained £500, and a grant of £2000 per annum out of their Irish lands "lying most conveniently to Dunmore House." It must have been this matter that Dorothy had heard of when she questions "whether she will get it when she comes there."

Francis Annesley, Lord Valentia, belonged to an ancient Nottinghamshire family, though he himself was born in Newport, Buckinghamshire. Of his daughter's marriage I can find nothing. Lord Valentia was at this time Secretary of State at Dublin.

Sir Justinian has at length found a second wife. Her name is Vere, and she is the daughter of Lord Leigh of Stoneleigh. Thus do Dorothy's suitors, one by one, recover and cease to lament her obduracy. When she declares that she would rather have chosen *a chain to lead her apes in* than marry Sir Justinian, she refers to an old superstition as to the ultimate fate of spinsters—

Women, dying maids, lead apes in hell,

runs the verse of an old play, and that is the whole superstition, the origin of which seems somewhat inexplicable. · The phrase is thrice used by Shakespeare, and constantly occurs in the old burlesques and comedies ; in one instance, . in a comedy entitled "Love's Convert" (1651), it is altered to "lead an ape in *heaven*." Many will remember the fate of "The

young Mary Anne" in the famous Ingoldsby legend,
" Bloudie Jacke : "—

So they say she is now leading apes—
Bloudie Jack,
And mends bachelors' smallclothes below.

No learned editor that I am acquainted with has
been able to suggest an explanation of this curious
expression.

SIR,—All my quarrels to you are kind ones, for,
sure, 'tis alike impossible for me to be angry as
for you to give me the occasion; therefore, when
I chide (unless it be that you are not careful
enough of yourself, and hazard too much a health
that I am more concerned in than my own), you
need not study much for/ excuses, I can easily
forgive you anything but want of kindness.   The
judgment you have made of the four lovers I
recommended to you does so perfectly agree with
what I think of them, that I hope it will not alter
when you have read their stories. *L'Amant Absent*
has (in my opinion) a mistress so much beyond
any of the rest, that to be in danger of losing her
is more than to have lost the others; *L'Amant
non Aimé* was an ass, under favour (notwithstand-
the *Princesse Cleobuline's* letter); his mistress had
caprices that would have suited better with our
Amant Jaloux than with anybody else; and the
Prince Artibie was much to blame that he outlived his *belle Leontine*.   But if you have met
with the beginning of the story of *Amestris and*

Aglatides, you will find the rest of it in this part
I send you now; and 'tis, to me, one of the
prettiest I have read, and the most natural.
They say the gentleman that writes this romance
has a sister that lives with him, a maid, and she
furnishes him with all the little stories that come
between, so that he only contrives the main
design; and when he wants something to entertain his company withal, he calls to her for
it. She has an excellent fancy, sure, and a great
wit; but, I am sorry to tell it you, they say 'tis
the most ill-favoured creature that ever was born.
And 'tis often so; how seldom do we see a person
excellent in anything but they have some great
defect with it that pulls them low enough to make
them equal with other people; and there is justice
in't. Those that have fortunes have nothing
else, and those that want it deserve to have it.
That's but small comfort, though, you'll say; 'tis
confessed, but there is no such thing as perfect
happiness in this world, those that have come
the nearest it had many things to wish; and,
—bless me, whither am I going? Sure, 'tis the
death's head I see stand before me puts me into
this grave discourse (pray do not think I meant
that for a conceit neither); how idly have I spent
two sides of my paper, and am afraid, besides,
I shall not have time to write two more. Therefore I'll make haste to tell you that my friendship
for you makes me concerned in all your relations;

that I have a great respect for Sir John, merely
as he is your father, and that 'tis much increased
by his kindness to you; that he has all my
prayers and wishes for his safety; and that you
will oblige me in letting me know when you hear
any good news from him. He has met with a
great deal of good company, I believe. My Lady
Ormond, I am told, is waiting for a passage, and
divers others; but this wind (if I am not mistaken) is not good for them. In earnest, 'tis a
most sad thing that a person of her quality should
be reduced to such a fortune as she has lived
upon these late years, and that she should lose
that which she brought, as well as that which
was her husband's. Yet, I hear, she has now got
some of her own land in Ireland granted her; but
whether she will get it when she comes there is, I
think, a question.

We have a lady new come into this country
that I pity, too, extremely. She is one of my
Lord of Valentia's daughters, and has married
an old fellow that is some threescore and ten,
who has a house that is fitter for the hogs than
for her, and a fortune that will not at all recompense the least of these inconveniences. Ah! 'tis
most certain I should have chosen a handsome
chain to lead my apes in before such a husband;
but marrying and hanging go by destiny, they
say. It was not mine, it seems, to have an
emperor; the spiteful man, merely to vex me,

has gone and married my countrywoman, my Lord Lee's daughter. What a multitude of willow garlands I shall weave before I die; I think I had best make them into faggots this cold weather, the flame they would make in a chimney would be of more use to me than that which was in the hearts of all those that gave them me, and would last as long. I did not think I should have got thus far. I have been so persecuted with visits all this week I have had no time to despatch anything of business, so that now I have done this I have forty letters more to write; how much rather would I have them all to you than to anybody else; or, rather, how much better would it be if there needed none to you, and that I could tell you without writing how much I am

Yours.

Letter 33.—Sir Thomas Peyton, we must remember, had married Dorothy's eldest sister; she died many years ago, and Sir Thomas married again, in 1648, one Dame Cicely Swan, a widow, whose character Dorothy gives us.

Lord Monmouth was the eldest son of the Earl of Monmouth, and was born in 1596. He was educated at Exeter College, Oxford. His literary work was, at least, copious, and included some historical writing, as well as the translations mentioned by Dorothy. He published, among other things, *An Historical Relation of the United Provinces*, a *History of the Wars in Flanders*, and a *History of Venice.*

Sir John Suckling, in the following doggerel, hails our noble author with a flunkey's enthusiasm,—

> It is so rare and new a thing to see
> Aught that belongs to young nobility
> In print, but their own clothes, that we must praise
> You, as we would do those first show the ways
> To arts or to new worlds.

In such strain writes the author of *Why so pale and wan, fond lover?* and both the circumstance and the doggerel should be very instructive to the snobologist.

The literary work of Lord Broghill is not unknown to fame, and Mr. Waller's verse is still read by us; but I have never seen a history of the Civil Wars from his pen, and cannot find that he ever published one.

Prazimene and *Polexander* are two romances translated from the French,—the former, a neat little duodecimo; the latter, a huge folio of more than three hundred and fifty closely-printed pages. The title-page of *Prazimene*, a very good example of its kind, runs as follows:—"Two delightful Novels, or the Unlucky Fair One; being the Amours of Milistrate and Prazimene, Illustrated with variety of Chance and Fortune. Translated from the French by a Person of Quality. London. Sold by Eben Tracy, at the Three Bibles, on London Bridge." *Polexander* was "done into English by William Browne, Gent.," for the benefit and behoof of the Earl of Pembroke.

William Fiennes, Lord Say and Sele, was one of the chiefs of the Independent party, a Republican, and one of the first to bear arms against the King. He had, for that day, extravagant notions of civil liberty, and on the disappointment of his hopes, he appears to have retired to the Isle of Lundy, on the coast of Devon, and continued a voluntary prisoner there until Cromwell's death.

After the Restoration he was made Lord Chamberlain of the Household, and Lord Privy Seal. He published some political tracts, none of which are now in existence; and Anthony Wood mentions having seen other things of his, among which, maybe, was the romance that Dorothy had heard of, but which is lost to us.

SIR,—Pray, let not the apprehension that others say fine things to me make your letters at all the shorter; for, if it were so, I should not think they did, and so long you are safe. My brother Peyton does, indeed, sometimes send me letters that may be excellent for aught I know, and the more likely because I do not understand them; but I may say to you (as to a friend) I do not like them, and have wondered that my sister (who, I may tell you too, and you will not think it vanity in me, had a great deal of wit, and was thought to write as well as most women in England) never persuaded him to alter his style, and make it a little more intelligible. He is an honest gentleman, in earnest, has understanding enough, and was an excellent husband to two very different wives, as two good ones could be. My sister was a melancholy, retired woman, and, besides the company of her husband and her books, never sought any, but could have spent a life much longer than hers was in looking to her house and her children. This lady is of a free, jolly humour, loves cards and company, and is never more pleased than when she sees a great

many others that are so too. Now, with both
these he so perfectly complied that 'tis hard to
judge which humour he is more inclined to in
himself; perhaps to neither, which makes it so
much the more strange. His kindness to his
first wife may give him an esteem for her sister;
but he was too much smitten with this lady to
think of marrying anybody else, and, seriously, I
could not blame him, for she had, and has yet,
great loveliness in her; she was very handsome,
and is very good (one may read it in her face at
first sight). A woman that is hugely civil to all
people, and takes as generally as anybody that
I know, but not more than my cousin Molle's
letters do, but which, yet, you do not like, you
say, nor I neither, I'll swear; and if it be
ignorance in us both we'll forgive it one another.
In my opinion these great scholars are not the
best writers (of letters, I mean); of books, perhaps
they are. I never had, I think, but one letter
from Sir Justinian, but 'twas worth twenty of
anybody's else to make me sport. It was the
most sublime nonsense that in my life I ever
read; and yet, I believe, he descended as low as
he could to come near my weak understanding.
'Twill be no compliment after this to say I like
your letters in themselves; not as they come from
one that is not indifferent to me, but, seriously, I
do. All letters, methinks, should be free and
easy as one's discourse; not studied as an oration,

nor made up of hard words like a charm. 'Tis an admirable thing to see how some people will labour to find out terms that may obscure a plain sense. Like a gentleman I know, who would never say "the weather grew cold," but that " winter began to salute us." I have no patience for such coxcombs, and cannot blame an old uncle of mine that threw the standish at his man's head because he writ a letter for him where, instead of saying (as his master bid him), "that he would have writ himself, but he had the gout in his hand," he said, " that the gout in his hand would not permit him to put pen to paper." The fellow thought he had mended it mightily, and that putting pen to paper was much better than plain writing.

I have no patience neither for these trans-lations of romances. I met with *Polexander* and *L'illustre Bassa* both so disguised that I, who am their old acquaintance, hardly know them; besides that, they were still so much French in words and phrases that 'twas impossible for one that under-stands not French to make anything of them. If poor *Prazimene* be in the same dress, I would not see her for the world. She has suffered enough besides. I never saw but four tomes of her, and was told the gentleman that writ her story died when those were finished. I was very sorry for it, I remember, for I liked so far as I had seen of it extremely. Is it not my good Lord of Monmouth, or some such honourable

L

personage, that presents her to the English ladies ? I have heard many people wonder how he spends his estate. I believe he undoes himself with printing his translations. Nobody else will undergo the charge, because they never hope to sell enough of them to pay themselves withal. I was looking t'other day in a book of his where he translates *Pipero* as piper, and twenty words more that are as false as this.

My Lord Broghill, sure, will give us something worth the reading. My Lord Saye, I am told, has writ a romance since his retirement in the Isle of Lundy, and Mr. Waller, they say, is making one of our wars, which, if he does not mingle with a great deal of pleasing fiction, cannot be very diverting, sure, the subject is so sad.

But all this is nothing to my coming to town, you'll say. 'Tis confest; and that I was willing as long as I could to avoid saying anything when I had nothing to say worth your knowing. I am still obliged to wait my brother Peyton and his lady coming. I had a letter from him this week, which I will send you, that you may see what hopes he gives. As little room as I have left, too, I must tell you what a present I had made me to-day. Two of the finest young Irish greyhounds that ere I saw ; a gentleman that serves the General sent them me. They are newly come over, and sent for by Henry Cromwell, he tells me, but not how he got them for me.

However, I am glad I have them, and much the more becauses it dispenses with a very unfit employment that your father, out of his kindness to you and his civility to me, was content to take upon him.

Letter 34.

SIR,—Jane was so unlucky as to come out of town before your return, but she tells me she left my letter with Nan Stacy for you. I was in hope she would have brought me one from you; and because she did not I was resolv'd to punish her, and kept her up till one o'clock telling me all her stories. Sure, if there be any truth in the old observation, your cheeks glowed notably; and 'tis most certain that if I were with you, I should chide notably. What do you mean to be so melancholy? By her report your humour is grown insupportable. I can allow it not to be altogether what she says, and yet it may be very ill too; but if you loved me you would not give yourself over to that which will infallibly kill you, if it continue. I know too well that our fortunes have given us occasion enough to complain and to be weary of her tyranny; but, alas! would it be better if I had lost you or you me; unless we were sure to die both together, 'twould but increase our misery, and add to that which is more already than we can well tell how to bear. You are more cruel than she regarding a life that's dearer to me than that of the whole world besides, and which makes all the happiness I have or ever shall be capable of. Therefore, by all our friendship I conjure you and, by the power you have given me, command you, to preserve yourself with the same care that you would have me live. 'Tis all the obedience I require of you, and will be the greatest testimony you can give me of your faith. When you have promised me this, 'tis not impossible that I may promise you shall see me shortly; though my brother Peyton (who says he will come down to fetch his daughter) hinders me from making the journey in compliment to her. Yet I shall perhaps find business enough to carry me up to town. 'Tis all the service I expect from two girls whose friends have given me leave to provide for, that some order I must take for the disposal of them may serve for my pretence to see you; but then I must find you pleased and in good humour, merry as you were wont to be when we first met, if you will not have me show that I am nothing akin to my cousin Osborne's lady.

But what an age 'tis since we first met, and how great a change it has wrought in both of us; if there had been as great a'one in my face, it could be either very handsome or very ugly. For God's sake, when we meet, let us design one day to remember old stories in, to ask one another by what degrees our friendship grew to this height 'tis at. In earnest, I am lost sometimes with thinking on't; and though I can never repent the share you have in my heart, I know not whether I gave it you willingly or not at first. No, to speak ingenuously, I think you got an interest there a good while before I thought you had any, and it grew so insensibly, and yet so fast, that all the traverses it has met with since has served rather to discover it to me than at all to hinder it. By this confession you will see I am past all disguise with you, and that you have reason to be satisfied with knowing as much of my heart as I do myself. Will the kindness of this letter excuse the shortness on't? For I have twenty more, I think, to write, and the hopes I had of receiving one from you last night kept me from writing this when I had more time; or if all this will not satisfy, make your own conditions, so you do not return it me by the shortness of yours. Your servant kisses your hands, and I am

Your faithful.

Letter 35.—This is written on the back of a letter of Sir Thomas Peyton to Dorothy, and is probably a postscript to *Letter* 34. Sir Thomas's letter is a good example of the stilted letter-writing in vogue at that time, which Dorothy tells us was so much admired. The affairs that are troubling him are legal matters in connection with his brother-in-law Henry Oxenden's estate. There is a multitude of letters in the MSS. in the British Museum referring to this business; but we are not greatly concerned with Oxenden's financial difficulties. Sir Edward Hales was a gentleman of noble family in Kent. There is one of the same name who in 1688 declares himself openly to be a Papist, and is tried under the Test Act. He is concerned in the same year in the escape of King James, providing him with a fishing-boat to carry him into France. This is in all probability the Sir Edward Hales referred to by Sir Thomas Peyton, unless it be a son of the same name. Here is the letter :—

"GOOD SISTER,—I am very sorry to hear the loss of our good brother, whose short time gives us a sad example of our frail condition. But I will not say the loss, knowing whom I write to, whose religion and wisdom is a present stay to support in all worldly accidents.

"'Tis long since we resolved to have given you a visit, and have relieved you of my daughter. But I have had the following of a most laborious affair, which hath cost me the travelling, though in our own country style, fifty . . . ; and I have been less at home than elsewhere ever since I came from London ; which hath vext me the more in regard I have been detained from the desire I had of being with you before this time. Such entertainment, however, must all those have that have to do with such a purse-proud and wilful person as Sir Edward Hales. This next week being Michaelmas week, we shall end all and I be at liberty, I hope, to consider my own contentments. In the meantime I know not what excuses to make for the trouble I have put you to already, of which I grow to be ashamed ; and I should much more be so if I did not know you to be as good as you are fair. In both which regards I have a great honour to be esteemed,

" My good sister,

"Your faithful brother and servant,

" THOMAS PEYTON.

"KNOWLTON, *Sept.* 22, 1653."

On the other side of Sir T. Peyton's Letter.

NOTHING that is paper can 'scape me when I have time to write, and 'tis to you. But that I am not willing to excite your envy, I would tell you how many letters I have despatched since I ended yours ; and if I could show them you 'twould be a certain cure for it, for they are all very short ones, and most of them merely compliments, which I am sure you care not for.

I had forgot in my other to tell you what Jane requires for the satisfaction of what you confess you owe her. You must promise her to be merry, and not to take cold when you are at the tennis court, for there she hears you are found.

Because you mention my Lord Broghill and his wit, I have sent you some of his verses. My brother urged them against me one day in a dispute, where he would needs make me confess that no passion could be long lived, and that such as were most in love forgot that ever they had

been so within a twelvemonth after they were
married; and, in earnest, the want of examples to
bring for the contrary puzzled me a little, so that
I was fain to bring out those pitiful verses of my
Lord Biron to his wife, which was so poor an argument that I was e'en ashamed on't myself, and
he quickly laughed me out of countenance with
saying they were just such as a married man's
flame would produce and a wife inspire. I send
you a love letter, too; which, simple as you see, it
was sent me in very good earnest, and by a person
of quality, as I was told. If you read it when you
go to bed, 'twill certainly make your sleep approved.

I am yours.

Letter 36.—My Lady Carlisle was, as Dorothy says,
'an extraordinary person." She was the daughter of
Henry Percy, Earl of Northumberland, and at the age
of eighteen, against her father's will and under somewhat
romantic circumstances, married James Hay, Earl of
Carlisle. Her sister married the Earl of Leicester, and
she is therefore aunt to Lady Sunderland and Algernon
Sydney. She was a favourite attendant of Queen
Henrietta, and there are evil rumours connecting her
name with that of Strafford. On Strafford's death, it
is asserted that she transferred her affections to Pym,
to whom she is said to have betrayed the secrets of the
Court. There seems little doubt that it was she who
gave notice to Pym of the King's coming to the House
to seize the five members. In 1648 she appears, however, to have assisted the Royalists with money for the
purpose of raising a fleet to attack England, and at the

Restoration she was received at Court, and employed herself in intriguing for the return of Queen Henrietta to England, which was opposed at the time by Clarendon and others. Soon after this, and in the year of the Restoration, she died suddenly. Poets of all grades, from Waller downwards, have sung of her beauty, vivacity, and wit; and Sir Toby Matthew speaks of her as "too lofty and dignified to be capable of friendship, and having too great a heart to be susceptible of love,"— an extravagance of compliment hardly satisfactory in this plain age.

My Lord Paget, at whose house at Marlow Mr. Lely was staying, was a prominent loyalist both in camp and council chamber. He married Frances, the eldest daughter of the Earl of Holland, my Lady Diana's sister.

Whether or not Dorothy really assisted young Sir Harry Yelverton in his suit for the hand of fair Lady Ruthin we cannot say, but they were undoubtedly married. Sir Harry Yelverton seems to have been a man of superior accomplishments and serious learning. He was at this time twenty years of age, and had been educated at St. Paul's School, London, and afterwards at Wadham College, Oxford, under the tutorship of Dr. Wilkins, Cromwell's brother-in-law, a learned and philosophical mathematician. He was admitted gentleman commoner in 1650, and it is said "made great proficiency in several branches of learning, being as exact a Latin and Grecian as any in the university of his age or time." He succeeded to his father's title soon after coming of age, and took a leading part in the politics of the day, becoming Knight of the Shire of Northampton in the Restoration Parliament. He was a high Tory, and a great defender of the Church and its ejected ministers, one of whom, Dr. Thomas Morton, the learned theologian, Bishop of Coventry and Lichfield, died in his house in 1659. He wrote a discourse on the "Truth and Reasonableness of the Religion delivered by Jesus Christ," a Preface to Dr. Morton's work on Episcopacy, and a vindication of the Church of England against the attacks of the famous Edward Bagshawe.

In this letter Dorothy describes some husbands whom she could *not* marry. See what she expects in a lover! Have we not here some local squires hit off to the life? Could George Eliot herself have done more for us in like space?

Sir,—Why are you so sullen, and why am I the cause? Can you believe that I do willingly defer my journey? I know you do not. Why, then, should my absence now be less supportable to you than heretofore? Nay, it shall not be long (if I can help it), and I shall break through all inconveniences rather than deny you anything that lies in my power to grant. But by your own rules, then, may I not expect the same from you? Is it possible that all I have said cannot oblige you to a care of yourself? What a pleasant distinction you make when you say that 'tis not melancholy makes you do these things, but a careless forgetfulness. Did ever anybody forget themselves to that degree that was not melancholy in extremity? Good God! how you are altered; and what is it that has done it? I have known you when of all the things in the world you would not have been taken for a discontent; you were, as I thought, perfectly pleased with your condition; what has made it so much worse since? I know nothing you have lost, and am sure you have gained a friend that is capable of the highest degree of friendship you can propound, that has already given an entire heart for that which she received, and 'tis no more in her will than in her power ever to recall it or divide it; if this be not enough to satisfy you, tell me what I can do more?

There are a great many ingredients must go to the making me happy in a husband. First, as my cousin Franklin says, our humours must agree; and to do that he must have that kind of breeding that I have had, and used that kind of company. That is, he must not be so much a country gentleman as to understand nothing but hawks and dogs, and be fonder of either than his wife; nor of the next sort of them whose aim reaches no further than to be Justice of the Peace, and once in his life High Sheriff, who reads no book but statutes, and studies nothing but how to make a speech interlarded with Latin that may amaze his disagreeing poor neighbours, and fright them rather than persuade them into quietness. He must not be a thing that began the world in a free school, was sent from thence to the university, and is at his furthest when he reaches the Inns of Court, has no acquaintance but those of his form in these places, speaks the French he has picked out of old laws, and admires nothing but the stories he has heard of the revels that were kept there before his time. He must not be a town gallant neither, that lives in a tavern and an ordinary, that cannot imagine how an hour should be spent without company unless it be in sleeping, that makes court to all the women he sees, thinks they believe him, and laughs and is laughed at equally. Nor a travelled Monsieur whose head is all feather inside and outside, that can talk of nothing but dances and duets, and has courage enough to wear slashes when every one else dies with cold to see him. He must not be a fool of no sort, nor peevish, nor ill-natured, nor proud, nor covetous; and to all this must be added, that he must love me and I him as much as we are capable of loving. Without all this, his fortune, though never so great, would not satisfy me; and with it, a very moderate one would keep me from ever repenting my disposal.

I have been as large and as particular in my descriptions as my cousin Molle is in his of Moor Park,—but that you know the place so well I would send it you,—nothing can come near his patience in writing it, but my reading on't. Would you had sent me your father's letter, it would not have been less welcome to me than to you; and you may safely believe that I am equally concerned with you in anything. I should be pleased to see something of my Lady Carlisle's writing, because she is so extraordinary a person.

I have been thinking of sending you my picture till I could come myself; but a picture is but dull company, and that you need not; besides, I cannot tell whether it be very like me or not, though 'tis the best I ever had drawn for me, and Mr. Lilly [Lely] will have it that he never took more pains to make a good one in his life, and that was it I think that spoiled it. He was condemned for making the first he drew for me a little worse than I, and in making this better he has made it as unlike as t'other. He is now, I think, at my Lord Pagett's at Marloe [Marlow], where I am promised he shall draw a picture of my Lady for me,—she gives it me, she says, as the greatest testimony of her friendship to me, for by her own rule she is past the time of having pictures taken of her. After eighteen, she says, there is no face but decays apparently; I would fain have had her excepted such as had never been beauties, for my comfort, but she would not.

When you see your friend Mr. Heningham, you may tell him in his ear there is a willow garland coming towards him. He might have sped better in his suit if he had made court to me, as well as to my Lady Ruthin. She has been my wife this seven years, and whosoever pretends there must ask my leave. I have now given my consent that she shall marry a very pretty little gentleman, Sir Christopher Yelverton's son, and I think we shall have a wedding ere it be long. My Lady her mother, in great kindness, would have recommended Heningham to me, and told me in a compliment that I was fitter for him than her daughter, who was younger, and therefore did not understand the world so well; that she was certain if he knew me he would be extremely taken, for I would make just that kind of wife he looked for. I humbly thanked her, but said I was certain he would not make that kind of husband I looked for,—and so it went no further.

I expect my eldest brother here shortly, whose fortune is well mended by my other brother's death, so as if he were satisfied himself with what he has done, I know no reason why he might not be very happy; but I am afraid he is not. I have not seen my sister since I knew she was so; but, sure, she can have lost no beauty, for I never saw any that she had, but good black eyes, which cannot alter. He loves her, I think, at the ordinary rate of husbands, but not enough, I believe, to marry her so much to his disadvantage if it were to do again; and that would kill me were I as she, for I could be infinitely better satisfied with a husband that had never loved me in hopes he might, than with one that began to love me less than he had done.

I am yours.

Letter 37.

Sir,—You say I abuse you; and Jane says you abuse me when you say you are not melancholy: which is to be believed? Neither, I think; for I could not have said so positively (as it seems she did) that I should not be in town till my brother came back: he was not gone when she writ, nor is not yet; and if my brother Peyton had come before his going, I had spoiled her prediction. But now it cannot be; he goes on Monday or Tuesday at farthest. I hope you did truly with me, too, in saying that you are not melancholy (though she does not believe it). I am thought so, many times, when I am not at all guilty on't. How often do I sit in company a whole day, and when they are gone am not able to give an account of six words that was said, and many times could be so much better pleased with the entertainment my own thoughts give me, that 'tis all I can do to be so civil as not to let them see they trouble me. This may be your disease. However, remember you have promised me to be careful of yourself, and that if I secure what you have entrusted me with, you will answer for the rest. Be this our bargain then; and look that you give me as good an account of one as I shall give you of t'other. In earnest, I was strangely vexed to see myself forced to disappoint you so, and felt your trouble and my own too.

How often I have wished myself with you, though but for a day, for an hour : I would have given all the time I am to spend here for it with all my heart.

You could not but have laughed if you had seen me last night. My brother and Mr. Gibson were talking by the fire; and I sat by, but as no part of the company. Amongst other things (which I did not at all mind), they fell into a discourse of flying; and both agreed it was very possible to find out a way that people might fly like birds, and despatch their journeys : so I, that had not said a word all night, started up at that, and desired they would say a little more on't, for I had not marked the beginning; but instead of that, they both fell into so violent a laughing, that I should appear so much concerned in such an art; but they little knew of what use it might have been to me. Yet I saw you last night, but 'twas in a dream; and before I could say a word to you, or you to me, the disorder my joy to see you had put me into awakened me. Just now I was interrupted, too, and called away to entertain two dumb gentlemen ;—you may imagine whether I was pleased to leave my writing to you for their company ;—they have made such a tedious visit, too ; and I am so tired with making of signs and tokens for everything I had to say. Good God! how do those that live with them always ? They are brothers; and the eldest is a baronet, has a good estate, a wife and three or four children.

He was my servant heretofore, and comes to see me still for old love's sake; but if he could have made me mistress of the world I could not have had him; and yet I'll swear he has nothing to be disliked in him but his want of tongue, which in a woman might have been a virtue.

I sent you a part of *Cyrus* last week, where you will meet with one Doralise in the story of Abradah and Panthée. The whole story is very good; but the humour makes the best part of it. I am of her opinion in most things that she says in her character of " *L'honnest homme* " that she is in search of, and her resolution of receiving no heart that had been offered to anybody else. Pray, tell me how you like her, and what fault you find in my Lady Carlisle's letter? Methinks the hand and the style both show her a great person, and 'tis writ in the way that's now affected by all that pretend to wit and good breeding; only, I am a little scandalized to confess that she uses that word faithful,— she that never knew how to be so in her life.

I have sent you my picture because you wished for it; but, pray, let it not presume to disturb my Lady Sunderland's. Put it in some corner where no eyes may find it out but yours, to whom it is only intended. 'Tis not a very good one, but the best I shall ever have drawn of me; for, as my Lady says, my time for pictures is past, and therefore I have always refused to part with this,

M

because I was sure the next would be a worse. There is a beauty in youth that every one has once in their lives; and I remember my mother used to say there was never anybody (that was not deformed) but were handsome, to some reasonable degree, once between fourteen and twenty. It must hang with the light on the left hand of it; and you may keep it if you please till I bring you the original. But then I must borrow it (for 'tis no more mine, if you like it), because my brother is often bringing people into my closet where it hangs, to show them other pictures that are there; and if he miss this long thence, 'twould trouble his jealous head.

You are not the first that has told me I knew better what quality I would not have in a husband than what I would; but it was more pardonable in them. I thought you had understood better what kind of person I liked than anybody else could possibly have done, and therefore did not think it necessary to make you that description too. Those that I reckoned up were only such as I could not be persuaded to have upon no terms, though I had never seen such a person in my life as Mr. Temple: not but that all those may make very good husbands to some women; but they are so different from my humour that 'tis not possible we should ever agree; for though it might be reasonably enough expected that I should conform mine to theirs (to my shame be it spoken), I could never do it. And I have lived so long in the world, and so much at my own liberty, that whosoever has me must be content to take me as they find me, without hope of ever making me other than I am. I cannot so much as disguise my humour. When it was designed that I should have had Sir Jus., my brother used to tell me he was confident that, with all his wisdom, any woman that had wit and discretion might make an ass of him, and govern him as she pleased. I could not deny that possibly it might be so, but 'twas that I was sure I could never do; and though 'tis likely I should have forced myself to so much compliance as was necessary for a reasonable wife, yet farther than that no design could ever have carried me; and I could not have flattered him into a belief that I admired him, to gain more than he and all his generation are worth.

'Tis such an ease (as you say) not to be solicitous to please others: in earnest, I am no more concerned whether people think me handsome or ill-favoured, whether they think I have wit or that I have none, than I am whether they think my name Elizabeth or Dorothy. I would do nobody no injury; but I should never design to please above one; and that one I must love too, or else I should think it a trouble, and consequently not do it. I have made a general confession to you; will you give me absolution?

Methinks you should; for you are not much better by your own relation; therefore 'tis easiest to forgive one another. When you hear anything from your father, remember that I am his humble servant, and much concerned in his good health.

I am yours.

Letter 38.—Lady Isabella is Lady Isabella Rich, my Lady Diana's eldest sister. She married Sir James Thynne. Many years ago she had an intrigue with the Duke of Ormond, by whom she had a son, but Dorothy speaks, I think, of some later scandal than this.

My Lady Pembroke was the daughter of the Earl of Cumberland. She first married Richard Earl of Dorset, and afterwards the Earl of Pembroke. She is described as a woman whose mind was endowed by nature with very extraordinary attributes. Lord Pembroke, on the other hand, according to Clarendon, pretended to no other qualification "than to understand horses and dogs very well, and to be believed honest and generous." His stables vied with palaces, and his falconry was furnished at immense expense; but in his private life he was characterized by gross ignorance and vice, and his public character was marked by ingratitude and instability. The life of Lady Pembroke was embittered by this man for near twenty years, and she was at length compelled to separate from him. She lived alone, until her husband's death, which took place in January 1650. One can understand that they were entirely unsuited to each other, when Lady Pembroke in her Memorials is found to write thus of her husband : " He was no scholar, having passed but three or four months at Oxford, when he was taken thence after his father's death. He was of quick apprehension, sharp understanding, very crafty withal; of a discerning spirit, but a choleric nature, increased by the office he held of Chamberlain to the King." Why, then, did the accomplished Lady Anne Clifford unite herself to so worthless a person? Does she not answer this question for us when she writes that he was "the greatest nobleman in England"?

It is of some interest to us to remember that Francis Osborne, Dorothy's uncle (her father's youngest brother), was Master of the Horse to this great nobleman.

Whether Lord and Lady Leicester were, as Dorothy says, "in great disorder" at this time, it is impossible to say. Lady Leicester is said to have been of a warm and irritable temper, and Lord Leicester is described by Clarendon as "staggering and irresolute in his nature." However, nothing is said of their quarrels; but, on the other hand, there is a very pathetic account in Lord Leicester's journal of his wife's death in 1659, which shows that, whatever this "disorder" may have been, a complete reconciliation was afterwards effected.

SIR,—You would have me say something of my coming. Alas! how fain I would have something to say, but I know no more than you saw in that letter I sent you. How willingly would I tell you anything that I thought would please you; but I confess I do not like to give uncertain hopes, because I do not care to receive them. And I thought there was no need of saying I would be sure to take the first occasion, and that I waited with impatience for it, because I hoped you had believed all that already; and so you do,

I am sure. Say what you will, you cannot but
know my heart enough to be assured that I wish
myself with you, for my own sake as well as
yours. 'Tis rather that you love to hear me say
it often, than that you doubt it; for I am no
dissembler. I could not cry for a husband that
were indifferent to me (like your cousin); no, nor
for a husband that I loved neither. I think
'twould break my heart sooner than make me
shed a tear. 'Tis ordinary griefs that make me
weep. In earnest, you cannot imagine how often
I have been told that I had too much *franchise*
in my humour, and that 'twas a point of good
breeding to disguise handsomely; but I answered
still for myself, that 'twas not to be expected I
should be exactly bred, that had never seen a
Court since I was capable of anything. Yet I
know so much,—that my Lady Carlisle would take
it very ill if you should not let her get the point
of honour; 'tis all she aims at, to go beyond
everybody in compliment. But are you not afraid
of giving me a strong vanity with telling me I
write better than the most extraordinary person
in the world? If I had not the sense to understand that the reason why you like my letters
better is only because they are kinder than hers,
such a word might have undone me.

But my Lady Isabella, that speaks, and looks,
and sings, and plays, and all so prettily, why cannot I say that she is free from faults as her sister

believes her? No; I am afraid she is not, and
sorry that those she has are so generally known.
My brother did not bring them for an example;
but I did, and made him confess she had better
have married a beggar than that beast with all
his estate. She cannot be excused; but certainly
they run a strange hazard that have such husbands as makes them think they cannot be more
undone, whatever course they take. Oh, 'tis ten
thousand pities! I remember she was the first
woman that ever I took notice of for extremely
handsome; and, in earnest, she was then the
loveliest lady that could be looked on, I think.
But what should she do with beauty now? Were
I as she, I should hide myself from all the world;
I should think all people that looked on me read
it in my face and despised me in their hearts; and
at the same time they made me a leg, or spoke
civilly to me, I should believe they did not think
I deserved their respect. I'll tell you who he
urged for an example though, my Lord Pembroke and my Lady, who, they say, are upon
parting after all his passion for her, and his
marrying her against the consent of all his
friends; but to that I answered, that though he
pretended great kindness he had for her, I never
heard of much she had for him, and knew she
married him merely for advantage. Nor is she a
woman of that discretion as to do all that might
become her, when she must do it rather as things

fit to be done than as things she inclined to.
Besides that, what with a spleenatick side and a
chemical head, he is but an odd body himself.

But is it possible what they say, that my Lord
Leicester and my Lady are in great disorder, and
that after forty years' patience he has now taken
up the cudgels and resolved to venture for the
mastery? Methinks he wakes out of his long
sleep like a froward child, that wrangles and
fights with all that comes near it. They say he
has turned away almost every servant in the
house, and left her at Penshurst to digest it as
she can.

What an age do we live in, where 'tis a miracle
if in ten couples that are married, two of them
live so as not to publish to the world that they
cannot agree. I begin to be of your opinion of
him that (when the Roman Church first pro-
pounded whether it were not convenient for
priests not to marry) said that it might be convenient enough, but sure it was not our Saviour's
intention, for He commanded that all should take
up their cross and follow Him; and for his part,
he was confident there was no such cross as a
wife. This is an ill doctrine for me to preach;
but to my friends I cannot but confess that I am
afraid much of the fault lies in us; for I have
observed that formerly, in great families, the men
seldom disagree, but the women are always scold-
ing; and 'tis most certain, that let the husband be

what he will, if the wife have but patience (which, sure, becomes her best), the disorder cannot be great enough to make a noise; his anger alone, when it meets with nothing that resists it, cannot be loud enough to disturb the neighbours. And such a wife may be said to do as a kinswoman of ours that had a husband who was not always himself; and when he was otherwise, his humour was to rise in the night, and with two bedstaves labour on the table an hour together. She took care every night to lay a great cushion upon the table for him to strike on, that nobody might hear him, and so discover his madness. But 'tis a sad thing when all one's happiness is only that the world does not know you are miserable.

For my part, I think it were very convenient that all such as intend to marry should live together in the same house some years of probation; and if, in all that time, they never disagreed, they should then be permitted to marry if they please; but how few would do it then! I do not remember that I ever saw or heard of any couple that were bred up so together (as many you know are, that are designed for one another from children), but they always disliked one another extremely; parted, if it were left in their choice. If people proceeded with this caution, the world would end sooner than is expected, I believe; and because, with all my wariness, 'tis not impossible but I may be caught, nor likely that I should be wiser than anybody else, 'twere best, I think, that I said no more on this point.

What would I give to know that sister of yours that is so good at discovering; sure she is excellent company; she has reason to laugh at you when you would have persuaded her the " moss was sweet." I remember Jane brought some of it to me, to ask me if I thought it had no ill smell, and whether she might venture to put it in the box or not. I told her as I thought, she could not put a more innocent thing there, for I did not find it had any smell at all; besides, I was willing it should do me some service in requital for the pains I had taken for it. My niece and I wandered through some eight hundred acres of wood in search of it, to make rocks and strange things that her head is full of, and she admires it more than you did. If she had known I had consented it should have been used to fill up a box, she would have condemned me extremely. I told Jane that you liked her present, and she, I find, is resolved to spoil your compliment, and make you confess at last that they are not worth the eating; she threatens to send you more, but you would forgive her if you saw how she baits me every day to go to London; all that I can say will not satisfy her. When I urge (as 'tis true) that there is a necessity of my stay here, she grows furious, cries you will die with melancholy, and confounds me so with stories of your ill-

humour, that I'll swear I think I should go merely
to be at quiet, if it were possible, though there
were no other reason for it. But I hope 'tis not
so ill as she would have me believe it, though I
know your humour is strangely altered from what
it was, and am sorry to see it. Melancholy must
needs do you more hurt than to another to whom
it may be natural, as I think it is to me ; therefore
if you loved me you would take heed on't. Can
you believe that you are dearer to me than the
whole world beside, and yet neglect yourself?
If you do not, you wrong a perfect friendship ;
and if you do, you must consider my interest in
you, and preserve yourself to make me happy.
Promise me this, or I shall haunt you worse than
she does me. Scribble how you please, so you make
your letter long enough; you see I give you good
example; besides, I can assure you we do perfectly
agree if you receive not satisfaction but from my
letters, I have none but what yours give me.

Letter 39.—Dorothy has been in London since her last
letter, but unfortunately she has either not met with
Temple, or he has left town suddenly whilst she was
there, on some unexplained errand. This would therefore seem a natural place to begin a new chapter; but
as we have very shortly to come to a series of unhappy
letters, quite distinct in their character from these, I
have thought fit to place in this long chapter yet a few
more letters after Dorothy's autumn visit to London.

Stephen Marshall was, like Hugh Peters, one of those

preachers who was able to exchange the obscurity of a country parish for the public fame of a London pulpit, by reason of a certain gift of rhetorical power, the value of which it is impossible to estimate to-day. Such of his sermons as are still extant are prosy, long-winded, dogmatic absurdities, overloaded with periphrastic illustrations in scriptural language. They are meaningless to a degree, which would make one wonder at the docility and patience of a seventeenth century congregation, if one had not witnessed a similar spirit in congregations of to-day.

There is no honest biography of Stephen Marshall. In the news-books and tracts of the day we find references to sermons preached by him, by command, before the Army of the Parliament, and we have reprints of some of these. I have searched in vain to find the sermon which Dorothy heard, but it was probably not a sermon given on any great occasion, and we may believe it was never printed. There is an amusing scandalous tract, called the *Life and Death of Stephen Marshall,* which is so full of "evil speaking, lying, and slandering," as to be quite unworthy of quotation. From this we may take it, however, that he was born at Gormanchester, in Cromwell's county, was educated at Emmanuel College, Cambridge, and that before he came to London his chief cure of souls was at Finchingfield in Essex. These, and the records of his London preaching, are the only facts in his life's history which have come to my notice.

My Lord Whitelocke did go to Sweden, as Dorothy surmises; setting sail from Plymouth with one hundred honest men, on October 26, 1653, or very soon afterwards, as one may read in his journal of the progress of the Embassy. That he should fill this office, appears to have been proposed to him by Cromwell in September of this year.

An Act of Parliament to abolish the Chancery was indeed passed in the August of this year. Well may Lord Keble sore lament, and the rest of the world rejoice, at such news. Joseph Keble was a well-known law reporter, a son of Serjeant Richard Keble. He was a Fellow of All Souls, and a Bencher of Gray's Inn; and, furthermore, was one of the Lords Commissioners of the Great Seal from 1648–1654. There was "some debate," says Whitelocke, "whether they should be styled 'Commissioners' or 'Lords Commissioners,'" and though the word *Lords* was far less acceptable at this time than formerly, yet that they might not seem to lessen their own authority, nor the honour of their office constituted by them, they voted the title to be "Lords Commissioners."

SIR,—If want of kindness were the only crime I exempted from pardon, 'twas not that I had the least apprehension you could be guilty of it; but to show you (by excepting only an impossible thing) that I excepted nothing. No, in earnest, I can fancy no such thing of you, or if I could, the quarrel would be to myself; I should never forgive my own folly that let me to choose a friend that could be false. But I'll leave this (which is not much to the purpose) and tell you how, with my usual impatience, I expected your letter, and how cold it went to my heart to see it so short a one. 'Twas so great a pain to me that I am resolv'd you shall not feel it; nor can I in justice punish you for a fault unwillingly committed. If I were your enemy, I could not use you ill when I saw Fortune do it too, and in gallantry and good nature both, I should think myself rather obliged to protect you from her injury (if it lay in my power) than double them upon you. These things considered, I believe this letter will be longer than ordinary,—kinder I think it cannot be. I always speak my heart to you; and that is so much your friend, it never furnishes me with anything to your disadvantage. I am glad you are an admirer of Telesile as well as I; in my opinion 'tis a fine Lady, but I know you will pity poor Amestris strongly when you have read her story. I'll swear I cried for her when I read it first, though she were but an imaginary person; and, sure, if anything of that kind can deserve it, her misfortunes may.

God forgive me, I was as near laughing yesterday where I should not. Would you believe that I had the grace to go hear a sermon upon a week day? In earnest, 'tis true; a Mr. Marshall was the man that preached, but never anybody was so defeated. He is so famed that I expected rare things of him, and seriously I listened to him as if he had been St. Paul; and what do you think he told us? Why, that if there were no kings, no queens, no lords, no ladies, nor gentlemen, nor gentlewomen, in the world, 'twould be no loss to God Almighty at all. This we had

over some forty times, which made me remember
it whether I would or not. The rest was much
at this rate, interlarded with the prettiest odd
phrases, that I had the most ado to look soberly
enough for the place I was in that ever I had in
my life. He does not preach so always, sure?
If he does, I cannot believe his sermons will do
much towards bringing anybody to heaven more
than by exercising their patience. Yet, I'll say
that for him, he stood stoutly for tithes, though,
in my opinion, few deserve them less than he;
and it may be he would be better without them.

Yet you are not convinced, you say, that to be
miserable is the way to be good; to some natures
I think it is not, but there are many of so
careless and vain a temper, that the least breath
of good fortune swells them with so much pride,
that if they were not put in mind sometimes by a
sound cross or two that they are mortal, they
would hardly think it possible; and though 'tis a
sign of a servile nature when fear produces more
of reverence in us than love, yet there is more
danger of forgetting oneself in a prosperous
fortune than in the contrary, and affliction may be
the surest (though not the pleasantest) guide to
heaven. What think you, might not I preach
with Mr. Marshall for a wager? But you could
fancy a perfect happiness here, you say; that is
not much, many people do so; but I never heard
of anybody that ever had it more than in fancy,

so that will not be strange if you should miss on't. One may be happy to a good degree, I think, in a faithful friend, a moderate fortune, and a retired life; further than this I know nothing to wish; but if there be anything beyond it, I wish it you.

You did not tell me what carried you out of town in such haste. I hope the occasion was good, you must account to me for all that I lost by it. I shall expect a whole packet next week. Oh, me! I have forgot this once or twice to tell you, that if it be no inconvenience to you, I could wish you would change the place of direction for my letters. Certainly that Jones knows my name, I bespoke a saddle of him once, and though it be a good while agone, yet I was so often with him about it,—having much ado to make him understand how I would have it, it being of a fashion he had never seen, though, sure, it be common,— that I am confident he has not forgot me. Besides that, upon it he got my brother's custom; and I cannot tell whether he does not use the shop still. Jane presents her humble service to you, and has sent you something in a box; 'tis hard to imagine what she can find here to present you withal, and I am much in doubt whether you will not pay too dear for it if you discharge the carriage. 'Tis a pretty freedom she takes, but you may thank yourself; she thinks because you call her fellow-servant, she may use you accordingly. I bred her better, but you have spoiled her.

Is it true that my Lord Whitlocke goes Ambassador where my Lord Lisle should have gone? I know not how he may appear in a Swedish Court, but he was never meant for a courtier at home, I believe. Yet 'tis a gracious Prince; he is often in this country, and always does us the favour to send for his fruit hither. He was making a purchase of one of the best houses in the county. I know not whether he goes on with it; but 'tis such a one as will not become anything less than a lord. And there is a talk as if the Chancery were going down; if so, his title goes with it, I think. 'Twill be sad news for my Lord Keble's son; he will have nothing left to say when " my Lord, my father," is taken from him. Were it not better that I had nothing to say neither, than that I should entertain you with such senseless things. I hope I am half asleep, nothing else can excuse me; if I were quite asleep, I should say fine things to you; I often dream I do; but perhaps if I could remember them they are no wiser than my wakening discourses. Good-night.

Letter 40.—A letter has been lost: whether Harrold or Collins, the two carriers, were either or both of them guilty of carelessness in the delivery of these letters, it is quite impossible to say now. Dorothy seems to think Harrold delivered the letter, and it was mislaid in London. Perhaps it was this letter, and what was written about it, that caused all those latent feelings of

N

despair and discontent to awaken in the breasts of the two lovers. Was this the spark that loneliness and absence fanned into flame? You shall judge for yourself, reader, in the next chapter.

SIR,—That you may be at more certainty hereafter what to think, let me tell you that nothing could hinder me from writing to you (as well for my own satisfaction as yours) but an impossibility of doing it; nothing but death or a dead palsy in my hands, or something that had the same effect. I did write it, and gave it Harrold, but by an accident his horse fell lame, so that he could not set out on Monday; but on Tuesday he did come to town; on Wednesday, carried the letter himself (as he tells me) where 'twas directed, which was to Mr. Copyn in Fleet Street. 'Twas the first time I made use of that direction; no matter and I had not done it then, since it proves no better. Harrold came late home on Thursday night with such an account as your boy gave you: that coming out of town the same day he came in, he had been at Fleet Street again, but there was no letter for him. I was sorry, but I did not much wonder at it because he gave so little time, and resolved to make my best of that I had by Collins. I read it over often enough to make it equal with the longest letter that ever was writ, and pleased myself, in earnest (as much as it was possible for me in the humour I was in), to think how by that time you had asked me pardon for the little reproaches you had made me, and that the kindness and length of my letter had made you amends for the trouble it had given you in expecting it. But I am not a little annoyed to find you had it not. I am very confident it was delivered, and therefore you must search where the fault lies.

Were it not that you had suffered too much already, I would complain a little of you. Why should you think me so careless of anything that you were concerned in, as to doubt that I had writ? Though I had received none from you, I should not have taken that occasion to revenge myself. Nay, I should have concluded you innocent, and have imagined a thousand ways how it might happen, rather than have suspected your want of kindness. Why should not you be as just to me? But I will not chide, it may be (as long as we have been friends) you do not know me so well yet as to make an absolute judgment of me; but if I know myself at all, if I am capable of being anything, 'tis a perfect friend. Yet I must chide too. Why did you get such a cold? Good God! how careless you are of a life that (by your own confession) I have told you makes all the happiness of mine. 'Tis unkindly done. What is left for me to say, when that will not prevail with you; or how can you persuade me to a cure of myself, when you refuse to give me the example? I have nothing in the world that gives me the least desire of preserving myself, but the opinion I have you would not be willing to lose me ; and yet, if you saw with what caution I live (at least to what I did before), you would reproach it to yourself sometimes, and might grant, perhaps, that you have not got the advantage of me in friendship so much as you imagine. What (besides your consideration) could oblige me to live and lose all the rest of my friends thus one after another ? Sure I am not insensible nor very ill-natured, and yet I'll swear I think I do not afflict myself half so much as another would do that had my losses. I pay nothing of sadness to the memory of my poor brother, but I presently disperse it with thinking what I owe in thankfulness that 'tis not you I mourn for.

Well, give me no more occasions to complain of you, you know not what may follow. Here was Mr. Freeman yesterday that made me a very kind visit, and said so many fine things to me, that I was confounded with his civilities, and had nothing to say for myself. I could have wished then that he had considered me less and my niece more; but if you continue to use me thus, in earnest, I'll not be so much her friend hereafter. Methinks I see you laugh at all my threatenings ; and not without reason. Mr. Freeman, you believe, is designed for somebody that deserves him better. I think so too, and am not sorry for it ; and you have reason to believe I never can be other than

Your faithful friend.

CHAPTER IV.

DESPONDENCY.   CHRISTMAS 1653.

THIS chapter of letters is a sad note, sounding out from among its fellows with mournful clearness.   There had seemed a doubt whether all these letters must be regarded as of one series, or whether, more correctly, it was to be assumed that Dorothy and Temple had their lovers' quarrels, for the well-understood pleasure of kissing friends again.   But you will agree that these lovers were not altogether as other lovers are, that their troubles were too real and too many for their love to need the stimulus of constant April shower quarrels ; and these letters are very serious in their sadness, imprinting themselves in the mind after constant reading as landmarks clearly defining the course and progress of an unusual event in these lovers' history—a misunderstanding.

The letters are written at Christmastide, 1653. Dorothy had returned from London to Chicksands, and either had not seen Temple or he had left London hurriedly whilst she was there.   There is a letter lost.   Dorothy's youngest brother is lately dead ; her niece has left her ; her companion Jane is sick ; her father, growing daily weaker and weaker, was sinking into his grave before her eyes.   No bright chance seemed to open before her, and their marriage seemed an impossibility.   For a moment she loses faith, not in Temple, but in fortune ; faith once gone, hope, missing her comrade, flies away in search of her. She is alone in the old house with her dying father, and with her brother pouring his unkind gossip into her unwilling ear, whilst the sad long year draws slowly to its close, and there is no sign of better fortune for the lovers ; can we wonder, then, that Dorothy, lonely and unaided, pacing in the damp garden beneath the bare trees, with all the bright summer changed into decay, lost faith and hope ?

Temple, when Dorothy's thoughts reach him, must have replied with some impatience. There are stories, too, set about concerning her good name by one Mr. B., to disturb Temple. Temple can hardly have given credence to these, but he may have complained of them to Dorothy, who is led to declare, " I am the most unfortunate woman breathing, but I was never false," though she forgives her lover " all those strange thoughts he has had " of her. Whatever were the causes of the quarrel, or rather the despondency, we shall never know accurately. Dorothy was not the woman to vapour for months about " an early and a quiet grave." When she writes this it is written in the deepest earnest of despair ; when this mood is over it is over for ever, and we emerge into a clear atmosphere of hope and content. The despondency has been agonizing, but the agony is sharp and rapid, and gives place to the wisdom of hope.

Temple now comes to Chicksands at an early date. There is a new interchange of vows. Never again will their faith be shaken by fretting and despair ; and these vows are never broken, but remain with the lovers until they are set aside by others, taken under the solemn sanction of the law, and the old troubles vanish in new responsibilities and a new life.

Letter 41.—Lady Anne Blunt was a daughter of the Earl of Newport. Her mother had turned Catholic in 1637, which had led to an estrangement between her and her husband, and we may conclude poor Lady Anne had by no means a happy home. There are two scandals connected with her name. She appears to have run away with one William Blunt, — the "Mr. Blunt" mentioned by Dorothy in her next letter; and on April 18, 1654, she petitioned the Protector to issue a special commission upon her whole case. Mr. Blunt pretended that she was contracted to him for the sake, it is said, of gaining money thereby. There being no Bishop's Court at this time, there are legal difficulties in the way, and we never hear the result of the petition. Again, in February 1655, one Mr. Porter finds himself committed to Lambeth House for carrying away the Lady Anne Blunt, and endeavouring to marry her without her father's consent.

SIR, — Having tired myself with thinking, I mean to weary you with reading, and revenge myself that way for all the unquiet thoughts you have given me. But I intended this a sober letter, and therefore, *sans raillerie*, let me tell you, I have seriously considered all our misfortunes, and can see no end of them but by submitting to that which we cannot avoid, and by yielding to it break the force of a blow which if resisted brings a certain ruin. I think I need not tell you how dear you have been to me, nor that in your kindness I placed all the satisfaction of my life; 'twas the only happiness I proposed to

myself, and had set my heart so much upon it
that it was therefore made my punishment, to let
me see that, how innocent soever I thought my
affection, it was guilty in being greater than is
allowable for things of this world.   'Tis not a
melancholy humour gives me these apprehensions
and inclinations, nor the persuasions of others;
'tis the result of a long strife with myself, before
my reason could overcome my passion, or bring
me to a perfect resignation to whatsoever is
allotted for me.   'Tis now done, I hope, and I
have nothing left but to persuade you to that,
which I assure myself your own judgment will
approve in the end, and your reason has often
prevailed with you to offer; that which you would
have done then out of kindness to me and point
of honour, I would have you do now out of
wisdom and kindness to yourself.   Not that I
would disclaim my part in it or lessen my obliga-
tion to you, no, I am your friend as much as
ever I was in my life, I think more, and I am
sure I shall never be less.   I have known you
long enough to discern that you have all the
qualities that make an excellent friend, and I shall
endeavour to deserve that you may be so to me;
but I would have you do this upon the justest
grounds, and such as may conduce most to your
quiet and future satisfaction.   When we have
tried all ways to happiness, there is no such thing
to be found but in a mind conformed to one's

condition, whatever it be, and in not aiming at anything that is either impossible or improbable; all the rest is but vanity and vexation of spirit, and I durst pronounce it so from that little knowledge I have had of the world, though I had not Scripture for my warrant. The shepherd that bragged to the traveller, who asked him, "What weather it was like to be?" that it should be what weather pleased him, and made it good by saying it should be what weather pleased God, and what pleased God should please him, said an excellent thing in such language, and knew enough to make him the happiest person in the world if he made a right use on't. There can be no pleasure in a struggling life, and that folly which we condemn in an ambitious man, that's ever labouring for that which is hardly got and more uncertainly kept, is seen in all according to their several humours; in some 'tis covetousness, in others pride, in some stubbornness of nature that chooses always to go against the tide, and in others an unfortunate fancy to things that are in themselves innocent till we make them otherwise by desiring them too much. Of this sort you and I are, I think; we have lived hitherto upon hopes so airy that I have often wondered how they could support the weight of our misfortunes; but passion gives a strength above nature, we see it in most people; and, not to flatter ourselves, ours is but a refined degree of madness. What can it

be else to be lost to all things in the world but
that single object that takes up one's fancy, to
lose all the quiet and repose of one's life in
hunting after it, when there is so little likelihood
of ever gaining it, and so many more probable
accidents that will infallibly make us miss on't?
And which is more than all, 'tis being mastered
by that which reason and religion teaches us to
govern, and in that only gives us a pre-eminence
over beasts. This, soberly consider'd, is enough
to let us see our error, and consequently to persuade us to redeem it. To another person, I
should justify myself that 'tis not a lightness in
my nature, nor any interest that is not common
to us both, that has wrought this change in me.
To you that know my heart, and from whom I
shall never hide it, to whom a thousand testimonies of my kindness can witness the reality of
it, and whose friendship is not built upon common
grounds, I have no more to say but that I impose
not my opinion upon you, and that I had rather
you took them up as your own choice than upon
my entreaty. But if, as we have not differed in
anything else, we could agree in this too, and
resolve upon a friendship that will be much the
perfecter for having nothing of passion in it,
how happy might we be without so much as a fear
of the change that any accident could bring. We
might defy all that fortune could do, and putting
off all disguise and constraint, with that which

only made it necessary, make our lives as easy to us as the condition of this world will permit. I may own you as a person that I extremely value and esteem, and for whom I have a particular friendship, and you may consider me as one that will always be

Your faithful.

This was written when I expected a letter from you, how came I to miss it? I thought at first it might be the carrier's fault in changing his time without giving notice, but he assures me he did, to Nan. My brother's groom came down to-day, too, and saw her, he tells me, but brings me nothing from her; if nothing of ill be the cause, I am contented. You hear the noise my Lady Anne Blunt has made with her marrying? I am so weary with meeting it in all places where I go; from what is she fallen! they talked but the week before that she should have my Lord of Strafford. Did you not intend to write to me when you writ to Jane? That bit of paper did me great service; without it I should have had strange apprehension, and my sad dreams, and the several frights I have waked in, would have run so in my head that I should have concluded something of very ill from your silence. Poor Jane is sick, but she will write, she says, if she can. Did you send the last part of *Cyrus* to Mr. Hollingsworth?

Letter 42.

SIR,—I am extremely sorry that your letter miscarried, but I am confident my brother has it not, as, cunning as he is, he could not hide from me, but that I should discover it some way or other. No; he was here, and both his men, when this letter should have come, and not one of them stirred out that day; indeed, the next day they went all to London. The note you writ to Jane came in one of Nan's, by Collins, but nothing else; it must be lost by the porter that was sent with it, and 'twas very unhappy that there should be anything in it of more consequence than ordinary; it may be numbered amongst the rest of our misfortunes, all which an inconsiderate passion has occasioned. You must pardon me I cannot be reconciled to it, it has been the ruin of us both. 'Tis true that nobody must imagine to themselves ever to be absolute master on't, but there is great difference betwixt that and yielding to it, between striving with it and soothing it up till it grows too strong for one. Can I remember how ignorantly and innocently I suffered it to steal upon me by degrees; how under a mask of friendship I cozened myself into that which, had it appeared to me at first in its true shape, I had feared and shunned? Can I discern that it has made the trouble of your life, and cast a cloud upon mine, that will help to cover me in my grave? Can I know that it wrought so upon us both as to make neither of us friends to one another, but agree in running wildly to our own destruction, and that perhaps of some innocent persons who might live to curse our folly that gave them so miserable a being? Ah! if you love yourself or me, you must confess that I have reason to condemn this senseless passion; that wheresoe'er it comes destroys all that entertain it; nothing of judgment or discretion can live with it, and it puts everything else out of order before it can find a place for itself. What has it brought my poor Lady Anne Blunt to? She is the talk of all the footmen and boys in the street, and will be company for them shortly, and yet is so blinded by her passion as not at all to perceive the misery she has brought herself to; and this fond love of hers has so rooted all sense of nature out of her heart, that, they say, she is no more moved than a statue with the affliction of a father and mother that doted on her, and had placed the comfort of their lives in her preferment. With all this is it not manifest to the whole world that Mr. Blunt could not consider anything in this action but his own interest, and that he makes her a very ill return for all her kindness; if he had loved her truly he would have died rather than have been the occasion of this misfortune to her. My cousin Franklin (as you observe very well) may say fine things now she is warm in Moor Park, but she is very much altered in her opinions since her marriage, if these be her own. She left a gentleman, that I could name, whom she had much more of kindness for than ever she had for Mr. Franklin, because his estate was less; and upon the discovery of some letters that her mother intercepted, suffered herself to be persuaded that twenty-three hundred pound a year was better than twelve hundred, though with a person she loved; and has recovered it so well, that you see she confesses there is nothing in her condition she desires to alter at the charge of a wish. She's happier by much than I shall ever be, but I do not envy her; may she long enjoy it, and I an early and a quiet grave, free from the trouble of this busy world, where all with passion pursue their own interests at their neighbour's charges; where nobody is pleased but somebody complains on't; and where 'tis impossible to be without giving and receiving injuries.

You would know what I would be at, and how I intend to dispose of myself. Alas! were I in my own disposal, you should come to my grave to be resolved; but grief alone will not kill. All that I can say, then, is that I resolve on nothing but to arm myself with patience, to resist nothing that is laid upon me, nor struggle for what I have no hope to get. I have no ends nor no designs,

nor will my heart ever be capable of any; but like
a country wasted by a civil war, where two opposing parties have disputed their right so long till
they have made it worth neither of their con-
quests, 'tis ruined and desolated by the long
strife within it to that degree as 'twill be useful
to none,—nobody that knows the condition 'tis
in will think it worth the gaining, and I shall not
trouble anybody with it. No, really, if I may be
permitted to desire anything, it shall be only that
I may injure nobody but myself,—I can bear
anything that reflects only upon me; or, if I
cannot, I can die; but I would fain die innocent,
that I might hope to be happy in the next world,
though never in this. I take it a little ill that
you should conjure me by anything, with a belief
that 'tis more powerful with me than your kindness. No, assure yourself what that alone cannot
gain will be denied to all the world. You would
see me, you say? You may do so if you please,
though I know not to what end. You deceive
yourself if you think it would prevail upon me
to alter my intentions; besides, I can make no
contrivances; it must be here, and I must endure
the noise it will make, and undergo the censures
of a people that choose ever to give the worst
interpretation that anything will bear. Yet if
it can be any ease to you to make me more
miserable than I am, never spare me; consider
yourself only, and nòt me at all,—'tis no more

than I deserve for not accepting what you offered me whilst 'twas in your power to make it good, as you say it then was. You were prepared, it seems, but I was surprised, I confess. 'Twas a kind fault though; and you may pardon it with more reason than I have to forgive it myself. And let me tell you this, too, as lost and as wretched as I am, I have still some sense of my reputation left in me,—I find that to my cost,— I shall attempt to preserve it as clear as I can; and to do that, I must, if you see me thus, make it the last of our interviews. What can excuse me if I should entertain any person that is known to pretend to me, when I can have no hope of ever marrying him? And what hope can I have of that when the fortune that can only make it possible to me depends upon a thousand accidents and contingencies, the uncertainty of the place 'tis in, and the government it may fall under, your father's life or his success, his disposal of himself and of his fortune, besides the time that must necessarily be required to produce all this, and the changes that may probably bring with it, which 'tis impossible for us to foresee? All this considered, what have I to say for myself when people shall ask, what 'tis I expect? Can there be anything vainer than such a hope upon such grounds? You must needs see the folly on't yourself, and therefore examine your own heart what 'tis fit for me to do, and what you can do

for a person you love, and that deserves your compassion if nothing else,—a person that will always
have an inviolable friendship for you, a friendship
that shall take up all the room my passion held
in my heart, and govern there as master, till death
come and take possession and turn it out.

Why should you make an impossibility where
there is none? A thousand accidents might have
taken me from you, and you must have borne it.
Why would not your own resolution work as
much upon you as necessity and time does infallibly upon people? Your father would take it
very ill, I believe, if you should pretend to love
me better than he did my Lady, yet she is dead
and he lives, and perhaps may do to love again.
There is a gentlewoman in this country that loved
so passionately for six or seven years that her
friends, who kept her from marrying, fearing her
death, consented to it; and within half a year
her husband died, which afflicted her so strongly
nobody thought she would have lived. She saw
no light but candles in three years, nor came
abroad in five; and now that 'tis some nine years
past, she is passionately taken again with another,
and how long she has been so nobody knows but
herself. This is to let you see 'tis not impossible
what I ask, nor unreasonable. Think on't, and
attempt it at least; but do it sincerely, and do not
help your passion to master you. As you have
ever loved me do this.

o

The carrier shall bring your letters to Suffolk House to Jones. I shall long to hear from you; but if you should deny the only hope that's left me, I must beg you will defer it till Christmas Day be past; for, to deal freely with you, I have some devotions to perform then, which must not be disturbed with anything, and nothing is like to do it as so sensible an affliction.   Adieu.

Letter 43.

Sir,—I can say little more than I did,—I am convinced of the vileness of the world and all that's in it, and that I deceived myself extremely when I expected anything of comfort from it. No, I have no more to do in't but to grow every day more and more weary of it, if it be possible that I have not yet reached the highest degree of hatred for it. But I thank God I hate nothing else but the base world, and the vices that make a part of it. I am in perfect charity with my enemies, and have compassion for all people's misfortunes as well as for my own, especially for those I may have caused; and I may truly say I bear my share of such. But as nothing obliges me to relieve a person that is in extreme want till I change conditions with him and come to be where he began, and that I may be thought compassionate if I do all that I can without prejudicing myself too much, so let me tell you, that if I could help it, I would not love you, and that as long as I live I shall strive against it as against that which had been my ruin, and was certainly sent me as a punishment for my sin. But I shall always have a sense of your misfortunes, equal, if not above, my own. I shall pray that you may obtain a quiet I never hope for but in my grave, and I shall never change my condition but with my life. Yet let not this give you a hope. Nothing ever can persuade me to enter the world again. I shall, in a short time, have disengaged myself of all my little affairs in it, and settled myself in a condition to apprehend nothing but too long a life, therefore I wish you would forget me; and to induce you to it, let me tell you freely that I deserve you should. If I remember anybody, 'tis against my will. I am possessed with that strange insensibility that my nearest relations have no tie upon me, and I find myself no more concerned in those that I have heretofore had great tenderness of affection for, than in my kindred that died long before I was born. Leave me to this, and seek a better fortune. I beg it of you as heartily as I forgive you all those strange thoughts you have had of me. Think me so still if that will do anything towards it. For God's sake do take any course that may make you happy; or, if that cannot be, less unfortunate at least than

Your friend and humble servant,

D. Osborne.

I can hear nothing of that letter, but I hear from all people that I know, part of my unhappy story, and from some that I do not know. A lady, whose face I never saw, sent it me as news she had out of Ireland.

Letter 44.

SIR,—If you have ever loved me, do not refuse the last request I shall ever make you; 'tis to preserve yourself from the violence of your passion. Vent it all upon me; call me and think me what you please; make me, if it be possible, more wretched than I am. I'll bear it all without the least murmur. Nay, I deserve it all, for had you never seen me you had certainly been happy. 'Tis my misfortunes only that have that infectious quality as to strike at the same time me and all that's dear to me. I am the most unfortunate woman breathing, but I was never false. No; I call heaven to witness that if my life could satisfy for the least injury my fortune has done you (I cannot say 'twas I that did them you), I would lay it down with greater joy than any person ever received a crown; and if I ever forget what I owe you, or ever entertained a thought of kindness for any person in the world besides, may I live a long and miserable life. 'Tis the greatest curse I can invent; if there be a greater, may I feel it. This is all I can say.

Tell me if it be possible I can do anything for you, and tell me how I may deserve your pardon for all the trouble I have given you. I would not die without it.

[Directed.] For Mr. Temple.

Letter 45.

Sir,—'Tis most true what you say, that few have what they merit; if it were otherwise, you would be happy, I think, but then I should be so too, and that must not be,—a false and an inconstant person cannot merit it, I am sure. You are kind in your good wishes, but I aim at no friends nor no princes, the honour would be lost upon me; I should become a crown so ill, there would be no striving for it after me, and, sure, I should not wear it long. Your letter was a much greater loss to me than that of Henry Cromwell, and, therefore, 'tis that with all my care and diligence I cannot inquire it out. You will not complain, I believe, of the shortness of my last, whatever else you dislike in it, and if I spare you at any time 'tis because I cannot but imagine, since I am so wearisome to myself, that I must needs be so to everybody else, though, at present, I have other occasions that will not permit this to be a long one. I am sorry it should be only in my power to make a friend miserable, and that where I have so great a kindness I should do so great injuries; but 'tis my fortune, and I must bear it; 'twill be none to you, I hope, to pray for you, nor to desire that you would (all passion laid aside) freely tell me my faults, that I may, at least, ask your forgiveness where 'tis not in my power to make you better satisfaction. I would fain make even with all the world, and be out of danger of dying in anybody's debt; then I have nothing more to do in it but to expect when I shall be so happy as to leave it, and always to remember that my misfortune makes all my faults towards you, and that my faults to God make all my misfortunes.

Your unhappy.

Letter 46.

SIR,—That which I writ by your boy was in so much haste and distraction as I cannot be satisfied with it, nor believe it has expressed my thoughts as I meant them. No, I find it is not easily done at more leisure, and I am yet to seek what to say that is not too little nor too much. I would fain let you see that I am extremely sensible of your affliction, that I would lay down my life to redeem you from it, but that's a mean expression; my life is of so little value that I will not mention it. No, let it be rather what, in earnest, if I can tell anything I have left that is considerable enough to expose for it, it must be that small reputation I have amongst my friends; that's all my wealth, and that I could part with to restore you to that quiet you lived in when I first knew you. But, on the other side, I would not give you hopes of that I cannot do. If I loved you less I would allow you to be the same person to me, and I would be the same to you as heretofore. But to deal freely with you, that were to betray myself, and I find that my passion would quickly be my master again if I gave it any liberty. I am not secure that it would not make me do the most extravagant things in the world, and I shall be forced to keep a continual war alive with it as long as there are any remainders of it left;—I think I might as well have said as long as I lived. Why should you give yourself over so unreasonably to it? Good God! no woman breathing can deserve half the trouble you give yourself. If I were yours from this minute I could not recompense what you have suffered from the violence of your passion, though I were all that you can imagine me, when, God knows, I am an inconsiderable person, born to a thousand misfortunes, which have taken away all sense of anything else from me, and left me a walking misery only. I do from my soul forgive you all the injuries your passion has done me, though, let me tell you, I was much more at my ease whilst I was angry. Scorn and despite would have cured me in some reasonable time,

which I despair of now.   However, I am not
displeased with it, and, if it may be of any
advantage to you, I shall not consider myself in
it; but let me beg, then, that you will leave off
those dismal thoughts.   I tremble at the desperate
things you say in your letter; for the love of God,
consider seriously with yourself what can enter
into comparison with the safety of your soul.
Are a thousand women, or ten thousand worlds,
worth it?   No, you cannot have so little reason
left as you pretend, nor so little religion.   For
God's sake let us not neglect what can only
make us happy for trifles.   If God had seen it
fit to have satisfied our desires we should have
had them, and everything would not have con-
spired thus to have crossed them.   Since He has
decreed it otherwise (at least as far as we are
able to judge by events), we must submit, and
not by striving make an innocent passion a sin,
and show a childish stubbornness.

I could say a thousand things more to this
purpose if I were not in haste to send this away,
—that it may come to you, at least, as soon as
the other.   Adieu.

I cannot imagine who this should be that Mr.
Dr. meant, and am inclined to believe 'twas a
story meant to disturb you, though perhaps not
by him.

Letter 47.

SIR,—'Tis never my humour to do injuries, nor
was this meant as any to you. No, in earnest, if
I could have persuaded you to have quitted a
passion that injures you, I had done an act of
real friendship, and you might have lived to
thank me for it; but since it cannot be, I will
attempt it no more. I have laid before you the
inconveniences it brings along, how certain the
trouble is, and how uncertain the reward; how
many accidents may hinder us from ever being
happy, and how few , there are (and those so
unlikely) to make up our desire. All this makes
no impression on you; you are still resolved to
follow your blind guide, and I to pity where I
cannot help. It will not be amiss though to let
you see that what I did was merely in consideration of your interest, and not at all of my own,
that you may judge of me accordingly; and, to
do that, I must tell you that, unless it were after
the receipt of those letters that made me angry,
I never had the least hope of wearing out my
passion, nor, to say truth, much desire. For to
what purpose should I have strived against it?
'Twas innocent enough in me that resolved never
to marry, and would have kept me company in
this solitary place as long as I lived, without
being a trouble to myself or anybody else. Nay,
in earnest, if I could have hoped you would be so

much your own friend as to seek out a happiness
in some other person, nothing under heaven could
have satisfied me like entertaining myself with
the thought of having done you service in diverting you from a troublesome pursuit of what is so
uncertain, and by that giving you the occasion of
a better fortune.   Otherwise, whether you loved
me still, or whether you did not, was equally the
same to me, your interest set aside.   I will not
reproach you how ill an interpretation you made
of this, because we will have no more quarrels.
On the contrary, because I see 'tis in vain to think
of curing you, I'll study only to give you what
ease I can, and leave the rest to better physicians,
—to time and fortune.   Here, then, I declare that
you have still the same power in my heart that
I gave you at our last parting ; that I will never
marry any other ; and that if ever our fortunes
will allow us to marry, you shall dispose of me as
you please ; but this, to deal freely with you, I do
not hope for.   No ; 'tis too great a happiness, and
I, that know myself best, must acknowledge I
deserve crosses and afflictions, but can never
merit such a blessing.   You know 'tis not a fear
of want that frights me.   I thank God I never
distrusted His providence, nor I hope never shall,
and without attributing anything to myself, I
may acknowledge He has given me a mind that
can be satisfied with as narrow a compass as that
of any person living of my rank.   But I confess

that I have an humour will not suffer me to expose myself to people's scorn. The name of love
is grown so contemptible by the folly of such as
have falsely pretended to it, and so many giddy
people have married upon that score and repented so shamefully afterwards, that nobody can
do anything that tends towards it without being
esteemed a ridiculous person. Now, as my young
Lady Holland says, I never pretended to wit in
my life, but I cannot be satisfied that the world
should think me a fool, so that all I can do for
you will be to preserve a constant kindness for
you, which nothing shall ever alter or diminish;
I'll never give you any more alarms, by going
about to persuade you against that you have for
me; but from this hour we'll live quietly, no more
fears, no more jealousies; the wealth of the whole
world, by the grace of God, shall not tempt me
to break my word with you, nor the importunity
of all my friends I have. Keep this as a testimony against me if ever I do, and make me a
reproach to them by it; therefore be secure, and
rest satisfied with what I can do for you.

You should come hither but that I expect my
brother every day; not but that he designed a longer
stay when he went, but since he keeps his horses
with him 'tis an infallible token that he is coming.
We cannot miss fitter times than this twenty in a
year, and I shall be as ready to give you notice of
such as you can be to desire it, only you would

do me a great pleasure if you could forbear writing, unless it were sometimes on great occasions. This is a strange request for me to make, that have been fonder of your letters than my Lady Protector is of her new honour, and, in earnest, would be so still but there are a thousand inconveniences in't that I could tell you. Tell me what you can do; in the meantime think of some employment for yourself this summer. Who knows what a year may produce? If nothing, we are but where we were, and nothing can hinder us from being, at least, perfect friends. Adieu. There's nothing so terrible in my other letter but you may venture to read it. Have not you forgot my Lady's book?

CHAPTER V.

THE LAST OF CHICKSANDS. FEBRUARY AND MARCH 1654.

THE quarrel is over, happily over, and Dorothy and Temple are more than reconciled again. Temple has been down to Chicksands to see her, and some more definite arrangement has been come to between them. Dorothy has urged Temple to go to Ireland and join his father, who has once again taken possession of his office of Master of the Rolls. As soon as an appointment can be found for Temple they are to be married—that is, as far as one can gather, the state of affairs between them; but it would seem as if nothing of this was as yet to be known to the outer world, not even to Dorothy's brother.

Letter 48.

SIR,—'Tis but an hour since you went, and I am writing to you already; is not this kind? How do you after your journey; are you not weary; do you not repent that you took it to so little purpose? Well, God forgive me, and you too, you made me tell a great lie. I was fain to say you came only to take your leave before you went abroad; and all this not only to keep quiet, but to keep him from playing the madman; for when he has the least suspicion, he carries it so strangely that all the world takes notice on't, and so often guess at the reason, or else he tells it. Now, do but you judge whether if by mischance he should discover the truth, whether he would not rail most sweetly at me (and with some reason) for abusing him. Yet you helped to do it; a sadness that he discovered at your going away inclined him to believe you were ill satisfied, and made him credit what I said. He is kind now in extremity, and I would be glad to keep him so till a discovery is absolutely necessary. Your going abroad will confirm him much in his belief, and I shall have nothing to torment me in this place but my own doubts and fears. Here I shall find all the repose I am capable of, and nothing will disturb my prayers and wishes for your happiness which only can make mine. Your journey cannot be to your disadvantage neither; you must needs be pleased to visit a place you are so much concerned in, and to be a witness yourself of your hopes, though I will believe you need no other inducements to this voyage than my desiring it. I know you love me, and you have no reason to doubt my kindness. Let us both have patience to wait what time and fortune will do for us; they cannot hinder our being perfect friends.

Lord, there were a thousand things I remembered after you were gone that I should have said, and now I am to write not one of them will come into my head. Sure as I live it is not settled yet! Good God! the fears and surprises, the crosses and disorders of that day, 'twas confused enough to be a dream, and I am apt to think sometimes it was no more. But no, I saw you; when I shall do it again, God only knows! Can there be a romancer story than ours would make if the conclusion prove happy? Ah! I dare not hope it; something that I cannot describe draws a cloud over all the light my fancy discovers sometimes, and leaves me so in the dark with all my fears about me that I tremble to think on't. But no more of this sad talk.

Who was that, Mr. Dr. told you I should marry? I cannot imagine for my life; tell me, or I shall think you made it to excuse yourself. Did not you say once you knew where good French tweezers were to be had? Pray send me a pair; they shall cut no love. Before you go I must have a ring from you, too, a plain gold one; if I ever marry it shall be my wedding ring; when I die I'll give it you again. What a dismal story this is you sent me; but who could expect better from a love begun upon such grounds? I cannot pity neither of them, they were both so guilty. Yes, they are the more to be pitied for that.

Here is a note comes to me just now, will you do this service for a fine lady that is my friend;

have not I taught her well, she writes better than her mistress? How merry and pleased she is with her marrying because there is a plentiful fortune; otherwise she would not value the man at all. This is the world; would you and I were out of it: for, sure, we were not made to live in it. Do you remember Arme and the little house there? Shall we go thither? that's next to being out of the world. There we might live like Baucis and Philemon, grow old together in our little cottage, and for our charity to some ship-wrecked strangers obtain the blessing of dying both at the same time. How idly I talk; 'tis because the story pleases me—none in Ovid so much. I remember I cried when I read it. Me-thought they were the perfectest characters of a contented marriage, where piety and love were all their wealth, and in their poverty feasted the gods when rich men shut them out. I am called away,—farewell!

Your faithful.

Letter 49.—The beginning of this letter is lost, and with it, perhaps, the name of Dorothy's lover who had written some verses on her beauty. However, we have the "tag" of them, with which we must rest content.

. . . 'Tis pity I cannot show you what his wit could do upon so ill a subject, but my Lady Ruthin keeps them to abuse me withal, and has

put a tune to them that I may hear them all
manner of ways; and yet I do protest I remember
nothing more of them than this lame piece,—

> A stately and majestic brow,
> Of force to make Protectors bow.

Indeed, if I have any stately looks I think he has
seen them, but yet it seems they could not keep
him from playing the fool. My Lady Grey told
me that one day talking of me to her (as he would
find ways to bring in that discourse by the head
and shoulders, whatsoever anybody else could
interpose), he said he wondered I did not marry.
She (that understood him well enough, but would
not seem to do so) said she knew not, unless it
were that I liked my present condition so well
that I did not care to change it; which she was
apt to believe, because to her knowledge I had
refused very good fortunes, and named some so
far beyond his reach, that she thought she had
dashed all his hopes. But he, confident still, said
'twas perhaps that I had no fancy to their persons
(as if his own were so taking), that I was to be
looked upon as one that had it in my power to
please myself, and that perhaps in a person I
liked would bate something of fortune. To this
my Lady answered again for me, that 'twas not
impossible but I might do so, but in that point
she thought me nice and curious enough. And
still to dishearten him the more, she took occa-

sion (upon his naming some gentlemen of the
county that had been talked of heretofore as of
my servants, and are since disposed of) to say
(very plainly) that 'twas true they had some of
them pretended, but there was an end of my
Bedfordshire servants she was sure there were
no more that could be admitted into the number.
After all this (which would have satisfied an
ordinary young man) did I this last Thursday
receive a letter from him by Collins, which he
sent first to London that it might come from
thence to me. I threw it into the fire; and do
you but keep my counsel, nobody shall ever know
that I had it; and my gentleman shall be kept
at such a distance as I hope to hear no more of
him. Yet I'll swear of late I have used him so
near to rudely that there is little left for me to do.
Fye! what a deal of paper I have spent upon this
idle fellow; if I had thought his story would have
proved so long you should have missed on't, and
the loss would not have been great.

I have not thanked you yet for my tweezers
and essences; they are both very good. I kept
one of the little glasses myself; remember my
ring, and in return, if I go to London whilst you
are in Ireland, I'll have my picture taken in little
and send it you. The sooner you despatch away
will be the better, I think, since I have no hopes
of seeing you before you go; there lies all your
business, your father and fortune must do all the

rest. I cannot be more yours than I am. You are mistaken if you think I stand in awe of my brother. No, I fear nobody's anger. I am proof against all violence; but when people haunt me with reasoning and entreaties, when they look sadly and pretend kindness, when they beg upon that score, 'tis a strange pain to me to deny. When he rants and renounces me, I can despise him; but when he asks my pardon, with tears pleads to me the long and constant friendship between us, and calls heaven to witness that nothing upon earth is dear to him in comparison of me, then, I confess, I feel a stronger unquietness within me, and I would do anything to evade his importunity. Nothing is so great a violence to me as that which moves my compassion. I can resist with ease any sort of people but beggars. If this be a fault in me, 'tis at least a well-natured one; and therefore I hope you will forgive it me, you that can forgive me anything, you say, and be displeased with nothing whilst I love you; may I never be pleased with anything when I do not. Yet I could beat you for writing this last strange letter; was there ever anything said like? If I had but a vanity that the world should admire me, I would not care what they talked of me. In earnest, I believe there is nobody displeased that people speak well of them, and reputation is esteemed by all of much greater value than life itself. Yet let me tell you soberly, that with all my vanity I could be very well contented nobody should blame me or any action of mine, to quit all my part of the praises and admiration of the world; and if I might be allowed to choose, my happiest part of it should consist in concealment, there should not be above two persons in the world know that there was such a one in it as your faithful.

Stay! I have not done yet. Here's another good side, I find; here, then, I'll tell you that I am not angry for all this. No, I allow it to your ill-humour, and that to the crosses that have been common to us; but now that is cleared up, I should expect you should say finer things to me. Yet take heed of being like my neighbour's servant, he is so transported to find no rubs in his way that he knows not whether he stands on his head or his feet. 'Tis the most troublesome, busy talking little thing that ever was born; his tongue goes like the clack of a mill, but to much less purpose, though if it were all oracle, my head would ache to hear that perpetual noise. I admire at her patience and her resolution that can laugh at his fooleries and love his fortune. You would wonder to see how tired she is with his impertinences, and yet how pleased to think she shall have a great estate with him. But this is the world, and she makes a part of it betimes. Two or three great glistening jewels have bribed her to wink at all his faults, and she hears him as unmoved and unconcerned as if another were to marry him.

What think you, have I not done fair for once, would you wish a longer letter? See how kind I grow at parting; who would not go into Ireland to have such another? In earnest now, go as soon as you can, 'twill be the better, I think, who am your faithful friend.

Letter 50.—Wrest, in Bedfordshire, where Dorothy met her importunate lover, was the seat of Anthony Grey, Earl of Kent. There is said to be a picture there of Sir William Temple, — a copy of Lely's picture. Wrest Park is only a few miles from Chicksands.

SIR, — Who would be kind to one that reproaches one so cruelly? Do you think, in earnest, I could be satisfied the world should think me a dissembler, full of avarice or ambition? No, you are mistaken; but I'll tell you what I could suffer, that they should say I married where I had no inclination, because my friends thought it fit, rather than that I had run wilfully to my own ruin in pursuit of a fond passion of my own. To marry for love were no reproachful thing if we did not see that of the thousand couples that do it, hardly one can be brought for an example that it may be done and not repented afterwards. Is there anything thought so indiscreet, or that makes one more contemptible? 'Tis true that I do firmly believe we should be, as you say, *toujours les mesmes;* but if (as you confess) 'tis that which hardly happens once in two ages, we are not to expect the world should discern we were not like the rest. I'll tell you stories another time, you return them so handsomely upon me. Well, the next servant I tell you of shall not be called a whelp, if 'twere not to give you a stick to beat myself with. I would confess that I looked upon the impudence of this fellow as a punishment upon me for my over care in avoiding the talk of the world; yet the case is very different, and no woman shall ever be blamed that an inconsolable person pretends to her when she gives no allowance to it, whereas none shall 'scape that owns a passion, though in return of a person much above her. The little tailor that loved Queen Elizabeth was suffered to talk out, and none of her Council thought it necessary to stop his mouth; but the Queen of Sweden's kind letter to the King of Scots was intercepted by her own ambassador, because he thought it was not for his mistress's honour (at least that was his pretended reason), and thought justifiable enough. But to come to my Beagle again. I have heard no more of him, though I have seen him since; we met at Wrest again. I do not doubt but I shall be better able to resist his importunity than his tutor was; but what do you think it is that gives him his encouragement? He was told I had thought of marrying a gentleman that had not above two hundred pound a year, only out of my liking to his person. And upon that score his vanity allows him to think he may pretend as far as another. Thus you see 'tis not altogether without reason that I apprehend the noise of the world, since 'tis so much to my disadvantage.

Is it in earnest that you say your being there keeps me from the town? If so, 'tis very unkind. No, if I had gone, it had been to have waited on my neighbour, who has now altered her resolution and goes not herself. I have no business there, and am so little taken with the place that I could sit here seven years without so much as thinking once of going to it. 'Tis not likely, as you say, that you should much persuade your father to what you do not desire he should do; but it is hard if all the testimonies of my kindness are not enough to satisfy without my publishing to the world that I can forget my friends and all my interest to follow my passion; though, perhaps, it will admit of a good sense, 'tis that which nobody but you or I will give it, and we that are concerned in't can only say 'twas an act of great kindness and something romance, but must confess it had nothing of prudence, discretion, nor sober counsel in't. 'Tis not that I expect, by all your father's offers, to bring my friends to approve it. I don't deceive myself thus far, but I would not give them occasion to say that I hid myself from them in the doing it; nor of making my action appear more indiscreet than it is. It will concern me that all the world should know what fortune you have, and upon what terms I marry you, that both may not be made to appear ten times worse than they are. 'Tis the general custom of all people to make those that are rich to have more mines of gold than are in the Indies, and such as have small fortunes to be beggars. If an action take a little in the world, it shall be magnified and brought into comparison with what the heroes or senators of Rome performed; but, on the contrary, if it be once condemned, nothing can be found ill enough to compare it with; and people are in pain till they find out some extravagant expression to represent the folly on't. Only there is this difference, that as all are more forcibly inclined to ill than good, they are much apter to exceed in detraction than in praises. Have I not reason then to desire this from you; and may not my friendship have deserved it? I know not; 'tis as you think; but if I be denied it, you will teach me to consider myself. 'Tis well the side ended here. If I had not had occasion to stop there, I might have gone too far, and showed that I had more passions than one. Yet 'tis fit you should know all my faults, lest you should repent your bargain when 'twill not be in your power to release yourself; besides, I may own my ill-humour to you that cause it; 'tis the discontent my crosses in this business have given me makes me thus peevish. Though I say it myself, before I knew you I was thought as well an humoured young person as most in England; nothing displeased, nothing troubled me. When I came out of France, nobody knew me again. I was so altered, from a cheerful humour that was always alike, never over merry but always pleased, I was grown heavy and sullen, froward and discomposed; and that country which usually gives people a jolliness and gaiety that is natural to the climate, had wrought in me so contrary effects that I was as new a thing to them as my clothes. If you find all this to be sad truth hereafter, remember that I gave you fair warning.

Here is a ring : it must not be at all wider than this, which is rather too big for me than otherwise; but that is a good fault, and counted lucky by superstitious people. I am not so, though : 'tis indifferent whether there be any word in't or not; only 'tis as well without, and will make my wearing it the less observed. You must give Nan leave to cut a lock of your hair for me, too. Oh, my heart! what a sigh was there! I will not tell you how many this journey causes; nor the fear and apprehensions I have for you. No, I long to be rid of you, am afraid you will not go soon enough : do not you believe this ? No, my dearest, I know you do not, whate'er you say, you cannot doubt that I am yours.

Letter 51.—Lady Newport was the wife of the Earl of Newport, and mother of Lady Anne Blunt of whom we heard something in former letters. She is mentioned as a prominent leader of London society. In March 1652 she is granted a pass to leave the country, on condition that she gives security to do nothing prejudicial to the State ; from which we may draw the inference that she was a political notability.

My Lady Devonshire was Christian, daughter of Lord Bruce of Kinloss. She married William Cavendish, second Earl of Devonshire. Her daughter Anne married Lord Rich, and died suddenly in 1638. Pomfret, Godolphin, and Falkland celebrated her virtues in verse, and Waller wrote her funeral hymn, which is still known to some of us,—

> The Lady Rich is dead.
> Heartrending news ! and dreadful to those few
> Who her resemble and her steps pursue,
> That Death should licence have to range among
> The fair, the wise, the virtuous, and the young.

It was the only son of Lady Rich who married Frances Cromwell.

Lord Warwick was the father of Robert, Lord Rich, and we may gather from this letter that, at Lady Devonshire's instigation, he had interfered in a proposed second marriage between his son and some fair unknown.

Parthenissa is only just out. It is the latest thing in literary circles. We find it advertised in *Mercurius Politicus,* 19th January 1654 :—" *Parthenissa,* that most famous romance, composed by the Lord Broghill, and dedicated to the Lady Northumberland." It is a romance of the style of *Cléopâtre* and *Cyrus,* to enjoy which in the nineteenth century would require a curious and acquired taste. *L'illustre Bassa* was a romance of Scudéri; and the passage in the epistle to which Dorothy refers,—we quote it from a translation by one Henry Cogan, 1652,—runs as follows: "And if you see not my hero persecuted with love by women, it is not because he was not amiable, and that he could not be loved, but because it would clash with civility in the persons of ladies, and with true resemblance in that of men, who rarely show themselves cruel unto them, nor in doing it could have any good grace."

Sir,—The lady was in the right. You are a very pretty gentleman and a modest; were there ever such stories as these you tell? The best on't is, I believe none of them unless it be that of my Lady Newport, which I must confess is so like her that if it be not true 'twas at least excellently well fancied. But my Lord Rich was not caught, tho' he was near it. My Lady Devonshire, whose daughter his first wife was, has engaged my Lord Warwick to put a stop to the business. Otherwise, I think his present want of fortune, and the little sense of honour he has, might have been prevailed on to marry her.

'Tis strange to see the folly that possesses the young people of this age, and the liberty they take to themselves. I have the charity to believe they appear very much worse than they are, and that the want of a Court to govern themselves by is in great part the cause of their ruin; though that was no perfect school of virtue, yet Vice there wore her mask, and appeared so unlike herself that she gave no scandal. Such as were really discreet as they seemed to be gave good example, and the eminency of their condition made others strive to imitate them, or at least they durst not own a contrary course. All who had good principles and inclinations were encouraged in them, and such as had neither were forced to put on a handsome disguise that they might not be out of countenance at themselves. 'Tis certain (what you say) that where divine or human laws are not positive we may be our own judges; nobody can hinder us, nor is it in itself to be blamed. But, sure, it is not safe to take all liberty that is allowed us,—there are not many that are sober enough to be trusted with the government of themselves ; and because others judge us with more severity than our indulgence to ourselves will permit, it must necessarily follow that 'tis safer being ruled by their opinions than by our own. I am disputing again, though you told me my fault so plainly.

I'll give it over, and tell you that *Parthenissa* is now my company. My brother sent it down, and I have almost read it. 'Tis handsome language; you would know it to be writ by a person of good quality though you were not told it ; but, on the whole, I am not very much taken with it. All the stories have too near a resem-

blance with those of other romances, there is
nothing new or *surprenant* in them; the ladies
are all so kind they make no sport, and I meet
only with one that took me by doing a handsome
thing of the kind. She was in a besieged town,
and persuaded all those of her sex to go out with
her to the enemy (which were a barbarous people)
and die by their swords, that the provisions of the
town might last the longer for such as were able
to do service in defending it. But how angry
was I to see him spoil this again by bringing out
a letter this woman left behind her for the
governor of the town, where she discovers a
passion for him, and makes *that* the reason why
she did it. I confess I have no patience for our
faiseurs de Romance when they make a woman
court. It will never enter into my head that 'tis
possible any woman can love where she is not
first loved, and much less that if they should do
that, they could have the face to own it. Methinks he that writes *L'illustre Bassa* says well
in his epistle that we are not to imagine his hero
to be less taking than those of other romances
because the ladies do not fall in love with him
whether he will or not. 'Twould be an injury to
the ladies to suppose they could do so, and a
greater to his hero's civility if he should put him
upon being cruel to them, since he was to love
but one. Another fault I find, too, in the style—
'tis affected. *Ambitioned* is a great word with

him, and *ignore; my concern,* or of *great concern,* is, it seems, properer than *concernment :* and though he makes his people say fine handsome things to one another, yet they are not easy and *naïve* like the French, and there is a little harshness in most of the discourse that one would take to be the fault of a translator rather than of an author. But perhaps I like it the worse for having a piece of *Cyrus* by me that I am hugely pleased with, and that I would fain have you read: I'll send it you. At least read one story that I'll mark you down, if you have time for no more. I am glad you stay to wait on your sister. I would have my gallant civil to all, much more when it is so due, and kindness' too.

I have the cabinet, and 'tis in earnest a pretty one; though you will not own it for a present, I'll keep it as one, and 'tis like to be yours no more but as 'tis mine. I'll warrant you would ne'er have thought of making me a present of charcoal as my servant James would have done, to warm my heart I think he meant it. But the truth is, I had been inquiring for some (as 'tis a commodity scarce enough in this country), and he hearing it, told the baily [bailiff?] he would give him some if 'twere for me. But this is not all. I cannot forbear telling you the other day he made me a visit, and I, to prevent his making discourse to me, made Mrs. Goldsmith and Jane sit by all the while. But he came better provided than I could have imagined. He brought a letter with him, and gave it me as one he had met with directed to me, he thought it came out of North-amptonshire. I was upon my guard, and suspecting all he said, examined him so strictly where he had it before I would open it, that he was hugely confounded, and I confirmed that 'twas his. I laid it by and wished that they would have left us, that I might have taken notice on't to him. But I had forbid it them so strictly before, that they offered not to stir farther than to look out of window, as not thinking there was any necessity of giving us their eyes as well as their ears; but he that saw himself discovered took that time to confess to me (in a whispering voice that I could hardly hear myself) that the letter (as my Lord Broghill says) was of *great concern* to him, and begged I would read it, and give him my answer. I took it up presently, as if I had meant it, but threw it, sealed as it was, into the fire, and told him (as softly as he had spoke to me) I thought that the quickest and best way of answering it. He sat awhile in great disorder, without speaking a word, and so ris and took his leave. Now what think you, shall I ever hear of him more?

You do not thank me for using your rival so scurvily nor are not jealous of him, though your father thinks my intentions were not handsome towards you, which methinks is another argument that one is not to be one's own judge; for I am very confident they were, and with his favour shall never believe otherwise. I am sure I have no ends to serve of my own in what I did,—it could be no advantage to me that had firmly resolved not to marry; but I thought it might be an injury to you to keep you in expectation of what was never likely to be, as I apprehended. Why do I enter into this wrangling discourse? Let your father think me what he pleases, if he ever comes to know me, the rest of my actions shall justify me in this; if he does not, I'll begin to practise on him (what you so often preached to me) to neglect the report of the world, and satisfy myself in my own innocency.

'Twill be pleasinger to you, I am sure, to tell you how fond I am of your lock. Well, in earnest now, and setting aside all compliments, I never saw finer hair, nor of a better colour; but cut no more on't, I would not have it spoiled for the world. If you love me, be careful on't. I am combing, and curling, and kissing this lock all day, and dreaming on't all night. The ring, too, is very well, only a little of the biggest. Send me a tortoise one that is a little less than that I sent for a pattern. I would not have the rule so absolutely true without exception that hard hairs be ill-natured, for then I should be so. But I can allow that all soft hairs are good, and so are you, or I am deceived as much as you are if you think I do not love you enough. Tell me,

my dearest, am I ? You will not be if you think
I am

Yours.

Letter 52.—It is interesting to find Dorothy reading
the good Jeremy Taylor's *Holy Living*, a book too little
known in this day. For amidst its old-fashioned piety
there are many sentiments of practical goodness, expressed with clear insistence, combined with a quaint
grace of literary style which we have long ago cast
aside in the pursuit of other things. Dorothy loved
this book, and knew it well. Compare the following
extract from the chapter on Christian Justice with what
Dorothy has written in this letter. Has she been
recently reading this passage ? Perhaps she has ; but
more probably it is the recollection of what is well
known that she is reproducing from a memory not
unstored with such learning. Thus writes Dr. Taylor :
" There is very great peace and immunity from sin in
resigning our wills up to the command of others : for,
provided our duty to God be secured, their commands
are warrants to us in all things else ; and the case of
conscience is determined, if the command be evident
and pressing : and it is certain, the action that is but
indifferent and without reward, if done only upon our
own choice, is an action of duty and of religion, and
rewardable by the grace and favour of God, if done in
obedience to the command of our superiors."

Little and Great Brickhill, where Temple is to receive
a letter from Dorothy, kindly favoured by Mr. Gibson,
stand due west of Chicksands some seventeen miles, and
about forty-six miles along the high-road from London
to Chester. Temple would probably arrange to stay
there, receive Dorothy's letter, and send one in return.

Q

Dorothy has apparently tired of Clarapede and Scudéri, of *Cléopâtre* and *Cyrus*, and has turned to travels to amuse her. Fernando Mendez Pinto did, I believe, actually visit China, and is said to have landed in the Gulf of Pekin. What he writes of China seems to bear some resemblance to what later writers have said. It is hard to say how and where his conversations with the Chinese were carried on, as he himself admits that he did not understand one word of the language.

Lady Grey's sister, Mrs. Pooley, is unknown to history. Of Mr. Fish we know, as has already been said, nothing more than that he was Dorothy's lover, and a native of Bedfordshire, probably her near neighbour. James B—— must be another lover, and he is altogether untraceable. Mrs. Goldsmith is, as you will remember, wife of the Vicar of Campton. The Valentine stories will date this letter for us as written in the latter half of February.

Sir,—They say you gave order for this waste-paper; how do you think I could ever fill it, or with what? I am not always in the humour to wrangle and dispute. For example now, I had rather agree to what you say, than tell you that Dr. Taylor (whose devote you must know I am) says there is a great advantage to be gained in resigning up one's will to the command of another, because the same action which in itself is wholly indifferent, if done upon our own choice, becomes an act of duty and religion if done in obedience to the command of any person whom nature, the laws, or ourselves have given a power over us ;

so that though in an action already done we can only be our own judges, because we only know with what intentions it was done, yet in any we intend, 'tis safest, sure, to take the advice of another. Let me practise this towards you as well as preach it to you, and I'll lay a wager you will approve on't. But I am chiefly of your opinion that contentment (which the Spanish proverb says is the best paint) gives the lustre to all one's enjoyment, puts a beauty upon things which without it would have none, increases it extremely where 'tis already in some degree, and without it, all that we call happiness besides loses its property. What is contentment, must be left to every particular person to judge for themselves, since they only know what is so to them which differs in all according to their several humours. Only you and I agree 'tis to be found by us in a true friend, a moderate fortune, and a retired life ; the last I thank God I have in perfection. My cell is almost finished, and when you come back you'll find me in it, and bring me both the rest I hope.

I find it much easier to talk of your coming back than your going. You shall never persuade me I send you this journey. No, pray let it be your father's commands, or a necessity your fortune puts upon you. 'Twas unkindly said to tell me I banish you ; your heart never told it you, I dare swear ; nor mine ne'er thought it.

No, my dear, this is our last misfortune, let's bear it nobly. Nothing shows we deserve a punishment so much as our murmuring at it; and the way to lessen those we feel, and to 'scape those we fear, is to suffer patiently what is imposed, making a virtue of necessity. 'Tis not that I have less kindness or more courage than you, but that mistrusting myself more (as I have more reason), I have armed myself all that is possible against this occasion. I have thought that there is not much difference between your being at Dublin or at London, as our affairs stand. You can write and hear from the first, and I should not see you sooner if you continued still at the last.

Besides, I hope this journey will be of advantage to us; when your father pressed your coming over he told you, you needed not doubt either his power or his will. Have I done anything since that deserves he should alter his intentions towards us? Or has any accident lessened his power? If neither, we may hope to be happy, and the sooner for this journey. I dare not send my boy to meet you at Brickhill nor any other of the servants, they are all too talkative. But I can get Mr. Gibson, if you will, to bring you a letter. 'Tis a civil, well-natured man as can be, of excellent principles and exact honesty. I durst make him my confessor, though he is not obliged by his orders to conceal anything that is told him. But you must tell me then which Brickhill it is

you stop at, Little or Great; they are neither of
them far from us. If you stay there you will
write back by him, will you not, a long letter? I
shall need it; besides that, you owe it me for the
last being so short. Would you saw what letters
my brother writes me; you are not half so kind.
Well, he is always in the extremes; since our last
quarrel he has courted me more than ever he did
in his life, and made me more presents, which,
considering his humour, is as great a testimony of
his kindness as 'twas of Mr. Smith's to my Lady
Sunderland when he presented Mrs. Camilla.
He sent me one this week which, in earnest, is as
pretty a thing as I have seen, a China trunk, and
the finest of the kind that e'er I saw. By the
way (this puts me in mind on't), have you read
the story of China written by a Portuguese,
Fernando Mendez Pinto, I think his name is?
If you have not, take it with you, 'tis as diverting
a book of the kind as ever I read, and is as
handsomely written. You must allow him the
privilege of a traveller, and he does not abuse it.
His lies are as pleasant harmless ones, as lies can
be, and in no great number considering the scope
he has for them. There is one in Dublin now,
that ne'er saw much farther, has told me twice
as many (I dare swear) of Ireland. If I should
ever live to see that country and be in't, I should
make excellent sport with them. 'Tis a sister
of my Lady Grey's, her name is Pooley; her

husband lives there too, but I am afraid in no
very good condition.   They were but poor, and
she lived here with her sisters when I knew her;
'tis not half a year since she went, I think.   If
you hear of her, send me word how she makes a
shift there.

And hark you, can you tell me whether the
gentleman that lost a crystal box the 1st of
February in St. James' Park or Old Spring
Gardens has found it again or not, I have strong
curiosity to know?   Tell me, and I'll tell you
something that you don't know, which is, that I
am your Valentine and you are mine.   I did not
think of drawing any, but Mrs. Goldsmith and
Jane would need make me some for them and
myself; so I writ down our three names, and
for men Mr. Fish, James B., and you.   I cut
them all equal and made them up myself before
them, and because I would owe it wholly to my
good fortune if I were pleased.   I made both
them choose first that had never seen what was
in them, and they left me you.   Then I made
them choose again for theirs, and my name was
left.   You cannot imagine how I was delighted
with this little accident, but by taking notice that
I cannot forbear telling you it.   I was not half so
pleased with my encounter next morning.   I was
up early, but with no design of getting another
Valentine, and going out to walk in my night-
cloak and night-gown, I met Mr. Fish going a

hunting, I think he was; but he stayed to tell me I was his Valentine; and I should not have been rid on him quickly, if he had not thought himself a little too *negligée;* his hair was not powdered, and his clothes were but ordinary; to say truth, he looked then methought like other mortal people. Yet he was as handsome as your Valentine. I'll swear you wanted one when you took her, and had very ill fortune that nobody met you before her. Oh, if I had not terrified my little gentleman when he brought me his own letter, now sure I had had him for my Valentine!

On my conscience, I shall follow your counsel if be he comes again, but I am persuaded he will not. I writ my brother that story for want of something else, and he says I did very well, there was no other way to be rid on him; and he makes a remark upon't that I can be severe enough when I please, and wishes I would practise it somewhere else as well as there. Can you tell where that is? I never under-stand anybody that does not speak plain English, and he never uses that to me of late, but tells me the finest stories (I may apply them how I please) of people that have married when they thought there was great kindness, and how miser-ably they have found themselves deceived; how despicable they have made themselves by it, and how sadly they have repented on't. He

reckons more inconveniency than you do that
follows good nature, says it makes one credulous,
apt to be abused, betrays one to the cunning of
people that make advantage on't, and a thousand
such things which I hear half asleep and half
awake, and take little notice of, unless it be
sometimes to say that with all these faults I
would not be without it.   No, in earnest, nor I
could not love any person that I thought had it
not to a good degree.   'Twas the first thing I
liked in you, and without it I should never have
liked anything.   I know 'tis counted simple, but
I cannot imagine why.   'Tis true some people
have it that have not wit, but there are at least
as many foolish people I have ever observed to
be fullest of tricks, little ugly plots and designs,
unnecessary disguises, and mean cunnings, which
are the basest qualities in the world, and makes
one the most contemptible, I think ; when I once
discover them they lose their credit with me for
ever.   Some will say they are cunning only in their
own defence, and that there is no living in this
world without it; but I cannot understand how
anything more is necessary to one's own safety
besides a prudent caution; that I now think is,
though I can remember when nobody could have
persuaded me that anybody meant ill when it did
not appear by their words and actions.   I remember my mother (who, if it may be allowed me to
say it) was counted as wise a woman as most

in England,—when she seemed to distrust anybody, and saw I took notice on't, would ask if I
did not think her too jealous and a little ill-
natured. " Come, I know you do," says she, " if
you would confess it, and I cannot blame you.
When I was young as you are, I thought my
father-in-law (who was a wise man) the most
unreasonably suspicious man that ever was, and
disliked him for it hugely; but I have lived to see
it is almost impossible to think people worse than
they are, and so will you." I did not believe
her, and less, that I should have more to say to
you than this paper would hold. It shall never
be said I began another at this time of night,
though I have spent this idly, that should have
told you with a little more circumstance how
perfectly

I am yours.

Letter 53.—Dorothy's brother seems to have got hold
of a new weapon of attack in Temple's religious opinions,
which might have led to a strategic success in more
skilful hands. He only manages to exasperate Dorothy
with himself, not with Temple. As for Temple, he has
not altogether escaped the censure of the orthodox.
Gossiping Bishop Burnet, in one of his more ill-natured
passages, tells us that Temple was an Epicurean, thinking
religion to be fit only for the mob, and a corrupter of
all that came near him. Unkind words these, with just,
perhaps, those dregs of truth in them which make gossip
so hard to bear patiently. Was it true, as Courtenay
thinks, that jealousy of King William's attachment to

Temple disturbed the episcopal equipoise of soul, rendering his Lordship slanderous, even a backbiter?

Robin C. is probably one of the Cheeke family.

Bagshawe is Edward Bagshawe the Elder, B.A. of Brasenose, Oxford, and of the Middle Temple, barrister-at-law. In the early part of the century he had been a Puritan among Puritans, and in the old hall of the Middle Temple had delivered two lectures to show that bishops may not meddle in civil affairs, and that a Parliament may be held without bishops ; questions still unsettled. Laud appears to have prohibited these lectures. Bagshawe in after life joined the King at Oxford, and suffered imprisonment at the hands of his former friends in the King's Bench Prison from 1644 to 1646. Young Sir Harry Yelverton, Lady Ruthin's husband, broke a theological lance with his son, the younger Edward Bagshawe, to vindicate the cause of the Church of England. The elder Bagshawe died in 1662, and was buried at Morton Pinckney, in Northamptonshire. How and why he railed at love and marriage it is impossible now to know. Edward Bagshawe the younger published in 1671 an *Antidote against Mr. Baxter's Treatise of Love and Marriage.*

The preaching woman at Somerset House was, in all probability, Mrs. Hannah Trupnel. She, that in April of this year is spoken of, in an old news-book, as having "lately acted her part in a trance so many days at Whitehall." She appears to have been full of mystical, anti-Puritan prophecies, and was indicted in Cornwall as a rogue and vagabond, convicted and bound over in recognizances to behave herself in future. After this she abandoned her design of passing from county to county disaffecting the people with her prophecies, and we hear no more of her.

SIR, — 'Tis well you have given over your reproaches; I can allow you to tell me of my faults kindly and like a friend. Possibly it is a weakness in me to aim at the world's esteem, as if I could not be happy without it; but there are certain things that custom has made almost of absolute necessity, and reputation I take to be one of these. If one could be invisible I should choose that; but since all people are seen or known, and shall be talked of in spite of their teeth, who is it that does not desire, at least, that nothing of ill may be said of them, whether justly or otherwise? I never knew any so satisfied with their own innocence as to be content that the world should think them guilty. Some out of pride have seemed to contemn ill reports when they have found they could not avoid them, but none out of strength of reason, though many have pretended to it. No, not my Lady New-castle with all her philosophy, therefore you must not expect it from me. I shall never be ashamed to own that I have a particular value for you above any other, but 'tis not the greatest merit of person will excuse a want of fortune; in some degree I think it will, at least with the most rational part of the world, and, as far as that will read, I desire it should. I would not have the world believe I married out of interest and to please my friends; I had much rather they should know I chose the person, and took his fortune, because 'twas necessary, and that I prefer a competency with one I esteem infinitely before a vast estate in other hands. 'Tis much easier, sure, to get a good fortune than a good husband; but whosoever marries without any consideration of fortune shall never be allowed to do it, but of so reasonable an apprehension the whole world (without any reserve) shall pronounce they did it merely to satisfy their giddy humour.

Besides, though you imagine 'twere a great argument of my kindness to consider nothing but you, in earnest I believe 'twould be an injury to you. I do not see-that it puts any value upon men when women marry them for love (as they term it); 'tis not their merit, but our folly that is always presumed to cause it; and would it be any advantage to you to have your wife thought an indiscreet person? All this I can say to you; but when my brother disputes it with me I have other arguments for him, and I drove him up so close t'other night that for want of a better gap to get out at he was fain to say that he feared as much your having a fortune as your having none, for he saw you held my Lord Lt.'s [? Lieutenant's] principles. That religion and honour were things you did not consider at all, and that he was confident you would take any engagement, serve in employment, or do anything to advance yourself. I had no patience for this. To say you were a beggar, your father not worth

£4000 in the whole world, was nothing in comparison of having no religion nor no honour. I
forgot all my disguise, and we talked ourselves
weary; he renounced me, and I defied him, but
both in as civil language as it would permit, and
parted in great anger with the usual ceremony of
a leg and a courtesy, that you would have died
with laughing to have seen us.

The next day I, not being at dinner, saw him
not till night; then he came into my chamber,
where I supped but he did not. Afterwards Mr.
Gibson and he and I talked of indifferent things
till all but we two went to bed. Then he sat
half-an-hour and said not one word, nor I to him.
At last, in a pitiful tone, " Sister," says he, " I
have heard you say that when anything troubles
you, of all things you apprehend going to bed,
because there it increases upon you, and you lie
at the mercy of all your sad thought, which the
silence and darkness of the night adds a horror
to; I am at that pass now. I vow to God I
would not endure another night like the last to
gain a crown." I, who resolved to take no notice
what ailed him, said 'twas a knowledge I had
raised from my spleen only, and so fell into a
discourse of melancholy and the causes, and from
that (I know not how) into religion ; and we talked
so long of it, and so devoutly, that it laid all our
anger. We grew to a calm and peace with all
the world. Two hermits conversing in a cell they

equally inhabit, ne'er expressed more humble, charitable kindness, one towards another, than we. He asked my pardon and I his, and he has promised me never to speak of it to me whilst he lives, but leave the event to God Almighty; until he sees it done, he will always be the same to me that he is; then he shall leave me, he says, not out of want of kindness to me, but because he cannot see the ruin of a person that he loves so passionately, and in whose happiness he has laid up all his. These are the terms we are at, and I am confident he will keep his word with me, so that you have no reason to fear him in any respect; for though he should break his promise, he should never make me break mine. No, let me assure you this rival, nor any other, shall ever alter me, therefore spare your jealousy, or turn it all into kindness.

I will write every week, and no miss of letters shall give us any doubts of one another. Time nor accidents shall not prevail upon our hearts, and, if God Almighty please to bless us, we will meet the same we are, or happier. I will do all you bid me. I will pray, and wish, and hope, but you must do so too, then, and be so careful of yourself that I may have nothing to reproach you with when you come back.

That vile wench lets you see all my scribbles, I believe; how do you know I took care your hair should not be spoiled? 'Tis more than ere

you did, I think, you are so negligent on't, and
keep it so ill, 'tis pity you should have it. May
you have better luck in the cutting it than I had
with mine. I cut it two or three years agone, and
it never grew since. Look to it; if I keep the
lock you give me better than you do all the rest,
I shall not spare you; expect to be soundly
chidden. What do you mean to do with all my
letters ? Leave them behind you ? If you do,
it must be in safe hands, some of them concern
you, and me, and other people besides us very
much, and they will almost load a horse to carry.

Does not my cousin at Moor Park mistrust us
a little ? I have a great belief they do. I am
sure Robin C—— told my brother of it since I
was last in town. Of all things, I admire my
cousin Molle has not got it by the end, he that
frequents that family so much, and is at this
instant at Kimbolton. If he has, and conceals it,
he is very discreet; I could never discern by
anything that he knew it. I shall endeavour to
accustom myself to the noise on't, and make it as
easy to me as I can, though I had much rather it
were not talked of till there were an absolute
necessity of discovering it, and you can oblige me
in nothing more than in concealing it. I take it
very kindly that you promise to use all your
interest in your father to persuade him to endeavour our happiness, and he appears so confident
of his power that it gives me great hopes.

Dear! shall we ever be so happy, think you?
Ah! I dare not hope it. Yet 'tis not want of
love gives me these fears. No, in earnest, I
think (nay, I'm sure) I love you more than ever,
and 'tis that only gives me these despairing
thoughts; when I consider how small a proportion of happiness is allowed in this world, and
how great mine would be in a person for whom
I have a passionate kindness, and who has the
same for me. As it is infinitely above what I can
deserve, and more than God Almighty usually
allots to the best people, I can find nothing in
reason but seems to be against me; and, methinks,
'tis as vain in me to expect it as 'twould be to
hope I might be a queen (if that were really as
desirable a thing as 'tis thought to be); and it is-
just it should be so.

We complain of this world, and the variety of
crosses and afflictions it abounds in, and yet for
all this who is weary on't (more than in discourse),
who thinks with pleasure of leaving it, or prepar-
ing for the next? We see old folks, who have
outlived all the comforts of life, desire to continue
in it, and nothing can wean us from the folly of
preferring a mortal being, subject to great infirmity
and unavoidable decays, before an immortal one,
and all the glories that are promised with it. Is
this not very like preaching? Well, 'tis too good
for you; you shall have no more on't. I am afraid
you are not mortified enough for such discourse

to work upon (though I am not of my brother's
opinion, neither, that you have no religion in
you). In earnest, I never took anything he ever
said half so ill, as nothing, sure, is so great an
injury. It must suppose one to be a devil in
human shape. Oh, me! now I am speaking of
religion, let me ask you is not his name Bagshawe
that you say rails on love and women? Because
I heard one t'other day speaking of him, and
commending his wit, but withal, said he was a
perfect atheist. If so, I can allow him to hate us,
and love, which, sure, has something of divine in
it, since God requires it of us. I am coming into
my preaching vein again. What think you, were
it not a good way of preferment as the times are?
If you'll advise me to it I'll venture. The woman
at Somerset House was cried up mightily. Think
on't.

Dear, I am yours.

Letter 54.—Temple has really started on his journey,
and is now past Brickhill, far away in the north of
England. The journey to Ireland was made *via*
Holyhead in those days as it is now. It was a four
days' journey to Chester, and no good road after. The
great route through Wales to Holyhead was in such a
state that in 1685 the Viceroy going to Ireland was five
hours in travelling the fourteen miles from St. Asaph to
Conway; between Conway and Beaumaris he walked;
and his lady was carried in a litter. A carriage was
often taken to pieces at Conway, and carried to the

R

Menai Straits on the peasants' shoulders round the dangerous cliff of Penmaenmawr. Mr. B. and Mr. D. remain mysterious symbolic initials of gossip and scandalmongering. St. Gregory's, near St. Paul's, was a church entirely destroyed by the great fire.

Sir John Tufton of "The Mote," near Maidstone, married Mary, the third daughter and coheiress of Thomas Lord Wotton.

For your Master [seal with coat-of-arms],
        when your Mistress pleases.

SIR,—You bid me write every week, and I am doing it without considering how it will come to you. Let Nan look to that, with whom, I suppose, you have left the orders of conveyance. I have your last letter; but Jane, to whom you refer me, is not yet come down. On Tuesday I expect her; and if she be not engaged, I shall give her no cause hereafter to believe that she is a burden to me, though I have no employment for her but that of talking to me when I am in the humour of saying nothing. Your dog is come too, and I have received him with all the kindness that is due to anything you send. I have defended him from the envy and malice of a troop of greyhounds that used to be in favour with me; and he is so sensible of my care over him, that he is pleased with nobody else, and follows me as if we had been of long acquaintance. 'Tis well you are gone past my recovery.

My heart has failed me twenty times since you went, and, had you been within my call, I had brought you back as often, though I know thirty miles' distance and three hundred are the same thing. You will be so kind, I am sure, as to write back by the coach and tell me what the success of your journey so far has been. After that, I expect no more (unless you stay for a wind) till you arrive at Dublin. I pity your sister in earnest; a sea voyage is welcome to no lady; but you are beaten to it, and 'twill become you, now you are a conductor, to show your valour and keep your company in heart. When do you think of coming back again? I am asking that before you are at your journey's end. You will not take it ill that I desire it should be soon. In the meantime, I'll practise all the rules you give me. Who told you I go to bed late? In earnest, they do me wrong: I have been faulty in that point heretofore, I confess, but 'tis a good while since I gave it over with my reading o' nights; but in the daytime I cannot live without it, and 'tis all my diversion, and infinitely more pleasing to me than any company but yours. And yet I am not given to it in any excess now; I have been very much more. 'Tis Jane, I know, tells all these tales of me. I shall be even with her some time or other, but for the present I long for her with some impatience, that she may tell me all you have told her.

Never trust me if I had not a suspicion from the first that 'twas that ill-looked fellow B—— who made that story Mr. D—— told you. That which gave me the first inclination to that belief was the circumstance you told me of their seeing me at St. Gregory's. For I remembered to have seen B—— there, and had occasion to look up into the gallery where he sat, to answer a very civil salute given me from thence by Mr. Freeman, and saw B—— in a great whisper with another that sat next him, and pointing to me. If Mr. D—— had not been so nice in discovering his name, you would quickly have been cured of your jealousy. Never believe I have a servant that I do not tell you of as soon as I know it myself. As, for example, my brother Peyton has sent to me, for a countryman of his, Sir John Tufton,—he married one of my Lady Wotton's heirs, who is lately dead,—and to invite me to think of it. Besides his person and his fortune, without exception, he tells me what an excellent husband he was to this lady that's dead, who was but a crooked, ill-favoured woman, only she brought him £1500 a year. I tell him I believe Sir John Tufton could be content, I were so too upon the same terms. But his loving his first wife can be no argument to persuade me; for if he had loved her as he ought to do, I cannot hope he should love another so well as I expect anybody should that has me; and if he did not love her, I have less to expect he should me. I do not care for a divided heart; I must have all or none, at least the first place in it. Poor James, I have broke his. He says 'twould pity you to hear what sad complaints he makes; and, but that he has not the heart to hang himself, he would be very well contented to be out of the world.

That house of your cousin R—— is fatal to physicians. Dr. Smith that took it is dead already; but maybe this was before you. went, and so is no news to you. I shall be sending you all I hear; which, though it cannot be much, living as I do, yet it may be more than ventures into Ireland. I would have you diverted, whilst you are there, as much as possible; but not enough to tempt you to stay one minute longer than your father and your business obliges you. Alas! I have already repented all my share in your journey, and begin to find I am not half so valiant as I sometimes take myself to be. The knowledge that our interests are the same, and that I shall be happy or unfortunate in your person as much or more than in my own, does not give me that confidence you speak of. It rather increases my doubts, and I durst trust your fortune alone, rather than now that mine is joined with it. Yet I will hope yours may be so good as to overcome the ill of mine, and shall endeavour to mend my own all I can by striving to deserve it, maybe, better. My dearest, will you pardon me that I am forced to leave you so soon? The next shall be longer, though I can never be more than I am

Yours.

Letter 55.—This sad letter, fully dated 18th March 1654, was written after Sir Peter Osborne was buried in Campton Church. Even as Dorothy wrote this, the stone-mason might be slowly carving words that may be read to this day: "The maintainer of divine exercises, the friend to the poor." Her father is no longer living, and she is now even more lonely than before. To depend upon kindred that are not friends, to be under the protection of a brother who is her lover's avowed enemy, this is her lot in life, unless Temple can release her from it. Alas! poor Dorothy, who will now forbear to pity you?

March the 18th, 1654.

How true it is that a misfortune never comes single; we live in expectation of some one happiness that we propose to ourselves, an age almost, and perhaps miss it at the last; but sad accidents have wings to overtake us, and come in flocks like ill-boding ravens. You were no sooner gone but (as if that had not been enough) I lost the best father in the world; and though, as to himself, it was an infinite mercy in God Almighty to take him out of a world that can be pleasing to none, and was made more uneasy to him by many infirmities that were upon him, yet to me it is an affliction much greater than people judge it.

Besides all that is due to nature and the memory of many (more than ordinary) kindnesses received from him, besides what he was to all that knew him, and what he was to me in particular, I am left by his death in the condition (which of all others) is the most unsupportable to my nature, to depend upon kindred that are not friends, and that, though I pay as much as I should do to a stranger, yet think they do me a courtesy. I expect my eldest brother to-day; if he comes, I shall be able to tell you before I seal this up where you are likely to find me. If he offers me to stay here, this hole will be more agreeable to my humour than any place that is more in the world. I take it kindly that you used art to conceal our story and satisfy my nice apprehensions, but I'll not impose that constraint upon you any longer, for I find my kind brother publishes it with more earnestness than ever I strove to conceal it; and with more disadvantage than anybody else would. Now he has tried all ways to do what he desires, and finds it is in vain, he resolves to revenge himself upon me, by representing this action in such colours as will amaze all people that know me, and do not know him enough to discern his malice to me; he is not able to forbear showing it now, when my condition deserves pity from all the world, I think, and that he himself has newly lost a father, as well as I; but takes this time to torment me, which appears (at least to me) so barbarous a cruelty, that though I thank God I have charity enough perfectly to forgive all the injury he can do me, yet I am afraid I shall never look upon him as a brother more. And now do you judge whether I am not very unhappy, and whether that sadness in my face you used to complain of was not suited to my fortune. You must confess it; and that my kindness for you is beyond example, all these troubles are persecutions that make me weary of the world before my time, and lessen the concernment I have for you, and instead of being persuaded as they would have me by their malicious stories, methinks I am obliged to love you more in recompense of all the injuries they have done you upon my score. I shall need nothing but my own heart to fortify me in this resolution, and desire nothing in return of it but that your care of yourself may answer to that which I shall always have for your interests.

I received your letter of the 10th of this month; and I hope this will find you at your journey's end. In earnest, I have pitied your sister extremely, and can easily apprehend how troublesome this voyage must needs be to her, by knowing what others have been to me; yet, pray assure her I would not scruple at undertaking it myself to gain such an acquaintance, and would go much farther than where (I hope) she now is to serve her. I am afraid she will not think me a fit person to choose for a friend, that cannot agree with my own brother; but I must trust you to tell my story for me, and will hope for a better character from you than he gives me; who, lest I should complain, resolves to prevent me, and possess my friends first that he is the injured party. I never magnified my patience to you, but I begin to have a good opinion on't since this trial; yet, perhaps, I have no reason, and it may be as well a want of sense in me as of passion; however, you will not be displeased to know that I can endure all that he or anybody else can say, and that setting aside my father's death and your absence, I make nothing an affliction to me, though I am sorry, I confess, to see myself forc'd to keep such distances with one of his relations, because religion and nature and the custom of the world teaches otherwise. I see I shall not be able to satisfy you in this how I shall dispose of myself, for my brother is not come; the next will certainly tell you. In the meantime, I expect with great impatience to hear of your safe arrival. 'Twas a disappointment that you missed those fair winds. I pleased myself extremely with a belief that they had made your voyage rather a diversion than a trouble, either to you or your company, but I hope your passage was as happy, if not as sudden, as you expected it; let me hear often from you,

and long letters. I do not count this so. Have
no apprehensions from me, but all the care of
yourself that you please. My melancholy has no
anger in it; and I believe the accidents of my
life would work more upon any other than they
do upon me, whose humour is alway more
prepared for them than that of gayer persons.
I hear nothing that is worth your knowing; when
I do, you shall know it. Tell me if there's anything I can do for you, and assure yourself I am
perfectly

Yours.

Letter 56.—Temple has reached Dublin at last, and
begins to write from there. This letter also is dated,
and from this time forth there is less trouble in arrang-
ing the letters in order of date, as many of them have,
at least, the day of the month, if nothing more.

The Marquis of Hertford was the Duke of Somerset's
great-grandson. He married Lady Arabella Stuart,
daughter of Charles Stuart, Earl of Lennox, uncle of
King James I., for which matrimonial adventure he was
imprisoned in the Tower. His second wife was Frances,
daughter of Robert, Earl of Essex, and sister to the
great general of the Parliamentary Army. She was the
mother of young Lord Beauchamp, whose death Dorothy
deplores. He was twenty-eight years of age when he
died. He married Mary, daughter of Lord Capel of
Hadham, who afterwards married the Duke of Beaufort.

Baptist Noel, Viscount Camden, was a noted loyalist.
After the Restoration we find him appointed Lord-
Lieutenant of Rutland. Of his duel with Mr. Stafford

there seems to be no account. It did not carry him into the King's Bench Court, like Lord Chandos' duel, so history is silent about it.

April the 2nd, 1654.

SIR,—There was never any lady more surprised than I was with your last. I read it so coldly, and was so troubled to find that you were so forward on your journey; but when I came to the last, and saw Dublin at the date, I could scarce believe my eyes. In earnest, it transported me so that I could not forbear expressing my joy in such a manner as had anybody been by to have observed me they would have suspected me no very sober person.

You are safe arrived, you say, and pleased with the place already, only because you meet with a letter of mine there. In your next I expect some other commendation on't, or else I shall hardly make such haste to it as people here believe I will.

All the servants have been to take their leaves on me, and say how sorry they are to hear I am going out of the land; some beggar at the door has made so ill a report of Ireland to them that they pity me extremely, but you are pleased, I hope, to hear I am coming to you; the next fair wind expect me. 'Tis not to be imagined the ridiculous stories they have made, nor how J. B. cries out on me for refusing him and choosing his chamber-fellow; yet he pities me too, and swears I am condemned to be the miserablest person upon earth. With all his quarrel to me, he does not wish me so ill as to be married to the proudest, imperious, insulting, ill-natured man that ever was; one that before he has had me a week shall use me with contempt, and believe that the favour was of his side. Is not this very comfortable? But, pray, make it no quarrel; I make it none, I assure you. And though he knew you before I did, I do not think he knows you so well; besides that, his testimony is not of much value.

I am to spend this next week in taking leave of this country, and all the company in't, perhaps never to see it more. From hence I must go into Northamptonshire to my Lady Ruthin, and so to London, where I shall find my aunt and my brother Peyton, betwixt whom I think to divide this summer.

Nothing has happened since you went worth your knowledge. My Lord Marquis Hertford has lost his son, my Lord Beauchamp, who has left a fine young widow. In earnest, 'tis great pity; at the rate of our young nobility he was an extraordinary person, and remarkable for an excellent husband. My Lord Cambden, too, has fought with Mr. Stafford, but there's no harm done. You may discern the haste I'm in by my writing. There will come a time for a long letter again, but there will never come any wherein I shall not be

Yours.

[Sealed with black wax, and directed]
For Mr. William Temple,
at Sir John Temple's home
in Damask Street,
Dublin.

Thus Dorothy leaves Chicksands, her last words from her old home to Temple breathing her love and affection for him. It is no great sorrow at the moment to leave Chicksands, for its latest memories are scenes of sickness, grief, and death. And now the only home on earth for Dorothy lies in the future; it is not a particular spot on earth, but to be by his side, wherever that may be.

CHAPTER VI.

VISITING. SUMMER 1654.

THIS chapter opens with a portion of a letter written by Sir William Temple to his mistress, dated Ireland, May 18, 1654. It is the only letter, or rather scrap of letter, which we have of his, and by some good chance it has survived with the rest of Dorothy's letters. It will, I think, throw great light on his character as a lover, showing him to have been ardent and ecstatic in his suit, making quite clear Dorothy's wisdom in insisting, as she often does, on the necessity of some more material marriage portion than mere love and hope. His reference to the "unhappy differences" strengthens my view that the letters of the former chapter belong all to one date.

Letter 57.—Letter of Sir William Temple.

May 18*th*, 1654.

. . . I am called upon for my letter, but must have leave first to remember you of yours. For God's sake write constantly while I am here, or I am undone past all recovery. I have lived upon them ever since I came, but had thrived much better had they been longer. Unless you use to give me better measure, I shall not be in case to undertake a journey to England. The despair I was in at not hearing from you last week, and the belief that all my letters had miscarried (by some treachery among my good friends who, I am sorry, have the name of yours), made me press my father by all means imaginable to give me leave to go presently if I heard not from you this post. But he would never yield to that, because, he said, upon your silence he should suspect all was not likely to be well between us, and then he was sure I should not be in condition to be alone. He remembered too well the letters I writ upon our last unhappy differences, and would not trust me from him in such another occasion. But, withal, he told me he would never give me occasion of any discontent which he could remedy ; that if you desired my coming over, and I could not be content without, he would not hinder me, though he very much desired my company a month or two longer, and that in that time 'twas very likely I might have his as well.

Now, in very good earnest, do you think 'tis time for me to come or no ? Would you be very glad to see me there, and could you do it in less disorder, and with less surprise, than you did at Chicksands ?

I ask you these questions very seriously ; but

yet how willingly would I venture all to be with you. I know you love me still; you promised me, and that's all the security I can have in this world. 'Tis that which makes all things else seem nothing to it, so high it sets me; and so high, indeed, that should I ever fall 'twould dash me all to pieces. Methinks your very charity should make you love me more now than ever, by seeing me so much more unhappy than I used, by being so much farther from you, for that is all the measure can be taken of my good or ill condition. Justice, I am sure, will oblige you to it, since you have no other means left in the world of rewarding such a passion as mine, which, sure, is of a much richer value than anything in the world besides. Should you save my life again, should you make me absolute master of your fortune and your person too, I should accept none of all this in any part of payment, but look upon you as one behindhand with me still. 'Tis no vanity this, but a true sense of how pure and how refined a nature my passion is, which none can ever know except my own heart, unless you find it out by being there.

How hard it is to think of ending when I am writing to you; but it must be so, and I must ever be subject to other people's occasions, and so never, I think, master of my own. This is too true, both in respect of this fellow's post that is bawling at me for my letter, and of my father's

delays. They kill me; but patience,—would anybody but I were here! Yet you may command
me ever at one minute's warning. Had I not
heard from you by this last, in earnest I had
resolved to have gone with this, and given my
father the slip for all his caution. He tells me
still of a little time; but, alas! who knows not
what mischances and how great changes have
often happened in a little time?

For God's sake let me hear of all your motions,
when and where I may hope to see you. Let us
but hope this cloud, this absence that has overcast
all my contentment, may pass away, and I am
confident there's a clear sky attends us. My
dearest dear, adieu.

Yours.

Pray, where is your lodging? Have a care of
all the despatch and security that can be in our
intelligence. Remember my fellow-servant; sure,
by the next I shall write some learned epistle to
her, I have been so long about it.

Letter 58.—Dorothy is now in London, staying probably with that aunt whom she mentioned before as
one who was always ready to find her a husband other
than Temple. Of the plot against the Protector in
which my Lord of Dorchester is said to be engaged, an
account is given in connection with *Letter* 59; that is,
presuming it to be the same plot, and that Lord
Dorchester is one of the many persons arrested under

suspicion of being concerned in it. I cannot find anything which identifies him with a special plot.

Lady Sandis [Sandys], who seems so fond of race
meetings and other less harmless amusements, was the
wife of William Lord Sandys, and daughter of the Earl
of Salisbury. Lord Sandys' country house was Motes-
font or Mottisfont Priory, in Hampshire, "which the
King had given him in exchange for Chelsea, in Westminster." So says Leland, the antiquary and scholar, in
his *Itinerary;* but it is a little puzzling to the modern
mind with preconceived notions of Chelsea, to hear it
spoken of as a seat or estate in Westminster. Colonel
Tom Paunton is to me merely a name ; and J. Morton
is nothing more, unless we may believe him to be Sir
John Morton, Bart. of Milbourne, St. Andrew, in Nottinghamshire. This addition of a local habitation and a
name gives us no further knowledge, however, of the
scandal to which Dorothy alludes.

Mistress Stanley and Mistress Witherington have left
no trace of their identity that I can find, but Mistress
Philadelphia Carey is not wholly unknown. She was
the second daughter of Thomas Carey, one of the Earl
of Monmouth's sons, and readers may be pleased to
know that she did marry Sir Henry Littleton.

Of the scandal concerning Lord Rich I am not sorry
to know nothing.

May 25th [1654].

THIS world is composed of nothing but con-
trarieties and sudden accidents, only the proportions are not at all equal ; for to a great measure
of trouble it allows so small a quantity of joy, that
one may see tis merely intended to keep us alive

withal. This is a formal preface, and looks as if there were something of very useful to follow; but I would not wish you to expect it. I was only considering my own ill-humour last night, I had not heard from you in a week or more, my brother had been with me and we had talked ourselves both out of breath and patience too, I was not very well, and rose this morning only because I was weary of lying in bed. When I had dined I took a coach and went to see whether there was ever a letter for me, and was this once so lucky as to find one. I am not partial to myself I know, and am contented that the pleasure I have received with this, shall serve to sweeten many sad thoughts that have interposed since your last, and more that I may reasonably expect before I have another; and I think I may (without vanity) say, that nobody is more sensible of the least good fortune nor murmurs less at an ill than I do, since I owe it merely to custom and not to any constancy in my humour, or something that is better. No, in earnest, anything of good comes to me like the sun to the inhabitants of Greenland, it raises them to life when they see it, and when they miss it, it is not strange they expect a night of half a year long.

You cannot imagine how kindly I take it that you forgive my brother, and let me assure you I shall never press you to anything unreasonable. I will not oblige you to court a person that has

injured you.   I only beg that whatsoever he does
in that kind may be excused by his relation to
me, and that whenever you are moved to think
he does you wrong, you will at the same time
remember that his sister loves you passionately
and nobly ; that if he values nothing but fortune,
she despises it, and could love you as much a
beggar as she could do a prince ; and shall without question love you eternally, but whether with
any satisfaction to herself or you is a sad doubt.
I am not apt to hope, and whether it be the better
or the worse I know not.   All sorts of differences
are natural to me, and that which (if your kindness would give you leave) you would term a
weakness in me is nothing but a reasonable
distrust of my own judgment, which makes me
desire the approbation of my friends.   I never
had the confidence in my life to presume anything
well done that I had nobody's opinion in but my
own ; and as you very well observe, there are so
many that think themselves wise when nothing
equals their folly but their pride, that I dread
nothing so much as discovering such a thought in
myself because of the consequences of it.

Whenever you come you must not doubt your
welcome, but I can promise you nothing for the
manner on't.   I am afraid my surprise and disorder will be more than ever.   I have good
reason to think so, and none that you can take ill.
But I would not have you attempt it till your

father is ready for the journey too. No, really he deserves that all your occasions should wait for his; and if you have not much more than an ordinary obedience for him, I shall never believe you have more than an ordinary kindness for me; since (if you will pardon me the comparison) I believe we both merit it from you upon the same score, he as a very indulgent father, and I as a very kind mistress. Don't laugh at me for commending myself, you will never do it for me, and so I am forced to it.

I am still here in town, but had no hand, I can assure you, in the new discovered plot against the Protector. But my Lord of Dorchester, they say, has, and so might I have had if I were as rich as he, and then you might have been sure of me at the Tower;—now a worse lodging must serve my turn. 'Tis over against Salisbury House where I have the honour of seeing my Lady M. Sandis every day unless some race or other carry her out of town. The last week she went to one as far as Winchester with Col. Paunton (if you know such a one), and there her husband met her, and because he did so (though it 'twere by accident) thought himself obliged to invite her to his house but seven miles off, and very modestly said no more for it, but that he thought it better than an Inn, or at least a crowded one as all in the town were now because of the race. But she was so good a companion that she would not forsake her company. So he invited them too, but could prevail with neither. Only my Lady grew kind at parting and said, indeed if Tom Paunton and J. Morton and the rest would have gone she could have been contented to have taken his offer. Thus much for the married people, now for those that are towards it.

There is Mr. Stanley and Mrs. Witherington; Sir H. Littleton and Mrs. Philadelphia Carey, who in earnest is a fine woman, such a one as will make an excellent wife ; and some say my Lord Rich and my Lady Betty Howard, but others that pretend to know more say his court to her is but to countenance a more serious one to Mrs. Howard, her sister-in-law, he not having courage to pretend so openly (as some do) to another's wife. Oh, but your old acquaintance, poor Mr. Heningham, has no luck! He was so near (as he thought at least) marrying Mrs. Ger-herd that anybody might have got his whole estate in wagers upon't that would have ventured but a reasonable proportion of their own. And now he looks more like an ass than ever he did. She has cast him off most unhandsomely, that's the truth on't, and would have tied him to such con-ditions as he might have been her slave withal, but could never be her husband. Is not this a great deal of news for me that never stir abroad? Nay, I had brought me to-day more than all this : that I am marrying myself! And the pleasantness on't is that it should be to my Lord St. John.

Would he look on me, think you, that had pretty Mrs. Fretcheville? My comfort is, I have not seen him since he was a widower, and never spoke to him in my life. I found myself so innocent that I never blushed when they told it me. What would I give I could avoid it when people speak of you? In earnest, I do prepare myself all that is possible to hear it spoken of, yet for my life I cannot hear your name without discovering that I am more than ordinarily concerned in't. A blush is the foolishest thing that can be, and betrays one more than a red nose does a drunkard; and yet I would not so wholly have lost them as some women that I know has, as much injury as they do me.

I can assure you now that I shall be here a fortnight longer (they tell me no lodger, upon pain of his Highness's displeasure, must remove sooner); but when I have his leave I go into Suffolk for a month, and then come hither again to go into Kent, where I intend to bury myself alive again as I did in Bedfordshire, unless you call me out and tell me I may be happy. Alas! how fain I would hope it, but I cannot, and should it ever happen, 'twould be long before I should believe 'twas meant for me in earnest, or that 'twas other than a dream. To say truth, I do not love to think on't, I find so many things to fear and so few to hope.

'Tis better telling you that I will send my

letters where you direct, that they shall be as
long ones as possibly my time will permit, and
when at any time you miss of one, I give you
leave to imagine as many kind things as you
please, and to believe I mean them all to you.

Farewell.

Letter 59.—It is a little astonishing to read, as one
does in this and the last letter, of race meetings, and
Dorothy, habited in a mask, disporting herself at New
Spring Gardens or in the Park. It opens one's eyes to the
exaggerated gloom that has been thrown over England
during the Puritan reign by those historians who have
derived their information solely from State papers and
proclamations. It is one thing to proclaim amusements,
another to abolish them. The first was undoubtedly
done, but we doubt if there was ever any long-continued
effort to do the last; and in the latter part of Cromwell's
reign the gloom, and the strait-laced regulations that
caused it, must have almost entirely disappeared.

Spring Gardens seems at one time to have had no
very good reputation. Lady Alice Halkett, writing in
1644, tells us that "so scrupulous was I of giving any
occasion to speak of me as I know they did of others,
that though I loved well to see plays, and to walk in
the Spring Gardens sometimes (before it grew something scandalous by the abuses of some), yet I cannot
remember three times that ever I went with any man
besides my brother." However, fashions change in ten
years, and Spring Gardens is, doubtless, now quite
demure and respectable, or we should not find Dorothy
there. Spring Gardens was enclosed and laid out
towards the end of the reign of James I. The clump

of houses which still bears its name is supposed to indicate its position with tolerable exactness. Evelyn tells us that Cromwell shut up the Spring Gardens in 1649, and Knight thinks they were closed until the Restoration, in which small matter we may allow Dorothy to correct him. The fact of the old gardens having been closed may account for Dorothy referring to the place as "New Spring Gardens." Knight also quotes at second hand from an account of Spring Gardens, complaining that the author is unknown to him. This quotation is, however, from one of Somers' Tracts entitled "A Character of England as it was lately represented in a Letter to a Nobleman of France, 1659." The Frenchman by whom the letter is written —probably an English satirist in disguise—gives us such a graphic account of the Parks before the Restoration, that as the matter is fresh and bears upon the subject, I have no hesitation in quoting it at length :—

"I did frequently in the spring accompany my Lord N. into a field near the town which they call Hyde Park,—the place not unpleasant, and which they use as our '*Course*,' but with nothing that order, equipage, and splendour; being such an assembly of wretched jades and hackney coaches, as, next to a regiment of car-men, there is nothing approaches the resemblance. The Park was, it seems, used by the late King and nobility for the freshness of the air and the goodly prospect, but it is that which now (besides all other exercises) they pay for here in England, though it be free in all the world beside ; every coach and horse which enters buying his mouthful and permission of the publican who has purchased it, for which the entrance is guarded with porters and long staves.

"The manner is, as the company returns, to stop at the

Spring Gardens so called, in order to the Park as our
Thuilleries is to the *Course ;* the inclosure not disagree-
able for the solemnness of the groves, the warbling of
the birds, and as it opens into the spacious walks of
St. James. But the company walk in it at such a rate
as you would think all the ladies were so many Atalantas
contending with their wooers, and, my Lord, there was
no appearance that I should prove the Hippomenes,
who could with very much ado keep pace with them.
But, as fast as they run, they stay there so long, as if
they wanted not to finish the race, for it is usual here
to find some of the young company till midnight, and
the thickets of the garden seem to be contrived to all
the advantages of gallantry after they have refreshed
with the collation, which is here seldom omitted, at a
certain cabaret in the middle of this paradise, where the
forbidden fruits are certain trifling tarts, neats' tongues,
salacious meats, and bad Rhenish, for which the gallants
pay sauce, as indeed they do at all such houses throughout England ; for they think it a piece of frugality
beneath them to bargain or account for what they eat
in any place, however unreasonably imposed upon."

Dorothy is quite right in her correction concerning
Will Spencer. He was the first Earl of Sunderland,
and married Elizabeth, daughter of Lord Gerard.

June the 6th, 1654.

I SEE you know how to punish me. In earnest,
I was so frightened with your short letter as you
cannot imagine, and as much troubled at the
cause on't. What is it your father ails, and how
long has he been ill ? If my prayers are heard,
he will not be so long. Why do you say I failed

you? Indeed, I did not. Jane is my witness. She carried my letter to the White Hart, by St. James's, and 'twas a very long one too. I carried one thither since, myself, and the woman of the house was so very angry, because I desired her to have a care on't, that I made the coachman drive away with all possible speed, lest she should have beaten me. To say truth, I pressed her too much, considering how little the letter deserved it. 'Twas writ in such disorder, the company prating about me, and some of them so bent on doing me little mischiefs, that I know not what I did, and believe it was the most senseless, disjointed thing that ever was read.

I remember now that I writ Robin Spencer instead of Will. 'Tis he that has married, Mrs. Gerherd, and I admire their courage. She will have eight hundred pounds a year, 'tis true, after her mother's death; but how they will live till then I cannot imagine. I shall be even with you for your short letter. I'll swear they will not allow me time for anything, and to show how absolutely I am governed I need but tell you that I am every night in the Park and at New Spring Gardens, where, though I come with a mask, I cannot escape being known, nor my conversion being admired. Are you not in some fear what will become on me? These are dangerous courses. I do not find, though, that they have altered me yet. I am much the same person at heart I was in being   Yours.

Letter 60.

June 13*th* [1654].

You have satisfied me very much with this last
long letter, and made some amends for the short
one I received before. I am convinced, too,
happiness is much such a kind of thing as you
describe, or rather such a nothing. For there is
no one thing can properly be called so, but every
one is left to create it to themselves in something
which they either have or would have; and so far
it's well enough. But I do not like that one's
happiness should depend upon a persuasion that
this is happiness, because nobody knows how
long they shall continue in a belief built upon no
grounds, only to bring it to what you say, and to
make it absolutely of the same nature with faith.
We must conclude that nobody can either create
or continue such a belief in themselves; but
where it is there is happiness. And for my part
at this present, I verily believe I could find it in
the long walk at Dublin.

You say nothing of your father's sickness,
therefore I hope he is well again; for though I
have a quarrel to him, it does not extend so far
as to wish him ill. But he made no good return
for the counsel I gave you, to say that there
might come a time when my kindness might fail.
Do not believe him, I charge you, unless you
doubt yourself that you may give me occasion

to change; and when he tells you so again, engage what you please upon't, and put it upon my account. I shall go out of town this week, and so cannot possibly get a picture drawn for you till I come up again, which will be within these six weeks, but not to make any stay at all. I should be glad to find you here then. I would have had one drawn since I came, and consulted my glass every morning when to begin; and to speak freely to you that are my friend, I could never find my face in a condition to admit on't, and when I was not satisfied with it myself, I had no reason to hope that anybody else should. But I am afraid, as you say, that time will not mend it, and therefore you shall have it as it is as soon as Mr. Cooper will vouchsafe to take the pains to draw it for you.

I am in great trouble to think how I shall write out of Suffolk to you, or receive yours. However, do not fail to write, though they lie awhile. I shall have them at last, and they will not be the less welcome; and, though you should miss of some of mine, let it not trouble you; but if it be by my fault, I'll give you leave to demand satisfaction for it when you come. Jane kisses your hands, and says she will be ready in all places to do you service; but I'll prevent her, now you have put me into a jealous humour. I'll keep her in chains before she shall quit scores with me. Do not believe, sir, I beseech you, that the young heirs are for you; content yourself with your old mistress. You are not so handsome as Will Spencer, nor I have not so much courage nor wealth as his mistress, nor she has not so much as her aunt says by all the money. I should not have called her his mistress now they have been married almost this fortnight.

I'll write again before I leave the town, and should have writ more now, but company is come in. Adieu, my dearest.

Letter 61.—Lady Talmash was the eldest daughter of Mr. Murray, Charles I.'s page and whipping boy. She married Sir Lionel Talmash of Suffolk, a gentleman of noble family. After her father's death, she took the title of Countess of Dysart, although there was some dispute about the right of her father to any title. Bishop Burnet says : " She was a woman of great beauty, but of far greater parts. She had a wonderful quickness of apprehension, and an amazing vivacity in conversation. She had studied not only divinity and history, but mathematics and philosophy. She was violent in everything she set about,—a violent friend, but a much more violent enemy. She had a restless ambition, lived at a vast expense, and was ravenously covetous ; and would have stuck at nothing by which she might compass her ends. She had been early in a correspondence with Lord Lauderdale, that had given occasion to censure. When he was a prisoner after Worcester fight, she made him believe he was in great danger of his life, and that she saved it by her intrigues with Cromwell, which was not a little taken notice of. Cromwell was certainly fond of her, and she took care to entertain him in it ; till he, finding what was said upon it, broke it off. Upon the King's Restoration she thought that Lord Lauderdale made not those returns she expected. They lived for some years at a distance. But upon her husband's death she made up all quarrels ; so that Lord Lauderdale and she lived so much together that his Lady was offended at it and went to Paris, where she died about three years after." This was in 1672, and soon afterwards Lady Dysart and Lord Lauderdale were married. She had great power over him, and employed it in trafficking with such State patronage as was in Lord Lauderdale's power to bestow.

Cousin Hammond, who was going to take Ludlow's place in Ireland, would be the Colonel Robert Hammond who commanded Carisbrooke when the King was imprisoned there. He was one of a new council formed in August and sent into Ireland about the end of that month.

Lady Vavasour was Ursula, daughter of Walter Gifford of Chillington, Staffordshire. Her husband was Sir Thomas Vavasour, Bart. The Vavasours were a Roman Catholic family, and claimed descent from those who held the ancient office of King's Valvasour ; and we need not therefore be surprised to find Lady Vavasour engaged in one of the numerous plots that surrounded and endangered the Protector's power. The plot itself seems to have created intense excitement in the capital, and resulted in three persons being tried for high treason, and two executed,—John Gerard, gentleman, Peter Vowel, schoolmaster of Islington, and one Summerset Fox, who pleaded guilty, and whose life was spared. "Some wise men," writes one Thomas Gower in a contemporary letter (still unprinted) " believe that a couple of coy-ducks drew in the rest, then revealed all, and were employed to that purpose that the execution of a few mean persons might deter wiser and more considerable persons." This seems not improbable. On June 6th the official *Mercurius Politicus* speaks of this plot as follows :—" The traitorous conspiracy mentioned heretofore it appears every day more desperate and bloody. It is discovered that their design was to have destroyed his Highness's person, and all others at the helm of Government that they could have laid hands on. Immediately upon the villainous assassination, they intended to have proclaimed Charles Stuart by the assistance of a tumult," etc. etc. This with constant accounts of further arrests troubles the public mind at this time.

The passage of Cowley which Dorothy refers to is in the second book of Cowley's *Davideis.* It opens with a description of the friendship between David and Jonathan, and, upon that occasion, a digression concerning the nature of love. The poem was written by Cowley when a young man at Cambridge. One can picture Dorothy reading and musing over lines like these with sympathy and admiration :

> What art thou, love, thou great mysterious thing ?
> From what hid stock does thy strange nature spring ?
> 'Tis thou that mov'st the world through ev'ry part,
> And hold'st the vast frame close that nothing start
> From the due place and office first ordained,
> By thee were all things made and are sustained.
> Sometimes we see thee fully and can say
> From hence thou took'st thy rise and went'st that way,
> But oft'ner the short beams of reason's eye
> See only there thou art, not how, nor why.

His lines on love, though overcharged with quaint conceits, are often noble and true, and end at least with one fine couplet :

> Thus dost thou sit (like men e'er sin had framed
> A guilty blush), naked but not ashamed.

I PROMISED in my last to write again before I went out of town, and now I'll be as good as my word. They are all gone this morning, and have left me much more at liberty than I have been of late, therefore I believe this will be a long letter; perhaps too long, at least if my letters are as little entertaining as my company is. I was carried yesterday abroad to a dinner that was designed for mirth, but it seems one ill-humoured person in the company is enough to put all the rest out of tune; for I never saw people perform what they intended worse, and could not forbear telling them so: but to excuse themselves and silence my reproaches, they all agreed to say that I spoiled their jollity by wearing the most unreasonable looks that could be put on for such an occasion. I told them I knew no remedy but leaving me behind next time, and could have told them that my looks were suitable to my fortune, though not to a feast. Fye! I am got into my complaining humour that tires myself as well as everybody else, and which (as you observe) helps not at all. Would it would leave me, and then I could believe I shall not always have occasion for it. But that's in nobody's power, and my Lady Talmash, that says she can do whatsoever she will, cannot believe whatsoever she pleases. 'Tis not unpleasant, methinks, to hear her talk, how at such a time she was sick and the physicians told

T

her she would have the small-pox, and showed
her where they were coming out upon her; but
she bethought herself that it was not at all convenient for her to have them at that time; some
business she had that required her going abroad,
and so she resolved she would not be sick; nor
was not.   Twenty such stories as these she tells;
and then falls into discoveries of strength of
reason and the power of philosophy, till she
confounds herself and all that hear her.   You
have no such ladies in Ireland?

Oh me, but I heard to-day your cousin
Hammond is going thither to be in Ludlow's
place.   Is it true?   You tell me nothing what is
done there, but 'tis no matter.   The less one
knows of State affairs I find it is the better.   My
poor Lady Vavasour is carried to the Tower,
and her great belly could not excuse her, because
she was acquainted by somebody that there was a
plot against the Protector, and did not discover
it.   She has told now all that was told her, but
vows she will never say from whence she had
it : we shall see whether her resolutions are as
unalterable as those of my Lady Talmash.   I
wonder how she behaved herself when she was
married.   I never saw any one yet that did not
look simply and out of countenance, nor ever
knew a wedding well designed but one; and that
was of two persons who had time enough I confess to contrive it, and nobody to please in't but

themselves. He came down into the country where she was upon a visit, and one morning married her. As soon as they came out of the church they took coach and came for the town, dined at an inn by the way, and at night came into lodgings that were provided for them where nobody knew them, and where they passed for married people of seven years' standing.

The truth is I could not endure to be Mrs. Bride in a public wedding, to be made the happiest person on earth. Do not take it ill, for I would endure it if I could, rather than fail; but in earnest I do not think it were possible for me. You cannot apprehend the formalities of a treaty more than I do, nor so much the success on't. Yet in earnest, your father will not find my brother Peyton wanting in civility (though he is not a man of much compliment, unless it be in his letters to me), nor an unreasonable person in anything, so he will allow him out of his kindness to his wife to set a higher value upon her sister than she deserves. I know not how he may be prejudiced as to the business, but he is not deaf to reason when 'tis civilly delivered, and is as easily gained with compliance and good usage as anybody I know, but by no other way. When he is roughly dealt with, he is like me, ten times the worse for't.

I make it a case of conscience to discover my faults to you as fast as I know them, that you may consider what you have to do. My 'aunt told me no longer agone than yesterday that I was the most wilful woman that ever she knew, and had an obstinacy of spirit nothing could overcome. Take heed! you see I give you fair warning.

I have missed a letter this Monday : What is the reason ? By the next, I shall be gone into Kent, and my other journey is laid aside, which I am not displeased at, because it would have broken our intercourse very much.

Here are some verses of Cowley's. Tell me how you like them. 'Tis only a piece taken out of a new thing of his ; the whole is very long, and is a description of, or rather a paraphrase upon, the friendship of David and Jonathan. 'Tis, I think, the best I have seen of his, and I like the subject because 'tis that I would be perfect in.   Adieu.

Je suis vostre.

Letter 62.

June the 26th [1654].

I TOLD you in my last that my Suffolk journey was laid aside, and that into Kent hastened. I am beginning it to-day ; and have chosen to go as far as Gravesend by water, though it be very gloomy weather. If I drown by the way, this will be my last letter ; and, like a will, I bequeath all my kindness to you in it, with a charge never to bestow it all upon another mistress, lest my ghost rise again and haunt you. I am in such haste that I can say little else to you now. When you are come over, we'd think where to meet, for at this distance I can design nothing; only I should be as little pleased with the constraint of my brother's house as you. Pray let me know whether your man leaves you, and how you stand inclined to him I offer you. Indeed, I like him extremely, and he is commended to me, by people that know him very well and are able to judge, for a most excellent servant, and faithful as possible. I'll keep him unengaged till I hear from you. -Adieu.

My next shall make amends for this short one.

[*P.S.*]—I received your last of June 22nd since I sealed up my letter, and I durst not but make an excuse for another short one, after you have chid me so for those you have received already; indeed, I could not help it, nor cannot now, but if that will satisfy I can assure you I shall make a much better wife than I do a husband, if I ever am one. *Pardon, mon Cher Cœur, on m'attend. Adieu, mon Ame. Je vous souhait tout cé que vous desire.*

Letter 63.

July the 4th [1654].

BECAUSE you find fault with my other letters, this is like to be shorter than they; I did not intend it so though, I can assure you. But last night my brother told me he did not send his till ten o'clock this morning, and now he calls for mine at seven, before I am up ; and I can only be allowed time to tell you that I am in Kent, and in a house so strangely crowded with company that I am weary as a dog already, though I have been here but three or four days ; that all their mirth has not mended my humour, and that I am here the same I was in other places ; that I hope, merely because you bid me, and lose that hope as often as I consider anything but yours. Would I were easy of belief! they say one is so to all that one desires. I do not find it, though I am told I was so extremely when I believed you loved me. That I would not find, and you have only power to make me think it. But I am called upon. How fain I would say more ; yet 'tis all but the saying with more circumstance that I am

Yours.

[Directed.]   For your master.

Letter 64.

I SEE you can chide when you please; and with authority ; but I deserve it, I confess, and all I can say for myself is, that my fault proceeded from a very good principle in me.   I am apt

to speak what I think; and to you have so
accustomed myself to discover all my heart that
I do not believe it will ever be in my power to
conceal a thought from you.   Therefore I am
afraid you must resolve to be vexed with all my
senseless apprehensions as my brother Peyton is
with some of his wife's, who is thought a very
good woman, but the most troublesome one in
a coach that ever was.   We dare not let our
tongues lie more on one side of our mouths
than t'other for fear of overturning it.   You are
satisfied, I hope, ere this that I 'scaped drowning.
However, 'tis not amiss that my will made you
know now how to dispose of all my wealth whensoever I die.   But I am troubled much you
should make so ill a journey to so little purpose;
indeed, I writ by the first post after my arrival
here, and cannot imagine how you came to miss
of my letters.   Is your father returned yet, and
do you think of coming over immediately? How
welcome you will be.   But, alas! I cannot talk
on't at the rate that you do.   I am sensible that
such an absence is misfortune enough, but I dare
not promise myself that it will conclude ours;
and 'tis more my belief that you yourself speak
it rather to encourage me, and to your wishes
than your hopes.

My humour is so ill at present, that I dare say
no more lest you chide me again.   I find myself
fit for nothing but to converse with a lady below,

that is fallen out with all the world because her husband and she cannot agree. 'Tis the pleasantest thing that can be to hear us discourse. She takes great pains to dissuade me from ever marrying, and says I am the veriest fool that ever lived if I do not take her counsel. Now we do not absolutely agree in that point, but I promise her never to marry unless I can find such a husband as I describe to her, and she believes is never to be found; so that, upon the matter, we differ very little. Whensoever she is accused of maintaining opinions very destructive of society, and absolutely prejudicial to all the young people of both sexes that live in the house, she calls out me to be her second, and by it has lost me the favour of all our young gallants, who have got a custom of expressing anything that is nowhere but in fiction by the name of " Mrs. O——'s husband." For my life I cannot beat into their heads a passion that must be subject to no decay, an even perfect kindness that must last perpetually, without the least intermission. They laugh to hear me say that one unkind word would destroy all the satisfaction of my life, and that I should expect our kindness should increase every day, if it were possible, but never lessen. All this is perfect nonsense in their opinion; but I should not doubt the convincing them if I could hope to be so happy as to be

Yours.

Letter 65. — Of William Lilly, a noted and extraordinary character of that day, the following account is
taken from his own *Life and Times,* a lively book,
full of amusing lies and astrological gossip, in which
the author describes himself as a student of the Black
Art. He was born in 1602 at Diseworth, an obscure
town in the north of Leicestershire. His family
appear to have been yeomen in this town for many
generations. Passing over the measles of his infancy,
and other trivial details of childhood, which he describes
minutely, we find him as a boy at Ashby-de-la-Zouche,
where he is the pupil of one Mr. John Brinsley. Here
he learned Latin and Greek, and began to study
Hebrew. In the sixteenth year of his age he was
greatly troubled with dreams concerning his damnation
or salvation ; and at the age of eighteen he returned to
his father's house, and there kept a school in great
penury. He then appears to have come up to London,
leaving his father in a debtor's prison, and proceeded
in pursuit of fortune with a new suit of clothes and
seven shillings and sixpence in his pocket. In London
he entered the service of one Gilbert Wright, an
independent citizen of small means and smaller education. To him Lilly was both man - servant and
secretary. The second Mrs. Wright seems to have had
a taste for astrology, and consulted some of the quacks
who then preyed on the silly women of the city. She
was very fond of young Lilly, who attended her in her
last illness, and, in return for his care and attention, she
bequeathed to him several " sigils " or talismanic seals.
Probably it was the foolishness of this poor woman that
first suggested to Lilly the advantages to be gained
from the profession of astrology. Mr. Wright married a
third wife, and soon afterwards died, leaving his widow

comfortably off.   She fell in love with Lilly, who
married her in 1627, and for five years, until her death,
they lived happily together.   Lilly was now a man of
means, and was enabled to study that science which he
afterwards practised with so much success.   There were
a good many professors of the black art at this date,
and Lilly studied under one Evans, a scoundrelly ex-
parson from Wales, until, according to Lilly's own
account, he discovered Evans to be the cheat he
undoubtedly was.   Lilly, when he set up for himself,
wrote many astrological works, which seem to have
been very successful.   He was known and visited by all
the great men of the day, and probably had brains
enough only to prophesy when he knew.   His description of his political creed is beautifully characteristic of
the man: " I was more Cavalier than Roundhead, and
so taken notice of; but afterwards I engaged body and
soul in the cause of the Parliament, but still with much
affection to his Majesty's person and unto Monarchy,
which I ever loved and approved beyond any government whatsoever."   Lilly was, in a word, a self-seeking
but successful knave.   People who had been robbed,
women in love, men in debt, all in trouble and doubt,
from the King downwards, sought his aid.   He pretended
to be a man of science, not a man gifted with super-
natural powers.   Whether he succeeded in believing in
astrology and deceiving himself, it is impossible to say;
he was probably too clever for that, but he deceived
others admirably, and was one of the noted and most
successful of the old astrologers.

How long this letter will be I cannot tell.
You shall have all the time that is allowed me,
but upon condition that you shall not examine

the sense on't too strictly, for you must know
I want sleep extremely. The sun was up an
hour before I went to bed to-day, and this is not
the first time I have done this since I came
hither. 'Twill not be for your advantage that
I should stay here long; for, in earnest, I shall
be good for nothing if I do. We go abroad all
day and play all night, and say our prayers when
we have time. Well, in sober earnest now, I
would not live thus a twelvemonth to gain all
that the King has lost, unless it were to give it
him again. 'Tis a miracle to me how my brother
endures it. 'Tis as contrary to his humour as
darkness is to light, and only shows the power
he lets his wife have over him. Will you be so
good-natured? He has certainly as great a kindness for her as can be, and, to say truth, not
without reason; but of all the people that ever
I saw, I do not like his carriage towards her.
He is perpetually wrangling and finding fault, and
to a person that did not know him would appear
the worst husband and the most imperious in the
world. He is so amongst his children too, though
he loves them passionately. He has one son,
and 'tis the finest boy that e'er you saw, and has
a noble spirit, but yet stands in that awe of his
father that one word from him is as much as
twenty whippings.

You must give me leave to entertain you thus
with discourses of the family, for I can tell you

nothing else from hence. Yet, now I remember,
I have another story for you. You little think
I have been with Lilly, and, in earnest, I was, the
day before I came out of town; and what do you
think I went for? Not to know when you would
come home, I can assure you, nor for any other
occasion of my own; but with a cousin of mine
that had long designed to make herself sport with
him, and did not miss of her aim. I confess I
always thought him an impostor, but I could
never have imagined him so simple a one as we
found him. In my life I never heard so ridiculous
a discourse as he made us, and no old woman
who passes for a witch could have been more
puzzled to seek what to say to reasonable people
than he was. He asked us more questions than
we did him, and caught at everything we said
without discerning that we abused him and said
things purposely to confound him; which we did
so perfectly that we made him contradict himself
the strongest that ever you saw. Ever since
this adventure, I have had so great a belief
in all things of this nature, that I could not
forbear laying a peas-cod with nine peas in't
under my door yesterday, and was informed by
it that my husband's name should be Thomas.
How do you like that? But what Thomas,
I cannot imagine, for of all the servants I
have got since I came hither I know none of
that name.

Here is a new song,—I do not send it to you but to your sister; the tune is not worth the sending so far. If she pleases to put any to it, I am sure it will be a better than it has here. Adieu.

Letter 66.—"The Lost Lady" is a tragi-comedy by Sir William Berkely, and is advertised to be sold at the shop of the Holy Lamb in the year 1639, which we may take as the probable date of its publication. Dorothy would play Hermione, the heroine. We can imagine her speaking with sympathetic accent lines such as these :

> With what harsh fate does Heaven afflict me,
> That all the blessings which make others happy,
> Must be my ruin?

The five Portugals to whom Dorothy refers as being hanged were the Portuguese ambassador's brother, Don Pantaleon Sa, and four of his men. The *Mercurius Politicus* of November 1653 gives the following account of the matters that led to the execution; and as it is illustrative of the manners of the day, the account is here quoted at length :—

"NEW EXCHANGE IN THE STRAND. *November* 21.— In the evening there happened a quarrel between the Portugal ambassador's brother and two or three others of that nation with one Mr. Gerard, an English gentleman, whom they all fell upon; but he being rescued out of their hands by one Mr. Anstruther, they retired home, and within an hour after returned with about twelve more of their nation, armed with breastplates and headpieces; but after two or three hours taken there, not finding Anstruther, they went home again for that night.

"*November* 22.—At night the ambassador's brother and the rest returned again, and walking the upper Exchange, they met with one Col. Mayo, who, being a proper man, they supposed him to have been the same Anstruther that repelled them the night before; and so shooting off a pistol (which was as the watch-word), the rest of the Portugals (supposed about fifty) came in with drawn swords, and leaving a sufficient number to keep the stairs, the rest went up with the ambassador's brother, and there they fell upon Col. Mayo, who, very gallantly defending himself, received seven dangerous wounds, and lies in a mortal condition. They fell also upon one Mr. Greenway, of Lincoln's Inn, as he was walking with his sister in one hand and his mistress in the other (to whom, as I am informed, he was to have been married on Tuesday next), and pistoled him in the head, whereof he died immediately. They brought with them several earthen jars stuffed with gunpowder, stopped with wax, and fitted with matches, intending, it seems, to have done some mischief to the Exchange that they might complete their revenge, but they were prevented."

There is an account of their trial in the *State Trials*, of some interest to lawyers; it resulted in the execution of Don Pantaleon Sa and four of his servants. By one of those curious fateful coincidences, with which fact often outbids fiction, Mr. Gerard, who was the first Englishman attacked by the Portuguese, suffers on the same scaffold as his would-be murderers, his offence being high treason. Vowel, the other plotter, is also executed, but the third saves himself, as we know, by confession.

July 20th [1654 in pencil].

I AM very sorry I spoke too late, for I am confident this was an excellent servant. He was in the same house where I lay, and I had taken a great fancy to him, upon what was told me of him and what I saw. The poor fellow, too, was so pleased that I undertook to inquire out a place for him, that, though mine was, as I told him, uncertain, yet upon the bare hopes on't he refused two or three good conditions; but I shall set him now at liberty, and not think at all the worse of him for his good-nature. Sure you go a little too far in your condemnation on't. I know it may be abused, as the best things are most subject to be, but in itself 'tis so absolutely necessary that where it is wanting nothing can recompense the miss on't. The most contemptible person in the world, if he has that, cannot be justly hated, and the most considerable without it cannot deserve to be loved. Would to God I had all that good-nature you complain you have too much of, I could find ways enough to dispose on't amongst myself and my friends; but 'tis well where it is, and I should sooner wish you more on't than less.

I wonder with what confidence you can complain of my short letters that are so guilty yourself in the same kind. I have not seen a letter this month which has been above half a sheet. Never trust me if I write more than you that live in a desolated country where you might finish a romance of ten tomes before anybody interrupted you. I that live in a house the most filled of any since the Ark, and where, I can assure [you], one has hardly time for the most necessary occasions. Well, there was never any one thing so much desired and apprehended at the same time as your return is by me; it will certainly, I think, conclude me a very happy or a most unfortunate person. Sometimes, methinks, I would fain know my doom whatever it be; and at others, I dread it so extremely, that I am confident the five Portugals and the three plotters which were t'other day condemned by the High Court of Justice had not half my fears upon them. I leave you to judge the constraint I live in, what alarms my thoughts give me, and yet how unconcerned this company requires I should be; they will have me at my part in a play, "The Lost Lady" it is, and I am she. Pray God it be not an ill omen!

I shall lose my eyes and you this letter if I make it longer. Farewell.

I am, yours.

Letter 67.—Elizabeth, Queen of Bohemia, was the daughter of James I. She married the Elector Frederick, who was driven from his throne owing to his own misconduct and folly, when his wife was forced to return and live as a pensioner in her native country. She is said to have been gifted in a superlative degree with all that is considered most lovely in a woman's character. On her husband's death in 1632 she went to live at the Hague, where she remained until the Restoration. There is a report that she married William, Earl of Craven, but there is no proof of this. He was, however, her friend and adviser through her years of widowhood, and it was to his house in Drury Lane that she returned to live in 1661. She is said to have been a lover of literature, and Francis Quarles and Sir Henry Wotton were her intimate friends. The latter has written some quaint and elegant verses to his mistress; the last verse, in which he apostrophizes her as the sun, is peculiarly graceful. It runs thus:

> You meaner beauties of the night,
>   That poorly satisfy our eyes,
> More by your number than your light,—
>   You common people of the skies,
>   What are you when the sun shall rise?

But the sun is set, and the beautiful Queen's sad, romantic story almost forgotten.

Sir John Grenvile was a son of the valiant and loyal cavalier, Sir Bevil Grenvile, of Kelkhampton, Cornwall. He served the King successfully in the west of England, and was dangerously wounded at Newbury. He was entrusted by Charles II. to negotiate with General Monk. Monk's brother was vicar of Kelkhampton, so that Grenvile and Monk would in all probability be well acquainted before the time of the negotiation. We may remember, too, that Dorothy's younger brother was on intimate terms with General Monk's relations in Cornwall.

There must be letters missing here, for we cannot believe more than a month passed without Dorothy writing a single letter.

U

I WONDER you did not come before your last letter. 'Twas dated the 24th of August, but I received it not till the 1st of September. Would to God your journey were over! Every little storm of wind frights me so, that I pass here for the greatest coward that ever was born, though, in earnest, I think I am as little so as most women, yet I may be deceived, too, for now I remember me you have often told me I was one, and, sure, you know what kind of heart mine is better than anybody else.

I am glad you are pleased with that description I made you of my humour, for, though you had disliked it, I am afraid 'tis past my power to help. You need not make excuses neither for yours; no other would please me half so well. That gaiety which you say is only esteemed would be insupportable to me, and I can as little endure a tongue that's always in motion as I could the click of a mill. Of all the company this place is stored with, there is but two persons whose conversation is at all easy; one is my eldest niece, who, sure, was sent into the world to show 'tis possible for a woman to be silent; the other, a gentleman whose mistress died just when they should have married; and though 'tis many years since, one may read it in his face still. His humour was very good, I believe, before that accident, for he will yet say things pleasant enough, but 'tis so seldom that he speaks at all,

and when he does 'tis with so sober a look, that
one may see he is not moved at all himself when
he diverts the company most. You will not be
jealous though I say I like him very much. If
you were not secure in me, you might be so in
him. He would expect his mistress should rise
again to reproach his inconstancy if he made
court to anything but her memory. Methinks
we three (that is, my niece, and he and I) do
become this house the worst that can be, unless
I should take into the number my brother Peyton
himself too; for to say truth his, for another sort
of melancholy, is not less than ours. What can
you imagine we did this last week, when to our
constant company there was added a colonel and
his lady, a son of his and two daughters, a maid
of honour to the Queen of Bohemia, and another
colonel or a major, I know not which, besides all
the tongue they brought with them; the men the
greatest drinkers that ever I saw, which did not
at all agree with my brother, who would not be
drawn to it to save a kingdom if it lay at stake
and no other way to redeem it? But, in earnest,
there was one more to be pitied besides us, and
that was Colonel Thornhill's wife, as pretty a
young woman as I have seen. She is Sir John
Greenvil's sister, and has all his good - nature,
with a great deal of beauty and modesty, and
wit enough. This innocent creature is sacrificed
to the veriest beast that ever was. The first day

she came hither he intended, it seems, to have
come with her, but by the way called in to see
an old acquaintance, and bid her go on, he would
overtake her, but did not come till next night, and
then so drunk he was led immediately to bed,
whither she was to follow him when she had
supped. I blest myself at her patience, as you
may do that I could find anything to fill up this
paper withal. Adieu.

Letter 68.—In this scrap of writing we find that
Temple is again in England with certain proposals from
his father, and ready to discuss the "treaty," as Dorothy
calls it, with her brother Peyton. The few remaining
letters deal with the treaty. Temple would probably
return to London when he left Ireland, and letters
would pass frequently between them. There seems to
have been some hitch as to who should appear in the
treaty. Dorothy's brother had spoken of and behaved
to Temple with all disrespect, but, now that he is reconciled to the marriage, Dorothy would have him
appear, at least formally, in the negotiations. The last
letter of this chapter, which is dated October 2nd, calls
on Temple to come down to Kent, to Peyton's house;
and it is reasonable to suppose that at this interview
all was practically settled to the satisfaction of those
two who were most deeply concerned in the negotiation.

I DID so promise myself a letter on Friday that
I am very angry I had it not, though I know you
were not come to town when it should have been

writ. But did not you tell me you should not stay above a day or two? What is it that has kept you longer? I am pleased, though, that you are out of the power of so uncertain things as the winds and the sea, which I never feared for myself, but did extremely apprehend for you. You will find a packet of letters to read, and maybe have met with them already. If you have, you are so tired that 'tis but reasonable I should spare you in this. For, [to] say truth, I have not time to make this longer; besides that if I had, my pen is so very good that it writes an invisible hand, I think; I am sure I cannot read it myself. If your eyes are better, you will find that I intended to assure you I am

Yours.

Letter 69.

I am but newly waked out of an unquiet sleep, and I find it so late that if I write at all it must be now. Some company that was here last night kept us up till three o'clock, and then we lay three in a bed, which was all the same to me as if we had not gone to bed at all. Since dinner they are all gone, and our company with them part of the way, and with much ado I got to be excused, that I might recover a little sleep, but am so moped yet that, sure, this letter will be nonsense.

I would fain tell you, though, that your father is mistaken, and that you are not, if you believe

that I have all the kindness and tenderness for
you my heart is capable of.   Let me assure you
(whate'er your father thinks) that had you £20,000
a year I could love you no more than I do, and
should be far from showing it so much lest it
should look like a desire of your fortune, which,
as to myself, I value as little as anybody in the
world, and in this age of changes ; but certainly
I know what an estate is.   I have seen my father's
reduced, better than £4000, to not £400 a year,
and I thank God I never felt the change in anything that I thought necessary.   I never wanted,
nor am confident I never shall.   But yet, I would
not be thought so inconsiderate a person as not
to remember that it is expected from all people
that have sense that they should act with reason,
that to all persons some proportion of fortune is
necessary, according to their several qualities, and
though it is not required that one should tie oneself to just so much, and something is left for
one's inclination, and the difference in the persons
to make, yet still within such a compass,—and
such as lay more upon these considerations than
they will bear, shall infallibly be condemned by all
sober persons.   If any accident out of my power
should bring me to necessity though never so
great, I should not doubt with God's assistance
but to bear it as well as anybody, and I should
never be ashamed on't if He pleased to send it
me ; but if by my own folly I had put it upon

myself, the case would be extremely altered. If
ever this comes to a treaty, I shall declare that in
my own choice I prefer you much before any other
person in the world, and all that this inclination
in me (in the judgment of any persons of honour
and discretion) will bear, I shall desire may be
laid upon it to the uttermost of what they can
allow. And if your father please to make up the
rest, I know nothing that is like to hinder me
from being yours. But if your father, out of
humour, shall refuse to treat with such friends as
I have, let them be what they will, it must end
here ; for though I was content, for your sake, to
lose them, and all the respect they had for me,
yet, now I have done that, I'll never let them see
that I have so little interest in you and yours as
not to prevail that my brother may be admitted
to treat for me. Sure, when a thing of course
and so much reason as that (unless I did disclose
to all the world he were my enemy), it must be
expected whensoever I dispose of myself he should
be made no stranger to it. When that shall be
refused me, I may be justly reproached that I
deceived myself when I expected to be at all
valued in a family that I am a stranger to, or
that I should be considered with any respect
because I had a kindness for you, that made me
not value my own interests.

I doubt much whether all this be sense or not ;
I find my head so heavy. But that which I

would say is, in short, this : if I did say once that my brother should have nothing to do in't, 'twas when his carriage towards me gave me such an occasion as could justify the keeping that distance with him ; but now it would look extremely unhandsome in me, and, sure, I hope your father would not require it of me. If he does, I must conclude he has no value for me, and, sure, I never disobliged him to my knowledge, and should, with all the willingness imaginable, serve him if it lay in my power.

Good God! what an unhappy person am I. All the world is so almost. Just now they are telling me of a gentleman near us that is the most wretched creature made (by the loss of a wife that he passionately loved) that can be. If your father would but in some measure satisfy my friends that I might but do it in any justifiable manner, you should dispose me as you pleased, carry me whither you would, all places of the world would be alike to me where you were, and I should not despair of carrying myself so towards him as might deserve a better opinion from him.

I am yours.

Letter 70.

My doubts and fears were not at all increased by that which gives you so many, nor did I apprehend that your father might not have been prevailed with to have allowed my brother's being seen in the treaty; for as to the thing itself, whether he appears in't or not, 'twill be the same. He cannot but conclude my brother Peyton would not do anything in it without the others' consent.

I do not pretend to any share in your father's kindness, as having nothing in me to merit it; but as much a stranger as I am to him, I should have taken it very ill if I had desired it of him, and he had refused it me. I do not believe my brother has said anything to his prejudice, unless it were in his persuasions to me, and there it did not injure him at all. If he takes it ill that my brother appears so very averse to the match, I may do so too, that he was the same; and nothing less than my kindness for you could have made me take so patiently as I did his saying to some that knew me at York that he was forced to bring you thither and afterwards to send you over lest you should have married me. This was not much to my advantage, nor hardly civil, I think, to any woman; yet I never so much as took the least notice on't, nor had not now, but for this occasion; yet, sure, it concerns me to be at least as nice as he in point of honour. I think 'tis best for me to end here lest my anger should make me lose that respect I would always have for your father, and 'twere not amiss, I think, that I devoted it all towards you for being so idle as to run out of your bed to catch such a cold.

If you come hither you must expect to be
chidden so much that you will wish that you had
stayed till we came up, when perhaps I might
have almost forgot half my quarrel to you. At
this present I can assure you I am pleased with
nobody but your sister, and her I love extremely,
and will call her pretty ; say what you will, I
know she must be so, though I never saw more
of her than what her letters show. She shall
have two "spots" [carriage dogs] if she please (for
I had just such another given me after you were
gone), or anything else that is in the power of

Yours.

Letter 71.

Monday, October the 2nd [1654].

AFTER a long debate with myself how to
satisfy you and remove that rock (as you call it),
which in your apprehensions is of so great danger,
I am at last resolved to let you see that I value
your affections for me at as high a rate as you
yourself can set it, and that you cannot have
more of tenderness for me and my interests than I
shall ever have for yours. The particulars how
I intend to make this good you shall know when
I see you ; which since I find them here more
irresolute in point of time (though not as to
the journey itself) than I hoped they would have
been, notwithstanding your quarrel to me, and the
apprehension you would make me believe you

had that I do not care to see you, pray come hither and try whether you shall be welcome or not! In sober earnest now I must speak with you; and to that end if your occasions will [serve] come down to Canterbury. Send some one when you are there, and you shall have further directions.

You must be contented not to stay here above two or three hours. I shall tell you my reason when you come. And pray inform yourself of all that your father will do on this occasion, that you may tell it me only; therefore let it be plainly and sincerely what he intends and all.

I will not hinder your coming away so much as the making this letter a little longer might take away from your time in reading it. 'Tis enough to tell you I am ever

Yours.

CHAPTER VII.

THE END OF THE THIRD VOLUME.

THIS short series of notes was written, I think, during a visit to London after the formal betrothal and before the marriage. These notes were evidently written upon the trivial occasions of the day, more perhaps for the sake of writing something than for any more serious reason. The note in French is somewhat of a curiosity on account of its quaint orthography, which is purposely left uncorrected. Was Dorothy in London to purchase her *trousseau ?* Where did she and Jane spend their days, if that was the case, when Regent Street was green fields ? These questions cannot be satisfactorily answered ; but the notes themselves, without any history or explanation, are so full of interest, so fresh and vivacious, even for Dorothy, that they place themselves from the freedom and joy of their style and manner at the end of the third volume.

YOU are like to have an excellent housewife of me ; I am abed still, and slept so soundly, nothing but your letter could have waked me. You shall hear from me as soon as we have dined. Farewell ; can you endure that word ? No, out upon't. I'll see you anon.

FYE upon't I shall grow too good now, I am taking care to know how your worship slept to-night; better I hope than you did the last. Send me word how you do, and don't put me off with a bit of a note now; you could write me a fine long letter when I did not deserve it half so well.

YOU are mistaken if you think I am in debt for both these days. Saturday I confess was devoted to my Lady; but yesterday, though I ris with good intentions of going to church, my cold would not suffer me, but kept me prisoner all the day. I went to your lodging to tell you that visiting the sick was part of the work of the day, but you were gone, and so I went to bed again, where your letter found me this morning. But now I will rise and despatch some visits that I owe, that to-morrow may be entirely yours.

I FIND my conscience a little troubled till I have asked your pardon for my ill-humour last night. Will you forgive it me; in earnest, I could not help it, but I met with a cure for it; my brother kept me up to hear his learned lecture till after two o'clock, and I spent all my ill-humour upon him, and yet we parted very quietly, and look'd as if a little good fortune might make us good friends; but your special friend, my elder brother, I have a story to tell you of him. Will my cousin

F. come, think you? Send me word, it maybe
'twas a compliment; if I can see you this morning
I will, but I dare not promise it.

Sir,—This is to tell you that you will be expected to-morrow morning about nine o'clock at
a lodging over against the place where Charinge
Crosse stood, and two doors above Ye Goate
Taverne; if with these directions you can find it
out, you will there find one that is very much

Your servant.

Now I have got the trick of breaking my
word, I shall do it every day. I must go to Roehampton to-day, but 'tis all one, you do not care
much for seeing me. Well, my master, remember
last night you swaggered like a young lord. I'll
make your stomach come down; rise quickly, you
had better, and come hither that I may give you a
lesson this morning before I go.

Je n'ay guere plus dormie que vous et mes
songes n'ont pas estres moins confuse, au rest
une bande de violons que sont venu jouer sous
ma fennestre, m'ont tourmentés de tel façon que
je doubt fort si je pourrois jamais les souffrire
encore, je ne suis pourtant pas en fort mauvaise
humeur et je m'en-voy ausi tost que je serai

habillée voire ce qu'il est posible de faire pour vostre sattisfaction, après je viendre vous rendre conte de nos affairs et quoy qu'il en sera vous ne scaurois jamais doubté que je ne vous ayme plus que toutes les choses du monde.

I HAVE slept as little as you, and may be allowed to talk as unreasonably, yet I find I am not quite senseless; I have a heart still that cannot resolve to refuse you anything within its power to grant. But, Lord, when shall I see you? People will think me mad if I go abroad this morning after having seen me in the condition I was in last night, and they will think it strange to see you here. Could you not stay till they are all gone to Roehampton? they go this morning. I do but ask, though do what you please, only believe you do a great injustice if you think me false. I never resolv'd to give you an eternal farewell, but I resolv'd at the same time to part with all the comfort of my life, and whether I told it you or not I shall die yours.

Tell me what you will have me do.

HERE comes the note again to tell you I cannot call on you to-night; I cannot help it, and you must take it as patiently as you can, but I am engaged to-night at the Three Rings to sup and play. Poor man, I am sorry for you; in earnest, I shall be quite spoiled. I see no remedy; think whether it were not best to leave me and begin a new adventure.

And now we have finished. Dorothy Osborne is passing away, will soon be translated into Dorothy Temple; with the romance of her life all past history, and fast becoming as much a romance to herself, as it seems to us, looking back at it after more than two centuries. Something it is becoming to her over which she can muse and dream and weave into tales for the children who will gather round her. Something the reality of which will grow doubtful to her, if she find idle hours for dreaming and doubting in her new name. Her last lover's letter is written. We are ready for the marriage ceremony, and listen for the wedding march and happy jingle of village bells; or if we may not have these in Puritan days, at least we may hear the pompous magistrate pronounce the blessing of the State over its two happy subjects. But no! There is yet a moment of suspense, a last trial to the lover's constancy. The bride is taken dangerously ill, so dangerously ill that the doctors rejoice when the disease pronounces itself to be small-pox. Alas! who shall now say what are the inmost thoughts of our Dorothy? Does she not need all her faith in her lover, in herself, ay, and in God, to uphold her in this new affliction? She rises from her bed, her beauty of face destroyed; her fair looks living only on the painter's canvas, unless we may believe that they were etched in deeply bitten lines on Temple's heart. But the skin beauty is not the firmest hold she has on Temple's affections; this was not the beauty that had attracted her lover and held him enchained in her service for seven years of waiting and suspense; this was not the only light leading him through dark days of doubt, almost of despair, constant, unwavering in his troth to her. Other beauty not outward, of which we, too, may have seen something, mirrored darkly in these letters; which we, too, as well as Temple, may know existed in Dorothy. For it is not beauty of face and form, but of what men call the soul, that made Dorothy to Temple, in fact as she was in name,—the gift of God.

APPENDIX

LADY TEMPLE.

OF Lady Temple there is very little to be known, and what there is can be best understood by following the career of her husband, which has been written at some length, and with laboured care, by Mr. Courtenay. After her marriage, at the end of 1654 or the beginning of 1655, they lived for a year at the home of a friend in the country. They then removed to Ireland, where they lived for five years with Temple's father; Lady Giffard, Temple's widowed sister, joining them. In 1663 they were living in England. Lady Giffard continued to live with them through the rest of their lives, and survived them both. In 1665 Temple was sent to Brussels as English representative, and his family joined him in the following year. In 1668 he was removed from Brussels to the Hague, where the successful negotiations which led to the Triple Alliance took place, and these have given him an honourable place in history. There is a letter of Lady Temple's, written to her husband in 1670, which shows how interested she was in the part he took in political life, and how he must have consulted her in all State matters. It is taken from Courtenay's *Life of Sir William Temple,* vol. i. p. 345. He quotes it as the only letter written after Lady Temple's death which has come into his hands.

THE HAGUE, *October 31st*, 1670.

MY DEAREST HEART,—I received yours from Yarmouth, and was very glad you made so happy a passage. 'Tis a comfortable thing, when one is on this side, to know that such a thing can be done in spite of contrary winds. I have a letter from P., who says in character that you may take it from him that the Duke of Buckingham has begun a negotiation there, but what success in England he may have he knows not; that it were to be wished our politicians at home would consider well that there is no trust to be put in alliances with ambitious kings, especially such as make it their fundamental maxim to be base. These are bold words, but they are his own. Besides this, there is nothing but that the French King grows very thrifty, that all his buildings, except fortifications, are ceased, and that his payments are not so regular as they used to be. The people here are of another mind; they will not spare their money, but are resolved—at least the States of Holland—if the rest will consent, to raise fourteen regiments of foot and six of horse; that all the companies, both old and new, shall be of 120 men that used to be of 50, and every troop 80 that used to be of 45. Nothing is talked of but these new levies, and the young men are much pleased.   Downton says they have strong suspicions here you will come back no more, and that they shall be left in the lurch; that something is striking up with France, and that you are sent away because you are too well inclined to these countries; and my cousin Temple, he says, told him that a nephew of Sir Robert Long's, who is lately come to Utrecht, told my cousin Temple, three weeks since, you were not to stay long here, because you were too great a friend to these people, and that he had it from Mr. Williamson, who knew very well what he said.   My cousin Temple says he told it to Major Scott as soon as he heard it, and so 'tis like you knew it before; but there is such a want of something to say that I catch at everything. I am my best dear's most affectionate

D. T.

In the summer of 1671 there occurred an incident that reminds us considerably of the Dorothy Osborne of former days.   The Triple Alliance had lost some of its freshness, and was not so much in vogue as heretofore. Charles II. had been coquetting with the French King, and at length the Government, throwing off its mask, formally displaced Temple from his post in Holland. "The critical position of affairs," says Courtenay, "induced the Dutch to keep a fleet at sea, and the English Government hoped to draw from that circumstance an occasion of quarrel.   A yacht was sent for Lady Temple; the captain had orders to sail through the Dutch fleet if he should meet it, and to fire into the nearest ships until they should either strike sail to the flag which he bore, or return his shot so as to make a quarrel!

"He saw nothing of the Dutch Fleet in going over, but on his return he fell in with it, and fired, without warning and ceremony, into the ships that were next him.

"The Dutch admiral, Van Ghent, was puzzled; he seemed not to know, and probably did not know, what the English captain meant; he therefore sent a boat, thinking it possible that the yacht might be in distress; when the captain told his orders, mentioning also that he had the ambassadress on board. Van Ghent himself then came on board, with a handsome compliment to Lady Temple, and, making his personal inquiries of the captain, received the same answer as before. The Dutchman said he had no orders upon the point, which he rightly believed to be still unsettled, and could not believe that the fleet, commanded by an admiral, was to strike to the King's pleasure-boat.

"When the Admiral returned to his ship, the captain also, 'perplexed enough,' applied to Lady Temple, who soon saw that he desired to get out of his difficulty by her help; but the wife of Sir William Temple called forth the spirit of Dorothy Osborne. 'He knew,' she told the captain, 'his orders best, and what he was to do upon them, which she left to him to follow as he thought fit, without any regard to her or her children.' The Dutch and English commanders then proceeded each upon his own course, and Lady Temple was safely landed in England."

There is an account of this incident in a letter of Sir Charles Lyttelton to Viscount Hatton, in the Hatton Correspondence. He tells us that the poor captain, Captain Crow of *The Monmouth*, "found himself in the Tower about it;" but he does not add any further information as to the part which Dorothy played in the matter.

After their retirement to Sheen and Moor Park, Surrey, we know nothing distinctively of Lady Temple, and little is known of their family life. They had only two children living, having lost as many as seven in their infancy. In 1684 one of these children, their only daughter, died of small-pox; she was buried in Westminster Abbey. There is a letter of hers written to her father which shows some signs of her mother's affectionate teaching, and which we cannot forbear to quote. It is copied from Courtenay, vol. ii. p. 113.

Sir,—I deferred writing to you till I could tell you that I had received all my fine things, which I have just now done; but I thought never to have done giving you thanks for them. They have made me so very happy in my new clothes, and everybody that comes does admire them above all things, but yet not so much as I think they deserve; and now, if papa was near, I should think myself a perfect pope, though I hope I should not be burned as there was one at Nell Gwyn's door the 5th of November, who was set in a great chair, with a red nose half a yard long, with some hundreds of boys throwing squibs at it. Monsieur Gore and I agree mighty well, and he makes me believe I shall come to something at last; that is if he stays, which I don't doubt but he will, because all the fine ladies will petition for him. We are got rid of the workmen now, and our house is ready to entertain you. Come when you please, and you will meet nobody more glad to see you than your most obedient and dutiful daughter,

D. TEMPLE.

Temple's son, John Temple, married in 1685 a rich heiress in France, the daughter of Monsieur Duplessis Rambouillet, a French Protestant ; he brought his wife to live at his father's house at Sheen. After King William and Queen Mary were actually placed on the throne, Sir William Temple, in 1689, permitted his son to accept the office of Secretary at War. For reasons now obscure and unknowable, he drowned himself in the Thames within a week of his acceptance of office, leaving this writing behind him :—

"My folly in undertaking what I was not able to perform has done the King and kingdom a great deal of prejudice. I wish him all happiness and abler servants than John Temple."

The following letter was written on that occasion by Lady Temple to her nephew, Sir John Osborne. The original of it is at Chicksands :—

To Sir John Osborne, thanking him for his consolation on the death of her son.

SHEEN, *May 6th,* 1689.

DEAR NEPHEW,—I give you many thanks for your kind letter and the sense you have of my affliction, which truly is very great. But since it is laid upon me by the hand of an Almighty and Gracious God, that always proportions His punishments to the support He gives with them, I may hope to bear it as a Christian ought to do, and more especially one that is conscious to herself of having many ways deserved it.   The strange revolution we have seen might well have taught me what this world is, yet it seems it was necessary that I should have a near example of the uncertainty of all human blessings, that so having no tie to the world I may the better prepare myself to leave it; and that this correction may suffice to teach me my duty must be the prayer of your affectionate aunt and humble servant,

D. TEMPLE.

During the remaining years of her life, Lady Temple was honoured, to use the conventional phrase, by the friendship of Queen Mary, and there is said to have been a continuous correspondence between them, though I can find on inquiry no trace of its existence at the present day.

Early in the year 1695, after forty years of married life, and in the sixty-seventh year of her age, she died. She lies, with her husband and children, on the north side of the nave of Westminster Abbey, close to the little door that leads to the organ gallery.

> Her body sleeps in Capel's monument,
> And her immortal part with angels lives.

INDEX.

————o————

THE Index contains every name mentioned in the Letters, and every reference to that name. The figures in italics refer to the page on which there is a biographical or explanatory note.

Y

Lightning Source UK Ltd.
Milton Keynes UK
UKOW03f0316210514

232043UK00001B/82/P

9 781108 070553